SINS OF OMISSION

The Jewish Community's Reaction to
Domestic Violence

WHAT NEEDS TO BE DONE

CAROL GOODMAN KAUFMAN

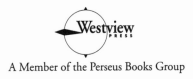

A Member of the Perseus Books Group

Published in the United States of America by Westview Press, A Member of the Perseus Books Group, 5500 Central Avenue, Boulder, Colorado 80301–2877, and in the United Kingdom by Westview Press, 12 Hid's Copse Road, Cumnor Hill, Oxford OX2 9JJ.

Find us on the world wide web at www.westviewpress.com

Westview Press books are available at special discounts for bulk purchases in the United States by corporations, institutions, and other organizations. For more information, please contact the Special Markets Department at the Perseus Books Group, 11 Cambridge Center, Cambridge, MA 02142, or call (617) 252–5298, (800) 255–1514 or email j.mccrary@perseusbooks.com.

A Cataloging-in-Publication data record for this book is available from the Library of Congress. ISBN 0–8133–4088–8

The paper used in this publication meets the requirements of the American National Standard for Permanence of Paper for Printed Library Materials Z39.48–1984.

Typeface used in this text: 11.5-point Bulmer MT Regular

10   9   8   7   6   5   4   3   2   1

*I dedicate this book to the memory of
my father, Isodore "Izzy" Goodman, who died
just weeks before the manuscript was completed.
Dad taught me that anything is possible.
May his memory be for a blessing.*

CONTENTS

ACKNOWLEDGMENTS

A BOOK LIKE THIS COULD NOT HAVE BEEN ATTEMPTED WITHOUT the cooperation of many, many people. To all of them I owe huge thanks. First, to Janet Hodos, who insisted that I cover the Jewish Women International *Shalom Bayit* conference at Brandeis University back in 1997, thank you for opening my eyes and my heart to the enormous problem of spousal abuse. To Dr. Jack Levin, for offering me the fellowship at the Brudnick Center on Violence and Conflict, which provided the seed money that launched the study, for critiquing my research design, and for generally providing moral support, thank you. To Dr. Gordana Rabrenovic, associate director of the Brudnick Center, who also critiqued the design, and became a friend in the process, thank you. Dr. Debra Kaufman of Northeastern University's Jewish Studies program generously gave me guidance and direction. Thank you. Lisa Molinelli, my editor at Westview Press, was judicious in her use of the blue pencil, and gentle in her criticism. Bless you. To Sgt. Vincent Gorgoglione, head of the Worcester Police Department Domestic Violence Unit, who let me ride along on some very cold and very frightening shifts, you and your officers are the greatest.

And, for all the people who participated in the study, but whose names must be kept confidential, I could not have done this without you. Thank you. You have done a great *mitzvah*.

Last but certainly not least, to my wonderful family: Joel, Seth, Avi, and Elana, who were the best moral support a woman could have. Thank you.

INTRODUCTION

IT IS MIDWAY THROUGH THE MORNING OF YOM KIPPUR, THE HOLIest day on the Jewish calendar. Despite the autumn chill outside, the air is already getting heavy with the closeness of bodies pressed together in prayer. The familiar, mournful strains of the High Holiday liturgy waft through the sanctuary. Surrounded by hundreds of my fellow congregants, I stand alone with my thoughts. My lower back hurts a bit, as I am wearing simple, flat canvas shoes in deference to the tradition of not wearing leather on the Day of Atonement. These modest shoes are symbolic of the humility with which we should view ourselves as we confess our failings over the past year.

On Yom Kippur Jews throughout the world beat their breasts for each sin they recite from a long list in the *Mahzor*, the High Holiday prayer book. These sins range from stubbornness to gluttony, having impure thoughts to spreading gossip, from sins of commission to sins of omission. Several aspects of this practice have always fascinated me. First, Jews do not have to have personally committed a particular sin to have to confess to it. We are held responsible as a community for these violations of God's laws. Community responsibility is a hallmark of Jewish tradition, and one that has helped this beleaguered people survive centuries of exile and persecution. Rabbi Hillel, the great Talmudic sage, once said, "Separate not yourself from the community,"[1] a precept that has guided Jewish life and buttressed the rationale for the Yom Kippur recitation.

Other Talmudic and biblical sources that support the concept of communal responsibility include "All Israel is responsible one for the other";[2] and, "If a person is found murdered and the assailant is unknown, the eld-

xii   INTRODUCTION

ers and leaders of the nearest community must declare, 'Our hands did not spill this blood, neither have our eyes seen it'" (Deut. 21:7).[3]

The second aspect of the Yom Kippur confessional is that, although one may make atonement for transgressions committed against the Almighty, God will not forgive trespasses committed against other people. For that damage, Jews must ask forgiveness from the person(s) hurt.

The sin that has always intrigued me is that of omission. I remember thinking as a young child, "How could one commit a sin by not doing something?" Jewish law had an answer for that question as well. "Do not stand idly by the blood of your neighbor," intones the Torah in Leviticus (19:16).[4]

The Talmud weighs in with, "Anyone who has the ability to correct a situation and is derelict in doing so, bears the responsibility for whatever results therefrom."[5]

Therefore, by standing by while a sin is being committed one also is in violation of Jewish law. In one of the most infamous examples in modern times, we saw in 1982 Israeli Defense Minister Ariel Sharon held responsible for massacres perpetrated in Lebanon, not by his own troops, but by Israel's Lebanese Christian militia allies. His guilt stemmed from the fact that he *should have known* that the Christian militia might carry out murders for vengeance against the Muslims. After a state inquiry found him indirectly responsible for the carnage, Sharon was forced to quit as defense minister. Again, one may not stand by either while a sin is being committed or if one knows one will be committed.

At around the same time I was having these thoughts about sins of omission, I was invited to Brandeis University to cover a historic conference for the *Jewish Chronicle* newspaper. In the spring of 1997, Jewish Women International had organized the first-ever national conference on the topic of domestic violence in the Jewish home. *Shalom Bayit* was the ironic name chosen for the meeting, as its meaning in Hebrew is "peace in the home." JWI had taken the lead among Jewish organizations in bringing domestic violence onto the radar screen of Jewish consciousness, and in fact had made domestic violence its main domestic agenda item.

One of the featured speakers at the *Shalom Bayit* conference was Rabbi Dr. Abraham Twerski, who is both an ordained rabbi and psychiatrist. Twerski first broke the silence about spousal abuse in Jewish homes with his book *The Shame Borne in Silence.*[6] Based on his knowledge of Jewish law, *halacha,* and his years of clinical experience, Twerski outlined the law regarding spousal abuse and summarized the situation of domestic violence in the Jewish community. When it comes to the subject of spousal abuse, one would assume that the same laws that apply to other crimes would hold true, and that the Jewish community's tolerance for these crimes would be low. However, according to Twerski, abuse occurs even among those who consider themselves the most devout, observant Jews.[7] Because abuse is not acknowledged, it is tolerated.

The statistics cited on spousal abuse are staggering. Although the community recites the old adage, *"der shiker is a goy"* (the drunk is a gentile) in its naive denial that Jewish men do not beat their wives, experts estimate that between 15 and 30 percent of all women are in abusive relationships. Even if Jews are on the low end of the range, that still leaves too many women who are being damaged. When I thought about this statistic in concrete terms, I realized that perhaps one in four to one in five of the women seated in the synagogue that Yom Kippur day were being abused.

The concept of *shalom bayit* is an ideal fostered by Jewish tradition. At virtually every point in Jewish history, the family was the only place of refuge, the only safe haven in a world bound and determined to eradicate the Jews. Unfortunately, ignorant people often cite *shalom bayit* to condone spousal abuse. They claim that it is the woman's responsibility to do her husband's will, attempting to bolster their argument with the saying, "A decent woman is one who does the wishes of her husband." This adage, claimed Twerski, is taken out of context and its meaning twisted to perverse ends. It was never intended to cause harm, and in fact would violate Torah law if it did.[8]

Twerski underscored that it is not just the wife who is responsible for peace in the home. The husband bears equal responsibility. And Twerski stated emphatically that sacrifice of human beings is not allowed. "To say that the Torah advocates a woman sacrificing herself to tolerate lifelong abuse is unconscionable."[9] Even the near sacrifice of Isaac, he wrote, was halted by God before it could be carried out.

At this point in my Yom Kippur reveries I realized that all my years of education and experience had brought me to this moment. Having received my doctorate in organizational psychology I was trained to look at organizational structure and culture and their effects on such important outcomes as member motivation and satisfaction. Any study on domestic violence approached from this perspective would then lead me to ask: How do these factors influence the organization's response, and that of its members, to events and trauma? More specific to my interest, what would the culture and structure of the Jewish community reveal about its response to domestic violence? I couldn't wait to get to the library after the holiday.

Once I began the literature search, I was surprised by the paucity of research that exists on the subject of spousal abuse within the Jewish community. A search of the PsychInfo database, covering 1,300 psychology related periodicals in twenty-five languages, yielded only four articles published in refereed academic journals. Considering the tiny Jewish community's history of persecution, a certain insularity and resistance to airing dirty laundry is not surprising. However, it was apparent to me that the community's silence has only served to exacerbate the problem.

In my consulting work with nonprofit Jewish organizations on how best to achieve their goals and objectives, I used to refer to their mission statement as the "*mezuzah*," an allusion to the scroll of the law that is fastened to the doorposts of Jewish homes. Contrary to popular opinion, the *mezuzah* is neither an amulet nor a good luck charm. It consists of the first and second paragraphs of the *Sh'ma*, the central prayer of the Jewish religion that proclaims the belief in one God. The *Sh'ma* also instructs Jews how to behave, and, since it is fastened to the doorpost of the house, reminds them how to behave when they both enter the home and leave it to participate in the workplace. To remind them of why they were there, I would have my clients, usually boards of directors, fasten their mission statement to the front of their board training manuals and encourage them to read it at the beginning of every board meeting.

In other words, the mission statement of the organization should guide its leaders and members in how to behave toward the organization and toward each other. Therefore, it seemed logical to me that the "mission statement" of the Jewish people should be tested for its validity and accuracy in predicting its behavior. Is the mission statement of the Jewish community visible to all, or has it become an invisible feature of the woodwork? Have the laws and prayers that saturate Jewish daily life become meaningless through rote repetition, or are they unintelligible to a population ignorant of the language? Has the education provided by the Jewish community, from its children to its professionals, addressed the topic of domestic life?

The Jewish community is guided by law and traditions that have grown over 4,000 years of its people's existence. It is a mission-driven organization, and ostensibly, it is the mission that sets the tone for all that happens within it—in this case, within the Jewish community as served by its synagogues, schools, agencies, charities, and volunteer organizations. And the Jews have organized their lives very well over the years. However, it is often the case that powerful and charismatic people within an organization drive its direction. They choose which items on the agenda to prioritize, and which to ignore. I have seen this behavior pattern in organizations as diverse as Fortune 500 corporations, community charity groups, and synagogue boards of directors.

Upon reviewing the literature on both abuse victims and abusers, it becomes apparent that looking at the problem at the microlevel has its limits. One of the biggest obstacles abuse victims face is the response of the organizations, and the people who represent these organizations, surrounding them. Psychotherapist Susan Weitzman, in her book *Not to People Like Us*,[10] tells the story of a woman of means who called a secular domestic violence shelter for help, but was told that she didn't need help because she had money; she had to be put on a waiting list. She called repeatedly for four years, desperate for assistance, but at the time Weitzman's book was published, had yet to receive a return call from the shelter. If organizations dedicated to helping abuse victims discriminate against and dismiss the victims, then we must look closely at these organizations.

This is not a book about why men abuse women. These issues can be explored elsewhere. Neither is it a profile of the victims of abuse. There are many excellent books that chronicle the struggles women have undergone and the obstacles they have had to overcome to be free of torment, although I did include some women's stories in terms of how they relate to their interaction with the organizations charged with caring for the community. Similarly, this is not a book about the children of violent marriages, although we know the tragic consequences for children reared in an abusive home. Neither is it a book about Jewish law, although I did explore that law as it pertains to the mission and accomplishments of the people. Virtually all of the written material to date on domestic violence among Jews has been focused on *halacha* and its historical development.

In this book I looked at the structure and processes of one specific organization—the Jewish community—in order to analyze it as a living organizational system. I wanted to study how that system impacts its members by looking at how it responds to the scourge of spousal abuse: its acknowledgment of the problem, its method(s) of dealing with it, and the funds it allocates to education, victim treatment, and prevention. I also wanted to prepare concrete recommendations for use in strategic planning by the communities.

I refer to the entire Jewish community as an "organization" for several reasons. First, unlike other religious or ethnic groups, the Jewish community is exceedingly small, numbering only 6 million in the United States and 13 million worldwide. Second, although the three Massachusetts communities I studied (Boston, Central Massachusetts, and the Berkshires) are organized slightly differently, given their enormous range in population and resources, they all adhere to some basic rules. Jewish life is founded on three main tenets: study, ritual, and acts of loving kindness. Study is for the most part covered by the synagogues and schools, although many organizations do have informal study groups. Ritual is handled by the synagogues, and acts of loving kindness are coordinated by virtually all the various agencies and charities that make up the community. After all, the mission of the Jewish organization is the mission of the Jewish faith. Quite often we see overlap among both membership rosters and programs and services offered, particularly in larger communities. The Jewish community needs, and has, multiple leaders because it has multiple goals.

Finally, the Jewish community is quite insular. The insularity is understandable when one looks at the history of persecution experienced by the Jews for thousands of years. Segregated into *shtetls* and ghettoes, kept apart from society in numerous countries, and prohibited from participating fully in economic and social life, the Jews developed their own culture and strong psychological defense mechanisms. Because they were so often oppressed by the ruling king or government or church, they developed their own *batei din*, or courts of justice, for dealing with violations of the law. Only when a life was at stake would the community go to the secular authorities. This approach is still followed today.

Airing one's dirty laundry would be embarrassing for a spousal abuse victim in two ways. First, within the small Jewish community, where everybody knows everybody else's business, people placed a high value on keeping private business private. In the case of observant Jews, domestic violence was considered a *shanda*, a shameful thing, that could affect the marriage prospects of the children of an abusive marriage. Second, the dominant community already had made life a living hell in many of the countries in which Jews lived. Letting the authorities know their personal problems could bring even greater suffering upon them.

Jews are known throughout the world as "The People of the Book." From the Ten Commandments to the *Sayings of the Fathers*[11] to Maimonides's *A Guide for the Perplexed*,[12] the Jews have led the world in ethical thinking. As evidenced by these sources, the Jews, through their writings, have promulgated the moral principle of communal responsibility, that "All Israel is responsible one for the other." How, then, does a people, organized around a set of laws dedicated to the joint mission of justice and *pikuah nefesh,* saving a life, respond when confronted with a blatant violation of the very precepts that define its faith?

Let us now begin to explore just how well the teachings accumulated over thousands of years have been translated into action, and how well the ethical mandates have been incorporated into modern communal behavior.

1

"OH, THAT I HAD WINGS LIKE A DOVE"[1]

SURVIVORS TELL THEIR STORIES

It is not an enemy who reviles me—I could bear that; It is not my foe who vaults himself against me—I could hide from him; But it is you, my equal, my companion, my friend; Sweet was our fellowship; we walked together in God's house"

—Psalms 55:13–15[2]

HEDDA NUSSBAUM. ELANA STEINBERG. LAURA JANE ROSENTHAL. Carol Neulander. Blima Zitrenbaum. These are the names of victims in some of the most infamous cases of domestic violence in recent years, cases that hit the headlines because they were so gruesome. Jewish women all, regardless of affiliation, they suffered the pain and humiliation of abuse, and ultimately, for most of them, death.

Hedda Nussbaum's common-law husband, Joel Steinberg, emotionally and physically battered her for years. Photographs of Hedda Nussbaum's bruised and flattened face caused revulsion and horror as they were splashed across New York newspapers. Hedda Nussbaum was "lucky," if you can call it that. She got out. Unfortunately, she didn't escape her relationship until after Steinberg murdered their six-year-old adopted daughter,

Lisa. Hedda herself has undergone countless surgeries to repair damage to her face.

Elana Steinberg, thirty-four, was stabbed twenty-six times as she slept in her suburban Phoenix home. Her husband, Steven, blamed Elana, claiming she was a "Jewish American Princess."

Richard Rosenthal beat his wife, Laura Jane, to death with a rock, dismembered her body, and then impaled her head on a stake. The Social Law Library, in reporting the trial results, didn't bother to include Laura Jane's name in their account. In effect, she was victimized a second time by a criminal justice system that could not manage to put an identity to a woman who died because she was unable to get out of her marriage. A recent search of the Internet for media references to the case found Laura Jane's name in only one, but Richard's name and profession (financial analyst) in all.

Rabbi Fred Neulander, the spiritual leader of a congregation of worshipers, hired two men to murder his wife, Carol. After his first experience with the criminal justice system ended in mistrial, he was subsequently convicted of murder. Joseph Zitrenbaum murdered his wife, Blima, causing shock and consternation among the New York *Hasidic* community in which they lived. While some people argue that murder for hire is not spousal abuse, I think that the distinction is fatuous. A woman was emotionally terrorized and died as a result of physical aggression.

These are the most prominent cases of domestic violence, those with the most horrific endings. But, what of the women who are still being abused, silently suffering at the hands of psychologically and physically abusive husbands and companions? How can we identify these women and get them help before it is too late?

Like the author of the psalm quoted at the beginning of this chapter, the women I met in my study cannot believe that their husbands, the men they loved and with whom they pledged to spend their lives, could deliberately hurt them. These survivors come from every walk of Jewish life. Although from all points on the economic scale, they are for the most part solidly middle and upper-middle class, proving that, although money can camouflage abuse, it does not protect against it. These women represent the range of religious observance, from unaffiliated to ultra-Orthodox. Further, an astonishing fifteen of the twenty-two women have postgraduate education, including master's degrees, M.D.'s, J.D.'s, and Ph.D.'s. Of those with

less education, most still have some college or other post–high school training. If we compare these statistics with those of the general population, we
see that the difference is remarkable. According to the U.S. Census Bureau,
only 7.8 percent of American women have an advanced degree, as compared with 68.2 percent of the women in this study.[3]

Wherever women would speak to me, I would drive, sometimes accu-
mulating up to a thousand miles a week. We met on hot, humid summer
days in the city and on crisp, riotously colored autumn afternoons. These
survivors of spousal abuse lived at points along the magnificent Mohawk
Trail, off exits from the Massachusetts Turnpike, Route 9, Route 128, and
in little towns and villages across the state. In coffee shops, franchise restau-
rants, one-of-a-kind diners, bungalows, apartments, and elegant Victorian
homes, I drank cups and cups of coffee, and I listened.

In the summer of 2001, the Brudnick Center on Violence and Conflict
at Boston's Northeastern University provided seed money for me to place
advertisements in Massachusetts's three major Jewish newspapers: the
Jewish Advocate, the *Jewish Chronicle,* and the *Berkshire Jewish Voice.*
These papers cover the three communities on which I focused my research, the areas served by the Jewish Federation of the Berkshires, the Jewish Federation of Central Massachusetts, and the Combined Jewish
Philanthropies (CJP) for Greater Boston. In addition, several synagogue
bulletins and secular newspapers printed press releases at no charge. The
ads solicited Jewish survivors of spousal abuse. The initial grant also paid
for a telephone line to be installed in my home office, dedicated solely to the
research study. It was important to have a confidential line to encourage
women who might otherwise have been afraid to call; privacy was essential
to earning their trust and encouraging participation. Then, I sat back to
wait for the volunteers I wasn't sure would materialize. After all, many
people had told me that because abuse "doesn't happen among Jews" I
would get no response. And, even if it did, nobody would call because it is a
shanda, a disgrace.

But the calls did come. Volunteers responded to the ads placed in
newspapers and synagogue bulletins, and posted at counseling centers,
health clubs, and women's rest rooms. Almost sixty women called to volunteer, and they were overwhelmingly bound and determined to tell their stories. From Texas to Florida, and Connecticut to New Hampshire, calls

came on the study telephone. However, either because the abuse took place in a community not part of the protocol, or because the women were still living with their abusive husbands, I was unable to include most of the volunteers in the sample. Then, a few women dropped out before they could be interviewed, leaving a total of twenty-two women who participated in the study. They all told me that even though it would be difficult to talk, it would be worth it if they could save even one woman from experiencing what they had gone through. They felt an obligation to help others.

Many women thanked me for doing this study, saying that it was "about time" somebody focused on the issue of violence in the Jewish community. The opinion they expressed over and over was that the Jewish community "keeps its head in the sand."

Although the purpose of my study was to analyze the Jewish community as an organization, in order to understand the women's experiences and perceptions of their communities, it was also vital to present their stories. Did they seek help from the Jewish community? Did the Jewish community offer the services they needed? What was the reaction of the Jewish professionals responsible for the health and well-being of their communities' members? These women's experiences with domestic violence are an indicator of how their own communities, and the general Jewish community, respond.

Throughout this book you will read of real experiences with abuse. However, because stalking and continued violence are all too often realities in their world, I have changed the names of the women whose stories fill these pages. Their words are their own. And I would be remiss if I did not state for the record that they are true heroines. These women, who suffered so greatly at the hands of their abusers, got out and made new lives for themselves. In addition, they did a true *mitzvah* by volunteering to share their experiences specifically in order to help other women avoid a similar fate. We all owe every one of them a debt of gratitude for speaking out.

About half of the women I interviewed wanted to meet in their own homes; the other half preferred to meet in a public place, such as a diner or coffee house. Their reasons varied. Some did not want their young children to overhear our conversation, whereas others seemed to be proclaiming their freedom from intimidation.

I met Paula at her rural Cape Cod style house. She was a small wraith of a woman and walked with a slight limp, her head down. Years of physical abuse at the hands of her husband had taken their toll on her health, and she suffered from a variety of serious illnesses. In fact, when I arrived at her home, a serviceman was busy installing a medical alarm system for her protection. Despite her disabilities, however, when she spoke, her vast intelligence shone through.

At the other end of the spectrum was the busy metropolitan restaurant where I met with Laura. Laura was an accomplished businesswoman who had married right out of college. As we ate, she spoke in a hoarse voice, about which I wondered to myself. I remembered that she had had the same laryngitis when we first spoke on the telephone, and was somewhat surprised that it hadn't yet healed. As if reading my mind, she then explained to me that the rasping was the result of years of stress.

Laura explained that what had attracted her to her husband was his intellect and charm. She expressed amazement that what seemed to be compatibility at every level of their relationship— "in tastes, interests, and backgrounds"—changed after the marriage. "We did very exciting things," but, she continued, "on our honeymoon I was grossly disappointed. Physically, he was warm and affectionate, but he had a low sex drive."

> I still can't put my finger on it, what was wrong. The ground felt as if it was shifting under me. I felt like I was being buried alive, in the vortex. The control was subtle. He was moving me away from things. He resented my friendships. He wouldn't pay the bills for things like the deck, the *bar mitzvah kiddush*, the decorator—just to embarrass me. He didn't pay the property taxes. I question how blind I was to him. I was so vested in the relationship. Then, one day his partner called to tell me that my husband had embezzled money from their firm, and from my customers. That precipitated the divorce.

As she did in insisting on meeting in a very public place, Laura displayed an admirable amount of strength and independence when, in response to her sister's suggestion that she move away from her home to Cape Cod, she answered, "Why should I? I did nothing wrong."

Jane was a tall, soft-spoken woman whose clear, makeup-free face was reminiscent of the flower children of the 1970s. Now, it was beginning to show signs of stress and aging. Fidgeting with her Diet Coke, she reflected on clues that she failed to pick up on before her marriage.

We were going on a trip and had two heavy suitcases. He told me to carry them, and took nothing himself. He walked ahead while I was dragging these bags. Looking back at that I realize that was the first hint that something was wrong. His sister told me he was selfish, but I didn't listen; I thought she was really rude to say that. He would blame me for things his parents had done, and I would blame myself.

Avital welcomed me into the large, beautifully decorated home that she shares with her second husband. She moved quickly and calmly around her kitchen to make us tea, and seemed at ease in her surroundings. Her effortlessness contrasted with the circumstances of her first marriage.

At first I didn't recognize what was happening. After we got married, it was like he didn't want to socialize at all. He tried to cut me off from my family. He tried to minimize contact with cousins I was very close with. If we were invited places, he'd say, "I'll give you a choice, I'll go to this one or that one, but I won't go to both." We were always arguing. It was absurd. There was no social life. At the end I would go out with friends, with other couples.

He would start to put me down for stupid things, like I would forget to bring his shirts to the cleaner. He once said to me, "You're always vacuuming and you think you're so fucking clean, you need to take the attachment and go along the edges. You're not getting the edges." He would call me a "lying, fucking cunt."

When I started to get involved with *Hadassah,* he was threatened. He would tell me I don't have the kind of money to be with those women, that I don't fit in. He told me I should be grateful that he wasn't out drinking or cheating on me.

It's interesting. I had the courage to speak up but not to leave. I never took it lying down, but it took me ten years of this marriage to leave.

Words can leave deeper scars than slaps.

A flashily dressed Stacy drove a distance to meet me in a bookstore café.

For a long time I knew something was wrong, but I didn't know what it was. Then, a friend gave me a book about verbal abuse. I had been going to counseling thinking I was the problem.

Chaya, too, didn't quite recognize what was happening to her. A petite, dark-haired woman with an old-fashioned eastern European beauty, she described her realization to me in such a way that indicated she was still surprised by the unexpectedness of the revelation.

I thought I must be provoking him. I didn't even realize I was being abused until I read an article in a magazine discussing domestic abuse. I was pregnant with my second kid, and I realized, "Oh, that's what this is. We're not just fighting. He's abusing me."

These women's experiences are not unique. One topic that came up over and over again throughout the interviews was that the women did not realize they were being abused. All but two told me that they didn't possess the words to describe what they were experiencing. Part of this misunderstanding is a failure of communication on the part of the very organizations that print the posters that hang in women's rest rooms across the country. The word *battering* to them meant blood and broken bones, not hurtful and demeaning words. Until it became physical, they described their experience with expressions such as "the ground kept shifting under me" and "I just knew that I always felt bad."

Too many people believe that if bruising, bleeding, and broken bones aren't involved, then it can't be abuse. However, as virtually every woman in this study sample told me, "The psychological abuse was much worse than almost anything he could have done physically." Nevertheless, lest anybody think that physical abuse does not occur in Jewish families, think again. Paula's experience shows us that this belief is simply not true.

We didn't have curtains or blinds on the windows for ten years because when he would get angry, he ripped the blinds. He threw things, swept the table clean. One day he pointed his rifle at my head and said he would shoot me.

Diane was a tall, thin woman with a quiet voice that spoke with firm resolve. Although not Jewish herself, she was married for twenty-two years to a Jewish professor at a local college, and raised her children as Jews. She explains her horrific experience with abuse almost as if it had happened to somebody else.

One Saturday evening I was getting ready for grocery shopping, which I always did on Sunday mornings. My husband's car was parked behind mine, so I asked him to move it so that we wouldn't have to do it in the morning. He became enraged, and began to beat me, forcing me to the floor, insisting over and over that I admit that I just wanted to make things more convenient for myself. He continued to hit me and kick me, and blocked my way out the door. My daughter shouted to me, "Mom, run to a neighbor and get help." My husband then shouted to one of the boys, "Stuff a rag down your sister's throat." He began to strangle me, still shouting at me. The police arrived just as I was beginning to fade. I was losing consciousness. I really thought I was going to die.

It was my twelve-year-old daughter telling me, her mother, the one who is supposed to be protecting her, to get help, that [made me realize] this had gone too far. I had to get out.

We can see from Diane's story that children can be harmed immeasurably by witnessing abuse. Her sons identified with their father and participated in the abuse, but her daughter helped her by, in effect, waking her up.

Avital managed to break free after half as many years of marriage, but her situation illustrates a parent-child influence just as strong.

At one point I was physically threatened. We had split up everything and there were these suitcases I had bought. I had the smaller one inside the larger one. I didn't give him one of those suitcases. I gave him some other ones because I really liked these, and he came back and said he was entitled to them. My daughter witnessed this. He had his

hands to my throat and said, "Are you going to tell me where the fucking suitcases are?" I told him, "No, I'm not." And I got up and called
911. And then he left. My daughter, who was six at the time, said,
"Why didn't you give him the suitcases?" And I said, "Because
they're not his and people can't just come in and take what they want
just because they rough you up."

I met Judith on a bright, sunny Sunday morning. Sitting at a pleasant
sidewalk café listening to her absorbing story, the busy traffic whizzing by
faded into mere background noise. She was the youngest and least educated of all the women in the study, with only a high school diploma and a
year of Israeli *yeshiva* learning.

After a week of verbal abuse, he came after me with full physical force.
He broke my jaw. I still have tendon and nerve damage. My husband
threatened to break my mother's legs and burn down her house.

The survivors spoke in even tones and calm voices in the recitation of
their experiences. Only a few times did I see overt displays of emotion. At
first I was a bit surprised at their collective composure, but on reflection I
realized what had happened. Although they had endured living nightmares, these women got out. They had survived. Even if their divorces were
not yet finalized, and despite the persistent anxiety over finances and child
custody their abusers caused, they were happier than they had been in their
marriages. They had rescued themselves and their children and were feeling empowered in their newfound freedom from abuse. But, did the Jewish
community help these women to rescue themselves?

I want to address one point before we get into the survey results. Two
people familiar with my research took issue with my use of the word survivor to describe the women presented in these pages. They felt strongly
that the term should be reserved for survivors of the *shoah*, the Holocaust. I
would like to take this space to respond to their concerns. Many of the
women referred to themselves as survivors. These Jewish women I met suffered mightily at the hands of their husbands, the people in whom they had
placed their trust and faith, and with whom they had taken vows under the
huppah, the wedding canopy, to love, honor, and cherish. Their trust was

shattered, and in some cases, their bones. Unfortunately, some of these women were victimized a second time, not by an outside enemy, but by their own established Jewish communities. These communities should have been there for them, but instead, either through ignorance, fear, or outright hostility, worked against them. That these women were able to find the courage to admit that there was a problem, leave all that was familiar, and summon the strength to make new lives for themselves and their children, is testament to their survivor attitude.

One of the advantages of doing an exploratory study is that, as the research protocol progresses, new and previously unanticipated topics come up in the course of conversation. In the case of this study, some of the most valuable information acquired came from chance remarks that triggered new series of questions. I have presented these serendipitous findings where appropriate to provide greater insight into the community experience of abused Jewish women. And, now, the results of the survey questions.

Did you speak to a rabbi about the abuse you were experiencing? Why?

Only half of the women I interviewed did speak to a rabbi, and in all cases they spoke to the rabbi at their own congregation. This percentage is high compared to that of the Jewish Women International data, which reports that only 10 percent of the women it surveyed sought help from rabbis.[4] It is important to note here that not all the women reported to the rabbis that they were being physically abused, even if they were. For example, while doing interviews preliminary to developing the questions for this main study, I spoke with Judy. A friendly, outgoing sprite of a woman carrying a terrible secret, Judy did not care for her own rabbi, so she made an appointment to speak with another, prominent rabbi in a nearby town. She went to his office seeking counsel, but did not tell him that she was being abused, both emotionally and physically. She was hoping that he would somehow divine her reason for being in his office and offer help; she was disappointed when he did not.

I saw this pattern of nondisclosure repeated over and over when women would seek help from either rabbis or counselors, but neglect to be open with them. As Yehudit learned from her experience, "Rabbis aren't psychic. You have to tell them what's going on." On the other hand, rabbis must be aware that abuse is a problem in their communities and should ask outright if their congregants are experiencing it.

Among the reasons they gave for contacting their rabbis, the women cited strong ties to their synagogue and to Judaism. Barbara said she felt that she was going through a major life event and that Judaism should have something to say about it. Other women cited the rabbi's personality, saying he was easy to talk to, and another felt safe with her rabbi and thought he would be able to help her without going to police. Two women contacted their rabbis only after leaving their husbands. Jane went at the suggestion of a friend, and Chaya told me, "It never occurred to me to go to anything but an Orthodox rabbi." Karen told me that she was "clueless" about what a rabbi could offer, and only went after her husband left the house but continued his abusive behavior. Paula approached her Reform rabbi because she knew that he had counseling experience from his years as a social worker prior to joining the rabbinate.

All but one of the women I interviewed had been in therapy, some for many years and with multiple counselors, but found that they were "getting nowhere" and needed to speak with someone who would both understand abuse and believe their stories. They thought that the rabbi would be the person to believe them and to help.

Why not?

Of the other half of the sample who did not speak to a rabbi, two women were unaffiliated with a congregation, making their choice not to seek rabbinical counsel understandable. Both of these women said that it would never have occurred to them to seek the help of a rabbi, and one said that she did not find the Jewish community welcoming.

However, of much greater interest are the other nine women who were affiliated with synagogues. Why did they not contact their rabbis for help? Avital told me, "I couldn't relate to the rabbi's personality, and I didn't see him as a skilled counselor. I really didn't think he could help." Luckily for Avital, a woman in her daughter's play group noticed something wrong with both her daughter's behavior and Avital's own demeanor.

Naomi told me, "I was scared. I didn't think of the rabbi as someone who could help." Yehudit said, "I'm not sure why I didn't go. I guess I didn't think it was part of [the rabbi's] job." Jill attributed her not asking for help to the "stigma, the shame, the blame. I had fought for five years to marry him. My parents did not care for his family. Then they finally gave up. I had to own the choice of the marriage." Laura described herself as the "queen of denial" in thinking her marriage was "no more problematic than others."

Judith's rabbi, on the other hand, took charge and got her the help she needed. Judith, unlike so many abused women, had a loving family, a supportive rabbi, and a lawyer who made house calls.

Tammy, a tall and strikingly attractive blond social worker, went to the *mikveh,* ritual bath, prior to her marriage to a prominent physician, and there developed a friendship with the superintendent. The *mikveh* requires a full immersion in water prior to marriage and every month after a woman's menstrual flow has ceased. The woman is naked, and must submit to inspection by the female superintendent to ensure that nothing impedes the water from reaching every part of the body. Tammy went to her friend when she could no longer tolerate the physical abuse in her marriage.

The *"mikveh* lady" is a potential source of rescue for the women who regularly use the ritual bath. Victims cannot hide their cuts and bruises from her. The Jewish community has an ideal opportunity, and indeed a responsibility, to train her to deal with situations involving physical abuse. (Unfortunately, although some community members agree with putting posters advertising help for abuse victims in the *mikveh,* a few rabbis and other communal leaders told me that they didn't want to interfere with a woman's "enjoyment" of the experience.)

Perhaps the biggest reason women did not go to their rabbis was that, prior to separation or divorce, not one had ever heard her own rabbi give a sermon on the topic of violence in the home. As Charlotte told me, "If I had heard him say something, then I would have known that what I was experiencing was not right. It would have validated what I was feeling. As it was, I felt so alone. I just knew I didn't feel good."

Many women reported that they felt their rabbis did not, or would not, believe their stories of abuse. In fact, many abusers are *machers,* or prominent men, in their communities, both secular and religious. They are respected by their clients, patients, and customers. They earn substantial livings and are very often generous to community institutions, including their synagogues. As Weitzman notes in her work on abuse in upscale marriages, well-heeled abusers are often charming to the outside world. Their behavior in the arena outside the home makes it difficult for rabbis, and the community at large, to believe that they could be capable of violence.[5]

Many of the husbands under discussion here were just such upscale men. They had used their brains and their charm to reach great professional heights. In view of perpetually strained synagogue finances, a rabbi might, correctly or not, tend to downplay a woman's concerns.

If you spoke to a rabbi, what was the rabbi's response? How did you feel about this response?

Six of the ten rabbis consulted by these survivors responded in what I would call a positive manner, whether the response was as simple as being sympathetic and supportive, or as hands-on as providing the names of support groups and professionals with experience in dealing with abuse problems. The women from these rabbis' congregations felt that their responses were "terrific, much more than I expected," "wonderful," "excellent, even though I got no concrete assistance." This last comment surprised me. The simple act of listening was enough to validate this woman's experience and provide moral support for the difficult decisions she would have to make to escape her marriage.

Debbie's rabbi told her bluntly, "Whatever you do, you cannot go back." As she recalled the encounter, she said, "God bless him. He really kept me on the straight and narrow. He was terrific."

Diane went to her Conservative rabbi when it became apparent that she needed help with not only her husband, but with her sons, who were acting out in inappropriate and violent ways. The rabbi was unable to gain compliance from the sons or support from the husband. However, when a new rabbi came to Diane's synagogue, she found tremendous help.

> The rabbi and his wife came with me to the emergency room, and stayed with me and my daughter there. They were very supportive. Then they came with us to the police department. The police asked me if I wanted to file a restraining order, and the rabbi stayed with me while I did. Then he came back to the house with me while I got the two youngest children, the kids' clothes and their school bags, and he stayed with me the whole time. Then he rode back with me to his house, where we stayed for two nights. They helped to find us a place to stay.

Despite the unseasonably hot June day, a delightful cross-breeze cooled us as we sat drinking coffee in the well-appointed kitchen of Karen's expansive, superbly decorated home. Although not particularly active in her Reform temple until that point, she approached her rabbi after her husband had left the house. Despite having a restraining order, he continued to harass her by telephone.

> I went to the rabbi with trepidation, and was actually surprised. I had an impression of her as being cold, almost arrogant, but she was extremely supportive. She sent me to a support group and gave me strategies to deal with my husband. She referred me to a tax professional who specializes in abuse cases. She gave me names and numbers of support groups. The best thing was a mentor connection. The rabbi set me up with somebody who had already gone through a divorce. She was there to lend support.

Unfortunately, four of the women who contacted rabbis reported disturbing responses to their pleas for help. Laura, upon learning of her husband's embezzlement and impending criminal trial, filed for divorce. Due to the precarious nature of her family's finances, she applied to her Reform temple for an abatement of her dues. The temple refused her. Laura recalled, "My synagogue was demeaning me in my request. I felt as if my religion was failing me." While a rabbi probably does not sit on the finance committee, he or she most certainly could have intervened on behalf of a member in trouble.

Chaya's experience with several rabbis made me wonder why she would even remain affiliated at all with the Jewish community.

> Very late into my experience after I had already gotten a restraining order against my husband, that's when I spoke to a rabbi. I really went to three. I didn't really want to go, to tell the honest truth. I had a strong sense that rabbis wouldn't be very sympathetic to me. I grew up in the Orthodox community, so I expected this kind of treatment. People were urging me to go to them, so I went, but not because I wanted to. I don't think they are at the level where they can deal honestly and fairly with women in general but with these kinds of women in particular.
>
> First I went to synagogue [X] because my husband immediately ran to [the rabbi] there. He knew he'd find a home there. He was no

help. The other was a Lubavitch rabbi who my friend thought would be helpful—not. The third was from the *beit din* [the Jewish court], when I needed my *get* [Jewish divorce decree], which I was able to achieve.

I've cut myself off from the Orthodox now.

All three of them knew about the abuse before I got there, one because my husband ran to him. On the surface they said, "Oh, no, you can't stay with him. You know we don't condone this." But they were really insensitive, they don't get it.

Here's an example. When I went to the Lubavitch rabbi, he asked me how old I was. At the time I was thirty-nine. His reaction was, like, "Oh, no, you'll never get remarried." It was very offensive.

Another rabbi would go off and on being sensitive and then insensitive. I'd tell him that I really thought my husband was trying to kill me—he *was* trying to kill me, my abuse was brutal, both physical and psychological, and the rabbi would say, "You mustn't defame anybody's character. We're all going to die." I said, "Yes, but I don't want to die now. I don't want to be murdered."

I completely expected this; I was not surprised.

The worst thing which I have never recovered from had to do with my kids. They were in [a Jewish day school] and when this came to light the principal, who is a rabbi, engaged in such psychological warfare against my son it was a nightmare. Eventually they suspended him.

At this point I asked, "They suspended the rabbi?"

Oh, no, of course they wouldn't suspend the rabbi. They [the school] suspended my son indefinitely. They [the administration] wouldn't go near him [the rabbi].

Once it [the abuse and the divorce] came to light I decided to tell them what was going on. The social worker was there and I asked them just to give him a break, to give him some time to get over this. They tormented my son; they would drag him out in the middle of *tefillot* [prayers] and say, "Just because your father is like this doesn't mean you can be." Eventually he just cracked up and they suspended him permanently. I put him in public school and he didn't have one bad day. He's an honor student, he's on the dean's list; he's a great, beautiful kid.

My little guy, a year after they threw my big one out, they threw him out, saying, "He's too stupid, we don't want him here."

I had to tell you that story because that killed me. That killed me. I knew that they would be jerks to me. I didn't expect them to attack my kids. And, I just couldn't be a part of the Jewish community after that. I sort of tried, but I just couldn't.

Chaya's brief reference to the *get* points out a unique problem faced by Jewish women. The divorce decree is essential to a complete Jewish divorce, but it is under the control of the husband. If he refuses to give the *get*, then the woman is considered an *agunah*, a chained woman. She can neither remarry nor have legitimate children. Withholding the *get* is just another form of manipulation and control by the abusive husband. Other than a small nucleus of activist rabbis, the established rabbinic community has done little to move forward on the issue. If for no other reason than facilitating procurement of the *get*, the Jewish community should be involved in the campaign against spousal abuse.

After years of unsuccessful therapy, Jane went to see her rabbi at her large Conservative synagogue. She went at the suggestion of a close friend who knew that she had not been happy with the counselors she had seen.

At first, the rabbi was very nice when he met with me; he was supportive, although he still didn't recognize that [what I was telling him] was abuse. We met once or twice and he recommended a counselor. When we were meeting with the rabbi for our son's bar mitzvah, he sided with my husband. I called the rabbi after he [my husband] punched my son, but he didn't believe me. He never once followed up with a phone call to see how we were doing. I felt terrible. I cried. My husband increased his participation in the synagogue because of the rabbi's attentions. I don't feel I can go there any longer. My son won't go. My children are being driven away. The High Holidays are coming up and I don't know if I can step foot in that building.

Reizel continues to suffer the emotional and financial manipulations of her alcoholic ex-husband. She described to me how her former rabbi responded when she told him what was happening at home. She recalled that, at first, he failed to respond at all and chose to side with her husband, who happened also to be a rabbi. Then, his response became an act of malignant neglect.

> One night my husband wanted to make a *kiddush* [blessing over the wine] for *Shavuos* [a Jewish holiday that occurs seven weeks after Passover, in the spring], but there was not enough wine. He threw the bottle. I went to the rabbi's house with my kids, but then I decided I would not be thrown out of my own house, so I went back. He hit my oldest daughter and threatened to kill the kids. I told them to call the police, and he beat me. Nobody could stop him—the nanny, the kids. The police came. I walked to *shul* [synagogue] and called out to the rabbi, "Look at me!" I was bleeding. The rabbi walked away from me. I went back home and locked the door, and then I bought a gun.

Every time I read these words I feel chills run up my spine. Along with the description of Chaya's experience, it paints a disturbing picture of rabbi-congregant interaction.

Did the rabbi refer you to a shelter? Did you go to a shelter?

Not one of the women who consulted a rabbi was referred to a shelter by that rabbi. However, several women from the total sample did try to contact hotlines, shelters, or both on their own, although none ever did ultimately stay in one. "It's not for me," one woman told me bluntly. This reaction to the prospect of shelter living is not unusual. In talks with the directors of two battered women's service providers in central and western Massachusetts, one told me that she does not recall ever having seen Jewish women at her agency, and in fact had only seen one middle-class woman at all. The other director recalled having seen a few Jewish women as outpatient clients, but never in the shelter.

One alarming finding was that several of the women tried to call shelters but got no return calls, despite repeated attempts at multiple agencies. Was it merely a coincidence that nobody was staffing the telephones when these women happened to call? Or, was this a case like that presented by

Weitzman, in which her upscale abuse victims encountered active rejection by hotline and shelter personnel because they were perceived to have money?[6] Whether shelters consciously choose not to serve middle- and upper-middle-class women is not a question for this study, but it is definitely one that should be addressed by the providers of services to battered women. Whether most Jewish women would or would not go to a shelter is irrelevant. If they call a hotline for help, they should at least be given the courtesy of a return call.

Chaya spoke for the survivors who suffered similar indignities, whether in dealing with shelters and hotlines, or in retaining legal advice.

> People forget that even if they're wealthy, their husbands have all the money. The women are cash-strapped. And they're usually being harassed by their husbands.

While some women went to family or friends, most remained in their own homes, relying on the power of a restraining order to keep their abusers at bay. However, as a number of judges, lawyers, and police detectives have told me directly, "Restraining orders are only as good as the paper they are written on." Although some of the women described their ex-husbands as being afraid of authority and compliant with the criminal justice system, others described repeated violations of restraining orders, including violent physical assault.

Sarah told me that, in her desperation to flee her husband, she tried to get into a shelter but was turned away because her son was over twelve and was considered a danger to the younger children there. At the hospital where Diane was treated, emergency room personnel called a shelter on her behalf. The shelter staff wanted her to stay away from her job and to take her children out of their schools. This, Diane felt, would have been too disruptive given the upheaval already in their lives. Instead, she fled the state to stay with friends.

Rivka, whom we meet below, was lucky to have her family nearby.

> One night when [my husband] was coming over in an enraged state, we fled. One of my kids was about nine or so, and he left his shoes at home because I said to the kids, "Quickly, we've gotta get out of here,

Daddy's coming and he's very angry." And the kids were great, they didn't argue with me, they just literally dropped whatever they were doing and this kid walked out of the house without his shoes. This same child is now fourteen and keeps a pair of shoes at the back door just in case we have to run again.

Did the rabbi refer you to a counselor?

Five of the women reported that their rabbis did refer them to counselors, although for general marital problems, not for abuse-related issues. Two rabbis did not refer because they knew the women already had arranged for therapy on their own, although one did suggest that the woman's children get counseling.

Virtually every woman I spoke with did go to counseling, whether recommended by her rabbi or not. They tried a variety of therapeutic styles, from individual psychotherapy to couples counseling to group therapy. None of the counseling seemed to have helped the women, their husbands, or the relationship, according to those who participated. Although this is admittedly a biased sample of women who have chosen to leave their abusers, I believe it demonstrates a void in therapists' training in distinguishing abusive relationships from simple marital problems. Rivka tried "as many as ten different therapists," both alone and as a couple. During couples counseling, her husband manipulated the sessions, blaming her for incidents in which he was at fault, and, at one point, instructing the therapist to "lower her [Rivka's] self-esteem." It wasn't until Rivka wound up in the emergency room after a particularly brutal beating that the medical staff person told Rivka that her husband was abusive. "It was the first time somebody had ever said that to me. Every other therapist I had spoken to had said, 'He's not abusive. He's just an angry man.'"

Because the only specifically Jewish counseling program in existence in Massachusetts is in Newton, a suburb of Boston, Judith expressed frustration that she had no access to it. "I was so emotionally tired, exhausted. You're so rock-bottom going through this, too tired to do anything. Having a satellite branch of the counseling service would have been so helpful to me."

Avital tried for years to get her husband to agree to attend counseling with her.

He wouldn't go to marital counseling. He was thinking that the counselor was going to blame him and that was too threatening. Finally he did go to an individual counselor, but I didn't see any changes. And the [counselor] was Jewish, but I didn't see any changes.

In the end, although the couple did go to counseling together, Avital realized it was too late. She wanted out of the marriage.

Jane describes her experience with counseling, an all too typical one in which the husband may agree to attend, but with a hidden agenda.

In the third year of our marriage he agreed to come to marriage counseling with me because, as he said, I had a problem and he would go to straighten me out.

Did the rabbi refer you to a lawyer?

Only three women were referred to lawyers by their rabbis. This result is not surprising, given rabbis' traditional preference for keeping the family together. Rabbis would consider a lawyer to be the last resort for a troubled marriage.

Did the rabbi provide spiritual counseling?

The response to this question perhaps surprised me most of all. Only four rabbis provided anything resembling spiritual counseling, according to the women who consulted them. When we look at the rabbis' responses, we will see that, because they do not feel sufficiently trained in counseling, they prefer to refer to professional therapists and agencies. They often express discomfort in dealing with abuse. However, considering that rabbis are the spiritual leaders of their congregations, why is it that they did not at least provide counseling in the area in which they supposedly do have training? As Barbara told me, "The situation had moral aspects. I am a Jew. The temple is a Jewish institution, and this [abuse and divorce] is a major life change. I wanted to let the support people [at the temple] know my situation. I needed support."

Did the rabbi tell you to leave your husband?

Only three women reported that their rabbis advised them to leave their husbands, while five specifically did not. Chaya consulted three different rabbis, each of whom gave conflicting advice.

Psychiatrist and rabbi Dr. Abraham Twerski, author of the breakthrough book *The Shame Borne in Silence*, has devoted a significant part of his career to helping Orthodox Jewish clients deal with abusive marriages. He writes that too many rabbis counsel their female congregants to return to their husbands in a tragic misunderstanding of the concept of *shalom bayit*, peace in the home.[7] As we discussed earlier, *shalom bayit* is a major tenet of Judaism and has traditionally been the purview of women. It has been credited with keeping the Jewish family strong and persevering through centuries of persecution. However, the notion conflicts directly with the precept of *pikuah nefesh*, the saving of a life. *Pikuah nefesh* takes precedence over all other commandments in the Jewish faith. Twerski says that rabbis should support a woman's obligation to save her own life and those of her children.

Do you have children?

Only three of the twenty-two women in the sample did not have children. However, of the three, only one woman left her marriage in less than a year. Of the other two, one stayed for three years, and the second remained nine years before leaving her abuser. Jane told me, "It would have been so easy to leave in the beginning when we had no children." Of course, she didn't leave. This unusual brand of loyalty typically brings up the question among laypeople, "Why did she stay?" As one lay leader active in domestic violence advocacy in Boston replied to that question, "The more appropriate question should be, 'Why didn't he stop beating her?'"

Virtually every woman with whom I spoke was afraid to uproot her children and worried that she could not support herself and them. These women initially believed that they would leave "after the children are gone" but admitted that, upon reflection, staying was worse for the children. That understanding is what ultimately led them to leave.

Many of the women I met were themselves orphans, only children, or estranged from their families. Evidence indicates that abusers seek out women fitting this profile so that the cumulative effects of their abusive behaviors and limiting of social networks makes it that much more difficult for abuse victims to find emotional support and, therefore, to leave.[8] And, as became evident from Reizel's story, the general Jewish community may intensify the isolating effect by "circling the wagons" against the abuse victim. She told me, "Even the rabbis' wives would ignore me and say, 'A bad marriage is better than no marriage.'" So, we see that the need for an abuse victim to belong to a community can in a sense serve as a prison, just as her abusive marriage does.

Other women also experienced exclusion by their communities. Chaya recalled, "On *Shabbes*, after *shul*, I found myself walking home alone. People avoided me. They wouldn't even make eye contact. People I thought were my friends ignored me." Judith, after experiencing kind and supportive help from her rabbi, found the congregants in her Orthodox synagogue judgmental and alienating. She left the synagogue of her youth to join a Lubavitch *shul*.

Were you aware of a Jewish support group in your area?

The overwhelming majority of the women were not aware of a Jewish support group in their area, and for good reason. *Kol Isha,* housed at the Jewish Family and Children's Service (JFCS) in suburban Boston, is a very recent addition to the social service scene in the area and is the only Jewish-community-funded group. Receiving only enough money to provide part-time staff, it offers counseling and referral services, as well as support groups for victims of abuse. Neither the Jewish communities of central Massachusetts nor the Berkshires have such support groups.

Were you aware of a Jewish shelter in your area?

Although one woman mistakenly believed that there was a shelter specifically targeted to Jewish women in the suburban Boston area, there isn't a single one in all of New England. Virtually all the women in the study, however, told me that they would seriously have considered going to a specifically Jewish safe house if one were available. As mentioned previously, Jewish women tend not to go to shelters, and there are several reasons for their reluctance. First, the vast majority of women who seek haven in a nondenominational battered women's shelter are from a different socioeconomic and ethnic profile. It is understandable that Jewish women, and middle-class women in general, would feel uncomfortable there. Indeed, every woman in my study expressed great discomfort with the idea of shelter living. Group living arrangements are far removed from their experience. To uproot them from the familiar and bring them to a vastly different culture would be difficult in the best of circumstances. In their desperate straits, it would cause great emotional upheaval.

Were you aware of a Jewish counseling program in your area, and if so, who operates it?

Both Boston and central Massachusetts have family services programs, although, as mentioned, only Boston has a program specifically designed for abuse victims, *Kol Isha*. The Jewish Family Service (JFS) of Worcester expressed interest in offering a support group for abuse victims, although it did not offer anything at the time of the interviews. Unfortunately, fewer than half the women were aware of the Jewish-sponsored counseling services in their areas, and only six of those women knew under whose auspices they operated.

Stacy attempted to get help from a series of counselors, although not from a Jewish-sponsored agency. Her words echo those of many other women who participated in therapy with their husbands, expressing great dissatisfaction with the therapists themselves.

> He would not go. Finally he did, but he could not control his verbally abusive behavior. We went to several counselors for about six months each. There was no change in his behavior. The problem with couples counseling is that men tend not to speak up so the counselors all tend to bend over backwards to accommodate them. He dug in his heels, and got worse.

Many of the survivors I interviewed complained that their counselors "don't get" the problem of abuse, and indeed, from my discussions with experts in the field of domestic violence, it appears that they perceive the situation correctly. Marital therapists consulted by the women in this study often appeared to assume automatically that the couples' problems stemmed from communication issues. They did not ask specifically about abuse in the marriage. Although it is true, as mentioned before, that a few of the women I spoke with never mentioned the physical abuse occurring in their marriages, they did speak of verbal and emotional abuse. This information should have sent up red flags to the counselors. Several interviewees stated that their counselors should be trained to ask outright whether abuse was occurring. Both professional associations and graduate programs should include specific abuse awareness and treatment training in their curricula so professionals and students can learn to read the signs of abuse.

Weitzman confessed in her book that she was surprised and shocked to discover that a young, attractive couple that came to her for marital counseling was involved in an abusive relationship. They didn't fit the image, according to Weitzman's own description. It wasn't until the wife came on her own later with her story of suffering that Weitzman realized that she had fallen for the stereotype of abuse not happening "to people like us." To Weitzman's credit, this experience impelled her to conduct her own research study, which has educated thousands about abuse in upscale marriages.[9]

Twerski urges counselors to separate a couple in therapy to discover if abuse is occurring. He writes that, too often, those who provide counsel keep the couple together for the entire session. If the counselor fails to separate the couple, he or she will likely not learn of the abuse. If the victim does speak up about the abuse she is suffering, it is highly likely that, upon returning home from the appointment, her husband will punish her.[10] Tammy reported attending joint couples counseling only to be beaten by her husband after each appointment. That same husband was charming for the therapist in the counseling sessions that had ended only minutes before.

That so many women in this sample did not approach their rabbis is disturbing. That so many of those who did seek help found a cold response and worse is profoundly sad. That so many found their therapists unable or unwilling to confront the problems of abusive relationships is deeply troubling.

I believe it is a combination of ignorance and blindness that exacerbates the issue of domestic violence in the Jewish community—ignorance of the facts and blind faith in the mythology of the Jewish husband. Victims of spousal abuse are desperately searching for validation of their experiences, and for a helping hand in getting out. They need to be met halfway with knowledgeable, caring, and trustworthy people.

Along with all the variations of abuse, Jewish women must cope with issues, such as that of the *get*, that women of other religions do not face. Jewish women need counsel and advice that view the issues through a Jewish lens. It is the responsibility of the Jewish community to educate its leaders and its constituents about the scourge of domestic violence and how to treat its victims.

The Jewish people have long depended on the foundation of the family for its strength. By ignoring facts and turning our backs on the victims of abuse, we perpetuate a dangerous myth that imperils future generations. The research literature has shown that children who grow up in abusive homes are far more likely to become abusers themselves. The tiny Jewish nation cannot afford to lose more of its people, especially at its own hand.

The issues surrounding domestic violence are complex and are not for deep discussion here. There are dozens of books on library and bookstore shelves describing individual women's struggles with abuse, research attempting to understand the reasons that men abuse, and programs to try to deal with abuse and its effects.

Now that we have heard from real women about their experiences with abuse, we can see that, although there are similarities, there are also many manifestations of that abuse. The survivors we have met were worn down by years of belittling and demeaning words, controlling behavior, and, often, financial blackmail. They were kept from their friends and family. They were told how to dress, when to wear makeup, and how much. They were informed that they were stupid and incompetent, and after a while, they began to believe what they were told. What's more, many were threatened, punched, cut, and strangled. In the next chapter we will learn more about the various forms that spousal abuse can take and why it is often misunderstood.

2

"WIFE BEATING IS A THING NOT DONE IN ISRAEL"[1]

THE MYTH OF *SHALOM BAYIT*

PAULA COMPOSED THESE WORDS AS PART OF A LONGER PIECE SHE read at a community vigil against domestic violence. She asked me to share it with my readers.

> Words hurt. Abusive words, profanity stings like the smarting of a yellow jacket's tail, piercing your skin. Actions are fearsome—a large, broadly framed spouse as compared to his slight wife, looking down upon her, his fiery eyes voicing, as the words resound in my fearful ears, "I could have made pulp out of you in a minute. You know that." Sometimes I wish he would. Sometimes getting bloody would at least, maybe, get the attention of a blue-uniformed policeman.

> We cringe when we read newspaper accounts of the beatings inflicted on women if they disagree with their husbands. We are repulsed to hear on the evening news that abuse has reached the ultimate point. And, when the name of the batterer is Cohen or Levy, we are ashamed and defensive and, often, in denial. "This doesn't happen among our people," we say. And, sometimes, we even say, "She must have provoked him," as if burned pasta could explain away Laura Jane Rosenthal's dismembered body.

Survivor Linda's response, below, to the possibility of spousal abuse among Jews is typical and fits with Weitzman's findings on societal perceptions of abuse among upscale families.[2]

> I didn't think of myself as a battered woman. I didn't even know the term. Every once in a while you'd see a story in the newspaper of those kinds of things, but I always attributed it to people who might be in some different socioeconomic class or who might be inner-city drunks coming home beating their wives. I was completely clueless about that stuff.

The most obvious form of abuse is that of actual physical battering. In fact, if you ask most people, they will tell you that spousal abuse consists of beating, punching, and other actions that cause physical harm, because that is what we read about in the newspapers.

Linda did experience physical abuse on several occasions. In the following account, she describes the particularly bizarre ways in which her husband assaulted her.

> I was in a lot of pain [as the result of a back injury], and I had to move very, very carefully. Any small, wrong movement could send huge lightning-bolt sheets of pain. I remember walking up a long flight of stairs . . . and we were about halfway up and he's behind me and he kept poking me in a way that was producing those bolts of pain. The only thing I could think was that I was going to fall down these stairs. I'm not going to make it up to the top. And I kept saying, "Don't do that." For whatever reason, he kept doing it. It was a joke to him.
>
> Another time, we were having an argument. We had gone to [the grocery store]. We were in the parking lot around 8:30. It was in the winter and I wasn't really dressed very warmly; we had just popped in the car to get something. He went into the store and I was in the car waiting. I didn't have the car keys; I was in the passenger seat. He had taken the keys with him. It was cold and I'm waiting for him to come out, and I'm waiting and I'm waiting. And the store closes and I'm still waiting and I'm still waiting. I don't know what's going on. He must have left me there for an hour. I was freezing. This was the dead of winter. It was just crazy. He wanted to teach me a lesson, to make a point.

To understand abuse, it is important that we work from the same basic definitions. Therefore, some descriptions, provided by the National Violence Against Women (NVAW) Survey, which in turn adapted terms from the National Family Survey,[3] the National Women's Study, and the Violence Against Women in Canada Survey, as well as the Conflict Tactics Scale, are included below. We should note here that the NVAW Survey did not look at Jews when they considered minorities. We can only extrapolate their findings from the general population to the smaller one.

Physical assault is defined as "behaviors that threaten, attempt, or actually inflict physical harm." Specific operational definitions of physical assault include the following behaviors as uncovered in the questions, "Did any other adult, male or female, ever . . .

Throw something at you that could hurt?
Push, grab, or shove you?
Pull your hair?
Slap or hit you?
Choke or attempt to drown you?
Hit you with some object?
Beat you up?
Use a gun on you?
Use a knife or other weapon on you?
Threaten you with a gun?
Threaten you with a knife or other weapon?"[4]

Most of these behaviors are what people normally consider physical assault. However, note the final two items on the list. It is encouraging to see that those academic and government agencies involved in studying abuse recognize that there is an overlap between the physical and psychological aspects of abuse. Although the abuser is not technically battering a victim when threatening with a gun or knife, the fear engendered in that victim by threats of violence is so pronounced that it is considered under the heading of physical assault.

For many women, an abuser's threat to hurt them is as powerful a weapon as is the actual act and can in fact predict it. Hedin and Janson studied pregnant women in Sweden.[5] Almost one-quarter of these women re-

ported threats or actual acts of violence at the hands of their intimate partners, or both. The authors found that both "moderate" and "serious" threats
correlated highly with the actual execution of violent acts. Therefore, a victim can rightfully expect that a violent incident could follow a threat.

Among the women in my study, I heard several accounts of threats.
Paula told me that her husband pointed a rifle at her while they were out
hunting. He also threatened to "snap her like a twig" and "beat her to a
pulp." Diane's husband met her at the door with a butcher knife when she
was late returning from an art class.

Sarah told me about a "game" her husband liked to play to frighten her.
"He had this stupid flare gun that would shoot off a flare to get help. He
used to threaten me with that. He used to say it would blow a hole through
me if he ever shot me with it."

Another form of physical abuse is one that surprises many who hear of
it. While most people have come to acknowledge that sexual violence is yet
another form of control and dominance by the rapist against his victim,
there has been a long-held assumption that rape does not occur within the
bonds of matrimony. A husband, after all, is entitled to sex, whether or not
his wife wants to participate. Yet, the NVAW Survey defines rape as "an
event that occurred *without the victim's consent* [italics mine], that involved
the use or threat of force to penetrate the victim's vagina or anus by penis,
tongue, fingers, or object, or the victim's mouth by penis."[6] Therefore, even
if committed against a wife, it is still rape. It is also against Jewish law, as we
will learn more about later.

Many of the women with whom I spoke told me of their own experiences with marital rape. As Sarah described it, "There was one other piece
to the abuse. It was a sexual piece; it's hard to talk about. For one thing he
would rape me frequently, and for another it turned him on to hit me as a
prelude to sex. And he always told me that there was something wrong with
me that I didn't like that."

Consulting a medical or counseling professional doesn't necessarily
mean getting help, either. Sarah continued her story, saying, "At one point I
went to a psychiatrist to get help and he told me that I liked that [the vio-
lence]. At that point, I gave up looking for any kind of outside help around
that issue." Another rape victim, Rivka, resigned herself to the abuse, telling
me, "I knew that if I resisted [sex] he would beat me up."

Even with physical abuse, we don't always see the evidence, as in the invisible scars of rape. When the abuser is clever, he smacks his victim in places that only the abuser and victim know about because her clothing covers the bruises. Nobody will see the black-and-blue marks turn their ugly shade of green over time.

Unfortunately, many posters that hang in rest rooms and advertise emergency hot lines have left people under the impression that physical battery is the only type that exists. After all, the word *battered* conjures up images of broken bones, a smashed jaw or nose, cut marks, and burns. The second half of the childhood rhyme "Sticks and stones can break my bones, but names can never hurt me" is wrong. Names do hurt, and after a prolonged period of hearing demeaning and belittling words, insulting names, and epithets, a woman feels diminished. She begins to believe the things her abuser tells her because, after all, this is the man whom she loves, with whom she has chosen to spend her life. He must know her better than any other person on earth, so he must be right. As a result, these abused women must endure unrelenting and severe psychological, social, and financial abuse that often goes unseen to the untrained, and even sometimes the trained, eye.

Psychological abuse takes many different forms, but they all have one thing in common: power over and control of the victim. Even if the abuser never lays a hand on his partner, he destroys her sense of self and place in the world just as certainly as if he had hit her. Linda's experience is an example of this. Her husband had their lives all planned out and in his control.

> The very first time I met him at a [Jewish Federation] dance . . . he really wanted to monopolize me . . . to the point that he kept joking that night about going away together for a weekend . . . it seemed really bizarre. But that was the level of intensity that he worked at.
>
> He seemed to have it all laid out in his mind, like we were going to get married, and we were going to do this and that. For whatever reasons, I had the right demographics and he had made this decision unilaterally, and it was just a question of when I would come around. And it's a tribute to his abilities to persuade someone to his line of thinking . . . that two weeks after the first time we dated we were engaged . . . After we were married he went into another mode and went

into this kind of place where he expected me to be some sort of traditional role-model wife.

For a while, Linda tried to comply with her husband's wishes. She believed that she could make things better by doing what her husband said he wanted.

I made a decision to completely commit myself 1000 percent to trying to make the marriage work, whatever that might take, and see if it could work, so I went back and told him that. And I did. I did whatever I could to be what he thought I should be. I made an attempt to do what he was hoping for, which was for me to be the traditional, dinner-on-the-table-in-the-evening wife. It worked out for a while but it didn't last. There was something really missing.

Another invisible way that abusers seize and maintain power and control is through manipulation and charm. They use this ability, which is really another form of psychological abuse, in everything from counseling sessions to court proceedings, convincing therapists and judges that, because they are accomplished professionals with stature in the community, they must be wonderful and fault free. Linda explains further.

He was incredibly charming. He could charm anybody into anything, and he did. He's extremely skilled at that, and prior to our marriage he pulled out all the stops to do whatever he had to do to acquire me. Up until the day when I made the decision to finally say no, he'd do his charming thing, which made me feel really stupid, made me feel like I'm making the wrong decision, making me mistrust my own judgment and my own thinking. He was really skilled at that, but he was charming in his way of manipulating, of turning my thinking around on its end, so that my way of thinking became faulty. I would find myself wondering whether I had thought it out clearly enough, and I started doubting my own feelings. It became like a chess game for him—checkmate, I've got you. And I wasn't skilled enough, I didn't know what to do with someone who was so charming and wouldn't take no for an answer.

He could play the role of being the good husband in therapy, the good patient role model, but when it finally came down to actual change, it never happened. I finally made a differentiation between playing that role and having some real action taken in the direction of change, but I was not strong enough to leave on my own. I needed help, and I was at a loss of where to find that help.

Virtually every woman in my study, and those in others' works, says that psychological abuse is worse than physical because one does not heal from it as one does from a bruise or broken bone. Interestingly, only one woman I interviewed for this study knew at the time she was married to her abuser that what he was doing to her when he wasn't hitting her was still abuse.

Yet another form of abuse invisible to outsiders is intimidation. The Domestic Abuse Intervention Project defines intimidation as "making her afraid by using looks, actions, gestures; smashing things, destroying her property, abusing pets, displaying weapons."[7] Paula's husband "ripped the blinds, threw things, and swept things off the table."

After repeated incidents, a victim develops what psychologists call a sensitization response. A gesture, such as a raised eyebrow, that has signaled prior violent episodes, can trigger a fear response. As a result, an abuser's clearing his throat can let his victim know she should be afraid. On one occasion, Rivka, upon receiving an unnerving phone call from her husband, grabbed her children and ran to her parents' home. She knew that the phrase "Daddy is angry" would be sufficient to mobilize her children to run.

A type of abuse that is almost completely invisible to the outside world is emotional abuse. The Domestic Abuse Intervention Project defines emotional abuse as, "Putting her down, making her feel bad about herself, calling her names, making her think she's crazy, playing mind games, humiliating her, making her feel guilty."[8]

Mind games are particularly vicious because they are aimed at making the woman feel as if she is losing her grip on reality. Rivka told me how her husband would take items of either financial or sentimental value to her, and then blame her for losing them. He then told her that she was crazy, and that nobody would ever believe her stories because she was "a hysterical woman" and everybody knew what a "pillar of the community" he was. Rivka's case is particularly disturbing when we consider the following story.

I spent $10,000 in keys and changing locks and alarm systems. I went out to a bar mitzvah party. [While getting ready] I was on the phone with a friend and said, "I'm going to this party tonight." [Husband] was invited. I've got all my tax return stuff ready. As soon as I get in . . . I'm going to do it so I can get the financial aid applications out. [Husband] made this whole big deal about going to the party, calling the kids to see if I was going to be home. He walked in front of me at the party and then he disappeared. An hour later the rabbi came up to me and said, "[Ex-husband's] outside. He wants to know if he can come inside because he knows there's a restraining order." So he had an alibi. When I came home I discovered all the papers were missing.

One type of psychological abuse, social isolation, is especially insidious because it can start off feeling good. According to the Domestic Abuse Intervention Project, the behaviors that characterize social isolation include "controlling what she does, who she sees and talks to, what she reads, where she goes, limiting her outside involvement, using jealousy to justify [his] actions."[9] During the early stages of a relationship, an abuser calls his girlfriend frequently "just to say 'Hi.'" She feels special as a result of the attention. Recall how Linda described her husband as "charming." As time goes on, he calls to ask where she's been. Sometimes his so-called concern can evolve into irrational jealousy, and he begins to accuse his wife of cheating on him. Often, an incipient abuser insists on getting married very soon after the relationship has begun. In hindsight, many women say that they were initially swept off their feet, flattered that someone could fall in love with them so quickly. They realized too late that what their partner wanted was to sweep them right into a trap. Or, another scenario: A husband says that he wants to spend more time with his wife, so they should cut down on their social engagements. A bit later, he will perhaps start to refuse to attend social functions, and then even family functions. Both Avital and Sarah experienced this progressively increasing isolation. When social isolation extends into prohibiting a wife to work outside the home or to volunteer in the community or to entertain, the victim no longer has any social contacts to turn to for guidance and support. Of course, forbidding her to work has the added effect of controlling her financially. Sarah describes this experience of social isolation.

He was very jealous. He didn't want me to work; he wanted me in the house sort of contained. I used to go folk dancing. He was very jealous, so I eventually stopped doing that. He had wanted to be a musician and failed at that, so he didn't like me pursuing my music, and I ended up giving it up. He discouraged me from seeing my parents.

Several women told me that their husbands would hang up the telephone if somebody called for them. Even a conversation with a friend or family member was threatening to these abusers.

In my study, I was stunned to learn through the course of conversation how many of the survivors told me they were orphans, only children, or estranged from their families. For example, Sarah had only one brother, but he was in and out of psychiatric hospitals, unable to provide support. Avital was an only child. Diane was alone, with neither siblings nor parents.

Had their abusers chosen them for this very reason? Had they known that it would be easier to isolate a woman who already had a smaller support network than other women? Some experts believe that abusers have a sort of "radar" that homes in on vulnerable women.[10]

Naomi was one of the unlucky ones. Her parents not only did nothing to help her, they told her, "You made your bed, now you must lie in it," thereby giving carte blanche to her husband to abuse her. Even when he chased her through the neighborhood with a weapon she was alone. It took serious physical injury, in the form of permanent brain and hearing damage, before she left her husband.

Avital, on the other hand, was fortunate that, although she was an only child, her parents lived in the same town and provided tremendous moral support during her marriage. At one point she tells how her parents met with her husband's parents and told them that he had better shape up or she would leave him. The husband, after years of Avital's pleading, finally relented and agreed to marriage counseling, but, as she told me, "I realized as soon as I sat down that it was too little too late. I wanted out."

Often a woman will stay in an abusive marriage because she feels she has no way to support herself and her children if she should leave. As Twerski says, having money, and the ability to earn it, is the best insurance a woman can have.[11] But, even women who do earn a salary, and sometimes very high ones, can suffer from economic abuse. The Domestic Abuse

Intervention Project operationally defines economic abuse as "preventing her [the victim] from getting or keeping a job, making her ask for money, giving her an allowance, taking her money, not letting her know about or have access to family income."[12] To this list of operational definitions I would add forcing her to drop out of school, thereby drastically reducing her chance of making a living should she leave him. Sarah experienced textbook economic abuse.

> As far as what he was earning, I'd say we were upper-middle class, but he didn't bring his money home. He drank it away, or he'd spend it foolishly when he was drinking. He always bought boats that were no good and cost thousands of dollars to fix, stupid things like that. I had a continuing running battle with bill collectors the whole time we were married. I remember rolling up pennies from my penny jar to feed my kids one week, and he was making a good income. We had a house in a nice suburban town. And I didn't always have grocery money.

Other women, such as Karen and Jane, told me about how their husbands deleted all financial records from their computers (in both cases, even while the police were in the house supposedly supervising their vacating), cleaned out their joint checking and investment accounts, canceled credit cards, and in Jane's case, removed furniture and sentimental items from their vacation home. Several women told me how their husbands doled out a weekly allowance, often barely enough to feed and clothe the family. If these women wanted some cash to go out to lunch with a friend, they had to beg for it. The reason? Their husbands said that they earned the money and therefore would determine how it was spent.

Despite the stereotype of the wealth and stature of the American Jewish community, poverty is by no means unknown. According to Bubis, writing for the American Jewish Committee, between 13 and 15 percent of Jews in this country live below the poverty line.[13] Many of these are single women raising children alone, quite often because their ex-husbands do not pay alimony or child support.

But, when an abuser happens to have a lot of money, he can make life a living hell even after he has agreed to divorce. Finding yet another way to abuse his wife financially, Rivka's husband used the legal system to delay an examination of his finances. This, it turned out, was disastrous for Rivka.

> He drove it [the divorce] to trial. What I didn't know at the time was that it gave him the opportunity to hide all our assets. My lawyer did freeze the assets, but the way he ran his business . . . I had an idea but didn't know everything. It cost me $300,000 in legal fees to get divorced because he continued to abuse the legal system. He wrote all these ridiculous letters and he canceled depositions and scheduled depositions.
>
> He made $300,000 the year before we separated. By the time we got to trial he told the judge he was making $60,000 and he hadn't filed tax returns for three years. Therefore, the judge had no basis for determining child support payments.
>
> I get about a third of what I should be getting in support. He doesn't pay health insurance for his kids. It's cost me about $100,000 since the divorce to get him to comply with the judgment. For us to go out for ice cream is a treat. I haven't been to a movie in seven years. And, he's going to Italy with his girlfriend.
>
> He went to Italy with [the girlfriend] for a week in June, and told his children he couldn't afford to pay the court-ordered support for tuition and things because he had a responsibility to her.

In the earliest days of television, wife beating was acceptable fodder for comedy. Ralph Cramden's weekly threats to hit wife Alice on *The Honeymooners* ("One of these days!" he would bellow) had audiences laughing themselves silly. We may look at the old television programs with nostalgia, pining for the good old days, but viewing them through rose-colored glasses minimizes the reality of abuse. Fortunately, society seems to have developed a greater understanding of abuse, and we are beginning to see it addressed in the media. From television's *Law and Order* to feature films, the subject is, more and more, being treated as the crime it really is.

The 1994 Paramount Pictures movie *Forrest Gump* features a scene in which the title character witnesses his childhood friend, Jenny, being beaten by her boyfriend, Wesley. The two had traveled to Washington, D.C., for an anti–Vietnam War rally.

FORREST: He should not have been hitting you, Jenny.
JENNY: He doesn't mean it when he does that.

The next day, as Jenny is getting ready to board the bus to leave the rally, Wesley approaches her.

WESLEY: Jenny, things got a little out of hand. It's just this war and that lying son-of-a-bitch Johnson. I would never hurt you. You know that.[14]

The above example describes the form of abuse called "minimizing, denying, and blaming." The Domestic Abuse Intervention Project defines this type of abuse as "making light of the abuse and not taking her concerns about it seriously, saying the abuse didn't happen, shifting responsibility for abusive behavior, saying she caused it."[15] Note how Wesley blames the president of the United States for his brutality. And, in denial about the state of her relationship with Wesley, Jenny defends Wesley.

Unfortunately, among abusers, self-awareness is not a strong suit. In fact, they typically blame their victims and then refuse to accept any responsibility for their own behavior. Many are able to manipulate their personae to become the Prince Charming I discussed earlier in certain situations (for example, in therapy) and actually believe that they are indeed the wonderful persons they portray. However, in a rare, revealing instance of self-perceptiveness, the much-married comedienne Roseanne, while a guest on Conan O'Brien's late night television show, said the following: "I didn't know being in a relationship meant you had to be nice. I thought it meant you had to hack away at the other person until they were beaten down and then were too afraid to leave."[16]

In real life, among the survivors in this study, one woman stands out as a victim of blaming. Jane describes several experiences during her marriage that illustrate blaming behavior. The first came at the beginning of the marriage, when Jane asked her husband to attend marital therapy with her. He agreed, but only as a way to "straighten her out." In another incident, her husband punched their son and blamed both her and the boy. A third time, he blamed Jane when he was written out of his parents' wills. In a fourth example, Jane describes a family dinner: "It had been a very tense day. We were all at the dinner table, and [husband] suddenly turned to the children and said, 'Your mother is suffering from borderline personality disorder. I am moving out.' He used blame frequently as his preferred form of abuse."

If one form of abuse could be considered more heinous than all the others, using children as pawns would be it. In Jane's experience, her husband not only physically battered their son and spoke through the children to announce he was leaving, he also tried to manipulate which therapist their son saw when the divorce was in progress. An abuser in this case manipulates a woman by threatening to hurt her children or to take them away, all to gain her compliance and capitulation in a divorce settlement. Or, conversely, he manipulates the children by pumping them for information about their mother, feeding them misinformation to harm their relationship with her, or both. Abusers use the children to control their partners, often picking one or more "buddy" to gang up on the mother. Children want to please their father and do not realize they are being manipulated.

Using the children has features in common with emotional abuse. Several women told stories of how their husbands charmed judges, lawyers, and *guardians ad litem* (GALs)[17] into believing that the women were crazy and that they did not deserve to have custody of the children. Both Karen and Jane told me that their husbands threatened to use the fact that they had stayed so long in their marriages as evidence that they were crazy and a risk to the children. They did not deserve to have custody of children that they had put in harm's way. (This reminds me of the old story about the man who murders his parents and then begs for mercy from the court because he is an orphan.) Ironically, these women often believe that they are staying for the good of the children and the family. It is only when the kids are hurt or threatened that they may find the courage to leave, and then they may have to face the real threat of being accused of child endangerment.

Although women have suffered for years from their abusers following and harassing them—even after their divorces were finalized—it was only fairly recently that the law finally recognized stalking as a serious form of psychological abuse. Stalking is defined as "a course of conduct directed at a specific person that involves repeated (two or more occasions) visual or physical proximity; nonconsensual communication; verbal, written, or implied threats; or a combination thereof that would cause fear in a reasonable

person."[18] The operational definitions of stalking include the following behaviors as asked in the questions, "Not including bill collectors, telephone
solicitors, or other salespeople, has anyone, male or female, ever . . .

> Followed or spied on you?
> Sent you unsolicited letters or written correspondence?
> Made unsolicited phone calls to you?
> Stood outside your home, school, or workplace?
> Showed up at places you were even though he or she had no busi-
> ness being there?
> Left unwanted items for you to find?
> Tried to communicate in other ways against your will?
> Vandalized your property or destroyed something you loved?"[19]

The NVAW Survey reported that 8.1 percent of American women have
been stalked at some point in their lives. Rivka not only experienced the
break-in and theft of her tax documents, but tells how her husband used her
credit cards fraudulently, tapped her telephone, and showed up at places he
should not have been, given the restraining order out against him. Reizl's ex-
husband forbade her new husband from attending their grandson's *brit
milah,* circumcision ceremony. He patrolled their daughter's house, throwing "a fit" when she and her new husband went there to deliver boxes.

Every abuse victim suffers. We've just seen how many forms of abuse
there are that produce immense suffering for all victims. However, the Jewish woman must endure a unique form of psychological abuse known as the
withholding of a *get,* the Jewish divorce decree. Throughout the millennia
of Jewish existence, men have held the sole right to dissolve a marriage,
often leaving a woman unable to remarry and have legitimate children.
Twerski claims, based on his experience, "Without exception, every case of
agunah, every case of a husband's refusal to give a *get,* will reveal a history
of a woman's having been abused during the marriage."[20] As one Orthodox
rabbi expounded:

> Clearly in the Orthodox community in particular, aside from the es-
> cape from physical and emotional battering that's involved, there's an-
> other issue which we have to confront, the issue of the religious

divorce, which is much more complicated and is something that has to be dealt with because we need the cooperation of the husband in order to make it happen.

The *get* is not considered kosher if it is given under duress. Ironically, the duress under which the woman exists, in neither slavery nor freedom, is viewed with sympathy but, until recently, not given much attention by the rabbinate. It has taken some of the sharpest civil and legal minds in the Jewish world to try to solve this problem. We will discuss the law and its maneuverings in Chapter 3.

We've seen the many different and malicious ways abuse can be carried out, but what does this look like in the daily life of women experiencing it? Psychologist Lenore Walker was first to document a cycle of abuse that is almost universal in its appearance.[21] The cycle begins with a build-up of tension. The victim, after exposure to a number of abusive incidents, has learned to tread lightly, hoping to avoid provoking an outburst. But, no matter how softly she steps, the second stage, the explosion, is bound to come. And it does come. The actual abuse incident can last anywhere from minutes to days and can include punching, kicking, or worse. Walker writes that unpredictability and lack of control both characterize the second stage. Here I disagree with Walker; I am not so sure that the batterers have lost control. They seem to know that outside the home they must be accountable for their behavior, and they do behave there. It is while inside the home, when they have nobody to answer to, that they let themselves go. In stage three, the abuser comes back sheepishly, after the incident is over, to apologize and promise that it will never happen again (see Wesley from *Forest Gump,* as quoted earlier in the chapter). Often, he carries flowers or other gifts in hand. However, as Weitzman notes in her book, and I found in my interviews, upscale men tend not to apologize. Virtually every woman in this study said that her husband never apologized. After all, these men are used to being in the driver's seat. Most, if not all, the men married to the women in my study are highly paid professionals, some in charge of large staffs of people whose job was to do their bidding. These abusers feel no need to apologize because they believe they are never wrong.

When one Orthodox rabbi asserted that abusive men cannot control themselves at home, I challenged him. Judging by their professional

achievement and status, it is apparent that they are quite capable of controlling their behavior in business or social settings. He replied:

> They assume that when they're home there are no consequences . . .
> and that's reinforced because they do it once and they get away with
> it, they do it three times and they get away with it. But, they've been
> doing it for five years and they're getting away with it. I'm reasonably
> confident that they didn't sit down and analyze it and say, "Here I
> can't get away with it and there is accountability." These are sick guys.
> Now, I'm not prepared to say that because they're sick that they're not
> guilty. I think that they're sick and they have to be dealt with.

So, who is dealing with these men? The victims themselves are caught
in the cycle of violence. They are at first in denial that abuse exists, and then
seem to experience a near paralysis at the prospect of seeking help. They
may be suffering in a parallel cycle in which they can deal with their abusers
on a survival basis only.

Regarding the so-called paralysis referred to above, Rivka's approach
to her situation illustrates the emotional roller coaster that a woman can go
through in attempting to escape. Rivka's children had witnessed ongoing
rages and physical beatings at the hands of her husband for years. "He hit
my nephew once. He emotionally abused the children." Here, she describes the incident that ultimately led to her breaking free.

> He became enraged . . . and he lost control, and he kicked me repeat-
> edly in the abdomen and then in the ribs. I couldn't breathe and I fell
> to the ground and he kicked me. I had huge bruises, all documented
> with the police.

She describes her ten-year-old son as saying, "Daddy, look what you
did. You need to get yourself a good psychiatrist." Rivka's story continues:

> Someone was waiting for me at the emergency room. She orchestrated
> me through the triage. While we were waiting, she sat with me and she
> said, "When your husband gets angry does he do X, Y, and Z?" and I
> said, "Yes," and she gave me a couple of different examples of his be-

havior, and she said to me, "Rivka, your husband's abusive and you need to get help." It was the first time that somebody had ever said that to me. Every other therapist that I had spoken to had said, "Oh, he's not abusive; he's just an angry man." This woman saved my life. That was when I left. I realized I had to go to the police. She convinced me to go to the police. I was just so afraid. She said, "You need to go there." By this time it's ten o'clock at night. They took pictures; they took the affidavit and they called the judge who was on call.

At this point I fully expected to hear that the husband was arrested and Rivka made her escape. I was naive. She continues:

> They were going to go arrest him. I said, "No, you can't do that; he'll be humiliated in front of his children." . . . I always put my kids first. And one of the reasons I was staying was because of my kids. They needed that nuclear family. And I had made this conscious decision. I have three kids who need to have a relationship with their father, because regardless of what he does to them they need to accept him for who he is and on the terms of what he can do for them. He controls them with the money.

Rivka's story demonstrates a classic pattern of confusing rationalizations. She fears losing her economic support, she believes that her abusive husband should still be in the picture for the good of the children, even when he has abused them, and she needs to protect him from humiliation that would ensue from an arrest.

Linda, on the other hand, describes her state of mind simply and succinctly: "I had become so befuddled being around my husband that I couldn't think clearly anymore. I didn't know what my feelings were even though I had them."

The women in this study are significantly better educated than the average American woman. So, if they are so smart and so well educated, why do they stay in abusive marriages? Why are they caught in the cycle of violence? There are two theories that attempt to explain this conundrum. First, as Weitzman demonstrates in her work, upscale women (highly educated, with good family incomes) battle on two fronts.[22] Her research sub-

jects were educated, accomplished women who were able to achieve just
about whatever they had set their minds to. When their marriages became
nightmares, she says, they believed they could "fix" the problem. After all,
they had been able to do so in other areas of their lives, such as school and
the workplace. When they could not "fix" the problems in their marriages,
they began to believe what their abusers had told them—that they are stupid, incompetent, and beneath contempt. In addition, Weitzman's upscale
women feared leaving their comfortable material lives, believing that they
would never be able to support themselves and their children. This fear was
made more pronounced by their abusers' constant haranguing that they
could never make it on their own. The women in my study were for the
most part employed in areas that easily could have helped support them in
a fine lifestyle, but they, too, feared leaving their marriages.

More specific to the Jewish experience, it is close to gospel that Jewish women feel obligated to maintain *shalom bayit*, peace in the home. I
do agree that this feeling of obligation may hold true among more traditional Jews who are familiar with the concept, but I also believe that the
bulk of American Jews are far too assimilated even to be aware of the
term. I would be more inclined to believe that the small size and insularity
of the Jewish community, in combination with the upscale woman's hesitance to draw attention to her plight, would intimidate women who are already in fear. They would more than likely be afraid that somebody
would discover, and perhaps reveal, their secrets. That would make it
very difficult to continue to live in the community that has been both their
home and their children's.

As we will see in Chapters 4 and 5 on rabbis and the community, neither of these two segments of community life are particularly aware of the
problem, and both are ill-equipped to deal with it. On the other hand, the
community cannot be aware of the problem if there are no physical signs,
and even if there are, it nevertheless hesitates to get involved.

One Conservative rabbi said straight out, "We have so many important
things to worry about. If I thought this was a real problem, then I would do
something about it. Show me some statistics." If the health and safety of the
family unit is not among the most important tenets in Judaism, then why are
we bothering with *Shabbat* observance? Why be so concerned about the
laws of *kashrut*, the Jewish laws regulating what foods are allowed to be

consumed, and how they are to be prepared, if human beings are treated with less respect than a cow going to slaughter? On the other hand, this rabbi had a point. Is the problem a real one, or simply a matter of overzealous reporting by a headline-seeking media?

If statistics are needed to quiet the naysayer, the following numbers should work. But first, a proviso: It is important to recognize that researchers use varying methods to measure the incidence of abuse. Consequently, estimates of the prevalence of domestic violence can vary widely. Some researchers look only at the twelve months prior to the study they are conducting, whereas others look at lifetime exposure to violence. In addition, most studies look only at physical violence and not the other forms that abuse can take. This approach is not surprising, since economic abuse, social isolation, and intimidation are not reported or documented.

The Uniform Crime Reports (UCR),[23] a national reporting system set up by the FBI, produces annual statistics on the top major crimes. Unfortunately, the UCR only reports arrests made, not convictions. In addition, police departments are not mandated to report their numbers to the FBI. Consequently, reporting is not always consistent or complete. One policewoman, speaking on condition of anonymity, told me that for several years, her police department did not report its numbers because there was no staff person assigned to do so. And, of course, nonphysical abuse is not considered a crime, so it is not reported (although one can get a restraining order or vacate order based on emotional abuse in some states). The only absolute in reporting is that of murder. Provided there is a body, murder must always be reported. Finally, medical personnel may not pick up on or may not report cases of physical abuse. In states where reporting abuse is not mandated by law, the absence of reporting is not surprising. But Plichta states, "Even when abuse is recognized, health care professionals often provide inappropriate, or even harmful treatment."[24]

Let us look at the data. The government found in its NVAW Survey that 1.3 million women are physically assaulted by an intimate partner (defined as a current or former husband, boyfriend, or date) every year. In their lifetimes, 22.1 percent of women had experienced violence at the hands of an intimate partner. The NVAW study discovered that an intimate partner, someone the women loved and trusted, committed 64 percent of all rape, physical assault, and stalking. The media-inspired image of a masked man jumping out of the bushes to assault or rape a woman is proved by the facts to be less prevalent than the stereotype would suggest.[25]

When it comes to Jewish women, there are virtually no scientific studies of domestic abuse that could give us reliable and valid statistics. In fact, I was surprised one day when an intern working at a Jewish domestic violence program called me to ask where I had found the statistics on rates of abuse in the Jewish community. "I got them from you," I answered with a sinking feeling in the pit of my stomach. When I went back to trace the source of the statistic, I realized that every single women's organization, every Jewish domestic violence program, had quoted either directly or indirectly, one article, published in a nonacademic newspaper.[26]

Guterman[27] questions the seminal master's thesis by Giller and Goldsmith,[28] whose work inspired the Los Angeles Jewish community to develop domestic abuse programming. Those authors, he points out, asked their research subjects if they had either experienced or known of instances of domestic violence. The form of the question led to unreliable and invalid results, he claims. I agree. Double-counting of victims is a real possibility given the vague wording of survey items. (That the programs developed from this study are busy is irrelevant.) Spitzer refers to a study conducted by the Jewish Board of Family Services in New York. That survey found that of 2,600 families seen by the agency, one in twenty wives was abused.[29] However, this number is misleading because families seeking help may not be representative of the general Jewish population. A second article Spitzer cites bases its statistics on anecdotal information, not research data.

Claims that between 15 and 35 percent of Jewish women are abused at some point in their lives, a rate comparable to estimates of abuse in the general population, may in fact be true. They may also be under- or overestimates. However, even if we flatter ourselves into thinking that Jewish men beat their wives at a lesser rate, that still leaves far too many abuse victims. If we say that only 10 percent of Jewish women suffer from abuse at the hands of their husbands, that means forty women in a congregation of four hundred family units are currently being abused. Even if only 1 percent of women is physically abused, that means four women are suffering. That is four too many women. What I am saying is that an unscientific study not only makes those working in the field appear unprofessional, it could quite possibly affect their mission. We have seen all too often in so many other fields (e.g., medicine, education) how headline-grabbing "discoveries" come to be discredited. The study of spousal abuse is much too serious a problem to be relegated to the trash heap because it relied on faulty research methods.

The Jewish community owes its attention to domestic violence because of the severe disruption and horrifying effects it has on women's lives. Take Linda, for example, whose health has suffered as a result of abuse.

> During the marriage there were a number of things that deteriorated, one of which was my health. My health deteriorated to the point . . . that my immune system from the stress had gotten so depleted that I actually had gotten allergic to everything. There was no food that I wasn't allergic to. My whole system was reactive and it manifested as a systemic inflammation of all my muscles and joints to the point where I barely could move . . . it was pretty painful . . . I was slowly getting worse, but maybe not that slowly if you can get deteriorated in the course of a year.

As science discovers more every day about the connection between mind and body, we learn new information about the physical and psychological effects of abuse. It may seem obvious that physical battering causes damage to the body. Some abusers break bones, beat their victims about the head, or cut them. What may not be as evident are the ramifications of verbal and psychological weapons. Whether abuse takes a physical or psychological form, there are consequences. Naomi to this day suffers from the brain damage her husband inflicted on her. She is hard of hearing and suffers from dizziness. Paula walks with a limp and has a medical monitoring device installed in her home due to the severe medical and psychiatric problems she now lives with due to her ex-husband's violence. Laura speaks with a constant hoarseness that resulted from years of stress.

The psychological effects of abuse, both physical and nonphysical, can be devastating. A study conducted by McCauley et al. compared women who had never been abused with those who had experienced what they termed "low-severity violence" and "high-severity violence."[30] They define low-severity violence as pushing, grabbing, or threatening to hurt a person or someone loved by that person in the twelve months prior to the study.

High-severity violence includes hitting, slapping, kicking, burning, chok-ing, and threatening or hurting with a weapon. The researchers looked at both the physical and psychological symptoms exhibited by 1,931 women aged eighteen years and older. They found that both physical symptoms and psychological distress increased with the severity of the violence. Among the psychological symptoms they measured were depression, anxi-ety, somatization (the conversion of anxiety into physical symptoms), and self-esteem. When looking only at the year prior to the study, 6.5 percent of the women participating reported having experienced either low- or high-severity abuse. However, when looking at total life experience, including childhood abuse, adult abuse, or both, the number skyrocketed to 34.9 percent of the women who reported having been battered.

The effects of psychological abuse can be just as devastating as those ex-perienced by women who have been primarily physically abused. Mechanic et al. studied both "relentlessly stalked" and "infrequently stalked" women to compare with other forms of abuse, as well as the physical and psycholog-ical effects they might be experiencing. The relentlessly stalked and battered women showed increased rates of depression and post-traumatic stress dis-order (PTSD) as compared with the infrequently stalked women.[31]

In one of the earlier studies on the effects of violence on psychiatric ill-ness, Carmen, Rieker, and Mills looked at 188 psychiatric patients who had experienced chronic physical abuse, sexual abuse, or both. They found that, similar to the figures from general statistics on rape, 90 percent of the victims not only knew the perpetrators, but were related to them. Long-term problems resulting from abuse included difficulty with anger manage-ment, impaired self-esteem, and an inability to trust others.[32] No stretch of the imagination is required to see how these symptoms can impact on the ability to lead a productive life, either in the workplace or at home.

The severity of abuse correlates highly with the number and severity of psychological and physical symptoms in the victim. But, what would hap-pen if the abuse stopped? Does time heal all wounds? Rollstin and Kern administered two standard psychological tests, the MMPI–2s and Conflict Tactic Scales, to fifty abused women, hypothesizing that distance in time from the abuse and the abuser would mitigate the consequences. Unfortu-nately, their hypothesis was not supported. Women in both groups suffered effects regardless of time since the abusive incidents occurred. Results significantly correlated with both types of abuse, but time away from the abuser did not moderate the response.[33]

In their study, Coker et al. found that partner abuse, and specifically sexual violence, may correlate with an increased risk of cervical dysplasia and cervical cancer.[34] The correlation was higher for women who endured physical as opposed to psychological violence, but the authors suggest that the psychological stress victims suffer may also increase the risk of developing these symptoms. We might also posit that, since many abusers commit adultery as a form of psychological abuse, they expose their wives to the human papilloma virus, which in turn can cause cervical disease.

Another harmful and long-term effect of both physical and psychological abuse comes in the form of Post Traumatic Stress Disorder. Normally when we think of PTSD, we think of war. Soldiers witnessing the deaths of their comrades, children viewing the rape and murder of their mothers and sisters, and POWs enduring months, or even years, of torture and isolation, these are the people whose experiences give rise to PTSD. Hollywood's version of PTSD includes flashbacks and nightmares, and many books have been published about the mental illness, homelessness, and suicide that have afflicted so many veterans. The survivors of spousal abuse, as well as their children, are also prone to develop the cluster of physical and psychological symptoms that define post-traumatic stress disorder. After all, they have been through a war zone themselves. Like soldiers in battle, they have felt the pain of physical attack, but they have not had the benefit of a potent defense. Like children in a war-torn territory, they have endured thunderous attacks at unexpected moments, always on the alert for a hint that more may be coming. And, like POWs, they have been held captive by a despotic ruler-of-the-roost who controlled their movements, doling out favors and punishments in an irrational manner designed to keep them off balance. But, unlike soldiers, they have endured their abuse in the one place they should feel safe and secure—their homes.

So, what exactly is PTSD? Davidson defines it as "a disorder in which one or more traumatic events give rise to four symptom clusters: recurrent and painful re-experiencing of the event; phobic avoidance of trauma-related situations and memories; emotional numbing and withdrawal, and hyperarousal."[35] Women in the United States are affected twice as often as men, and the author states that, on average, a person will suffer twenty years of active symptoms. The pain and suffering result in a loss of almost one day per week of work. Davidson goes on to say,

> Besides being associated with increased risk for depression, anxiety, alcohol or substance use disorders, PTSD is associated with higher rates of hypertension, bronchial asthma, and peptic ulcer and with other diseases of the cardiovascular, digestive, musculoskeletal, endocrine, respiratory, and nervous systems, as well as increased rates of infectious disease for up to twenty years following exposure to major trauma . . . The cost of PTSD exceeds that of all other anxiety disorders, and much of this expenditure is accounted for by direct costs of treatment seeking and medical evaluation.[36]

Having said that, Davidson then reveals that fewer than half of all physicians acknowledge the existence of the disorder, which often presents as a physical malady. To make matters worse, as few as 4 percent of those patients with the disorder are accurately diagnosed. Although PTSD can be treated successfully, it must be recognized before treatment can begin.

Street and Arias studied battered women to look at the relationship between physical and psychological abuse and PTSD.[37] By statistically controlling for the effects of physical abuse, the authors found that the effects of psychological abuse are *at least as damaging as those of physical abuse* (italics mine). Their results support previous similar findings. They also found shame and guilt to be important variables in predicting PTSD and urged physicians to pay close attention to these symptoms in order to help diagnose abuse and get women into early treatment.

And, what of the effects of spousal abuse on subsequent generations? The Family Violence Prevention Fund (FVPF) reported that Gallup Poll figures show that between 1.5 and 3.3 million children witness parental domestic violence every year. How do these children of abusive families fare in life?[38]

The biblical Book of Exodus states, "And that will by no means clear the guilty; visiting the iniquity of the fathers upon the children and upon the children's children, unto the third and fourth generation (34:6–7)."[39] As a child I thought the punishment to subsequent generations very unfair. After all, what had the children done to deserve the penalty for their parents' sins? It was only later, as an adult, that I realized it is not that children are punished for their parents' evil, but that they suffer the consequences of it. Not only do they endure the harsh life of the abusive home, they must function in a society that often debases them for having the bad luck to live in an abusive home. Either way, they suffer.

Whereas an acute disaster, such as an earthquake, can provoke a level of post-traumatic stress, continued and unrelenting stress, such as abuse, brings with it a whole host of other problems. According to Rossman, who summarized the research on longer-term response to abuse by children, several possible consequences can result from children witnessing one parent abuse another.[40]

It is impossible to separate out the various stressors in a violent family that could affect children; poverty, substance abuse, neighborhood influences, and physical and sexual abuse are just a few examples. But the fact remains that all of these elements could wreak cumulative havoc on the littlest victims. In fact, Appel and Holden note that, among children who live in parentally violent homes, 41 percent are physically abused themselves.[41] The FVPF reported on a sample of research studies, including one in Massachusetts, where, among two hundred substantiated child abuse cases, 48 percent also contained elements of adult abuse. Another study of more than 6,000 families found that 50 percent of men who frequently assaulted their wives also abused their children. And, the news gets worse. Women who are abused may then turn around and abuse their children.[42]

The FVPF paper corroborates Davidson's report on children and domestic violence. "There is growing evidence that domestic violence can have lasting negative consequences. As these child witnesses to domestic violence grow up, they are at greater risk for abusing alcohol or other drugs and for committing violent crimes of all types, eventually getting involved with the criminal justice system."[43] The FVPF goes on to quote the U.S. Advisory Board on Child Abuse and Neglect in stating that "domestic violence may be the *single major precursor* to child abuse and neglect in this country."[44]

What can that exposure do to children's fragile psyches? Appel and Holden say that anxiety and an inability to form interpersonal relationships are among the negative effects on children exposed to parental violence.[45] Heightened sensitivity to violence is a problem typical to children who witness violence in the home. They develop a heightened response to anything from a raised voice to a frowning face. In the example presented by the authors, the ramifications can go beyond an acute fear response. For example, if a child enters a room of rowdy, playful children, he may perceive the noise level as threatening. His reaction may be one of aggression, which confuses the children who meant no harm. They do not understand that he is simply responding to loud noises so as to protect himself, but they see a strange child and shun him. He then becomes more aggressive and antisocial due to the rejection. And, thus the path begins toward, perhaps, a life of aggression in his own relationships.

Domestic violence doesn't remain in the house. When one spouse batters another, it causes a ripple effect throughout society, and the health care system receives the brunt of it. Plichta found that abuse victims are more likely than nonvictims to have "poor health, chronic pain problems, depression, suicide attempts, addictions, and problem pregnancies. Abused women also use a disproportionate amount of health care services, including emergency room visits, primary care, and community mental health center visits."[46] As Weitzman describes, for a variety of reasons upscale women rarely use public health care facilities, preferring instead to pay private doctors. They do not usually charge psychological counseling services to their insurance providers, nor will they go to emergency rooms unless absolutely necessary.[47] Therefore, abused women's use of the health care system is probably even greater than Plichta suspects. Hedin and Janson found that an astounding 89.4 percent of their subjects—pregnant women—reported psychological abuse in the form of dominance and isolation by their partner, and 44.4 percent experienced emotional and verbal abuse. Sexual abuse also correlated highly with both physical and emotional abuse.[48]

Tjaden and Thoennes, reporting on the results of their work on the National Violence Against Women Survey, state that about one-third of women victimized by physical assault, rape, or both received medical treatment as a result of their most recent injury.[49] An important question related to this finding is, "Where are the other two-thirds of the injured and raped women going after their assaults, if they are not receiving medical treatment?"

Not surprisingly, Abbott found that domestic-violence-related illnesses and injuries are often seen in the hospital emergency room. However, he declares that many problems, including psychiatric and other medical complaints, seen in the emergency room may indeed have been caused by domestic violence, but have not been identified as such.[50] This is not an unexpected finding, given our survivors' experiences with doctors who never ask whether they had been abused. There appears to remain a great discomfort on the part of physicians to ask the questions that need to be asked. In the case of Jane's son, his pediatrician failed to report his abusive father's behavior to the Department of Social Services, even when told point blank *by the child* that he had been punched and kicked. (In the Commonwealth of Massachusetts, there is no requirement to report the abuse of an adult, but a physician is a mandated reporter of suspected child abuse.)

In another study of domestic violence in the emergency room, Roberts et al. looked at two groups of women, one self-identified as domestic violence victims, and one not. Victims visited the emergency room and outpatient clinic significantly more often than nonvictims and had more psychiatric problems. Victims of abuse attempted to commit suicide more often than nonvictims, and abused alcohol more than nonvictims.[51] As one domestic violence program director told me, the rate of serious mental illness among the abuse victims at her hospital is high. If not brought on by the abuse, it is certainly aggravated by it. Now, it is important to point out here that abusers will often say that the abuse victim is "crazy" and that the abuse she experiences is "all in her head." Abusers will use their manipulative charm to convince a judge and other professionals that the abuse victim is the perpetrator. So, in addition to the nightmare of an abusive marriage, the victim then enters a twilight zone of exploitation.

The reality is, just because a woman comes to an emergency room or to a private physician for treatment does not mean that she will be helped. And, specifically because of mandated abuse reporting, many women will not come for help. It is interesting to note that abuse victims differ significantly from those not abused, and from each other, in their opinions on whether to mandate reporting. Rodriguez et al. surveyed 1,218 emergency department patients on their opinions regarding mandatory reporting of domestic abuse to the police. Almost 56 percent of abuse victims supported mandated reporting, whereas more than 70 percent of nonabused patients supported the policy. Conversely, whereas about 44 percent of abuse victims were opposed to mandated reporting, only 29.3 percent of those not abused were opposed to it.[52]

Aside from abuse victims, other experts disagree on whether states should mandate reporting of abuse to police. Those in favor believe that it is important to get the abuser out of the house and away from the partner and any children who may live there. Opponents believe, just as strongly, that by releasing medical records to the authorities they are making abusers aware that their victims have "gone public." This information, they feel, puts abuse victims at even greater risk.

The opponents' point of view must be taken seriously, given the revolving-door history of batterers. Consider the following statistics: During the six months following an episode of domestic violence, 32 percent of battered women are victimized again.[53] Also, six months after obtaining a protection order, 34 percent of victims reported some type of problem with their abuser, either physical or psychological.[54] Buzawa and Buzawa, citing various studies on restraining orders, report that between 50 and 60 percent of women reported acts of abuse within one to two years after the entry of a protection order.[55] In one study, half of the abuse incidents were severe. Although reports to police of protection order violations were high, arrests were rare. Adams and Powell state that only 17 percent of violators in their study were arraigned for violation of an order, and only 6 percent were convicted of violating the order.[56] So we can see that the judge quoted earlier saying, "Restraining orders are only as good as the paper they are written on," was speaking from experience. It is no wonder women are afraid to report abuse.

In a paper discussing the privacy issues affecting battered women seeking health care, the Family Violence Prevention Fund cites further ramifications of reporting abuse including the loss of health insurance, employment, or both.[57] Fear of poverty and the inability to provide for their children prevents many women from escaping their own personal war zones, so the issue of mandated reporting needs much further discussion.

If the moral, religious, psychological, and medical effects are not persuasive enough an argument for taking community action against domestic violence, then perhaps the financial repercussions for business, and by extension, society, will persuade our leaders to do something. According to the American Institute on Domestic Violence (AIDV), intimate partners commit 13,000 acts of violence in the workplace every year. The AIDV states on its Web site,

> Employers lose between $3 and $5 billion every year for increased medical costs associated with battered workers. Businesses lose an additional $100 million in lost wages, sick leave, and absenteeism. Over 1,750,000 workdays are lost each year due to domestic violence. Domestic violence in the United States costs an estimated $67 billion annually.[58]

The AIDV also states that an astounding 96 percent of battered workers experience some sort of on-the-job problem due to abuse. For example, 74 percent of battered workers are harassed at work by their abuser, 54 percent are late to work, 28 percent have to leave work early, and 54 percent miss entire days of work—all due to violence.[59]

When a batterer shows up at the workplace to harass, stalk, or otherwise terrorize his partner, then coworkers and employers become witnesses. In fact, they can become protectors of and advocates for the victim. Moreover, the employer may find it in his or her best interest to do so, and not only for reasons of the cost of doing business. More and more victims and their estates are beginning to sue employers for their lack of action. Again, according to the AIDV, "Lawsuits against employers are rising and expensive. Average judgment is $2.2 million!"[60]

Granted, not all children of abusive families become abusive themselves. However, all the evidence points to the likelihood that, without treatment, we face the alarming possibility that a huge proportion of adults in every subsequent generation will be violent. What does this mean for the Jewish community? When compared to other religious or ethnic groups, the Jews are a tiny minority. They comprise less than 1 percent of the world's population. Add to that an intermarriage rate among the non-Orthodox that hovers at a startling 56 percent, and we have a recipe for a vanishing people.

Both lay and professional leadership have been bemoaning the high rate of assimilation into mainstream culture. "Jewish continuity" has become the rallying cry of the organized community, prompting the proliferation of programmatic efforts, ranging from Birthright Israel to Jewish dating services. But, a continuity of what? Is it continuation of more humiliation, degradation, pain, injury, and threats? Is this how the Jewish values of the pursuit of justice and valuing life have devolved?

In the next chapter, we will learn what both Jewish and secular law have had to say, both historically and in contemporary times, about abuse. From that perspective, perhaps we can gain some guidance in developing and supporting a new strategic vision for dealing with domestic violence in the Jewish community. The very future of the people depends on it.

3

"JUSTICE, JUSTICE SHALL YOU PURSUE"[1]

WHAT DOES JEWISH LAW SAY ABOUT ABUSE?

Jewish canon law, *HALACHA*, evolving now for more than 4,000 years, is a vast compendium of discussions of and decisions about a variety of topics, from the most minute ritual practice to the broadest ethical issue. However, in every discussion, from the earliest reference in the biblical book of Deuteronomy 16:20, quoted in this chapter's title, to modern rabbinic writing, justice is the goal. Perhaps that is why the yellow pages list so many Jewish lawyers. The *Tanach,* which comprises the Torah, Prophets, and Writings, provides ample proof of Judaism's opposition to violence, but it does not specifically mention spousal abuse. It does, nonetheless, provide a foundation on which was built an enormous, and still growing, body of law.

Is there a coherent set of Jewish laws on the books in regard to domestic violence? The short answer is "no." Judaism is not an undifferentiated whole. As Jews scattered to the four corners of the earth in the years following the destruction of the Temple they adapted to their situations. Over thousands of years of living, and trying to survive, in many countries, Jewish law has evolved in ways that mirror the people's environments and the sensibilities of their times, but not always in ways that one would expect from reading the basic texts. We can see the development of the religion and the people by reading the discussions and disputes among the sages about virtually every aspect of life and death. In regard to spousal abuse, we will see on reading just a sample of these texts that basic Torah laws were sometimes adhered to and just as often ignored.

What is most apparent is that spousal abuse is not a phenomenon unique to modern times, despite apologists' statements to the contrary. It is not simply that the lewd and lascivious ways of contemporary society have led to domestic violence. As Rabbi Julie Ringold Spitzer writes in her seminal work on rabbinic response to domestic violence, "It is safe to assume that if a law existed prohibiting an activity, that activity had been or was still being practiced" in ancient times.[2] In the writings to which she refers we see examples of spousal abuse ranging from social isolation to financial control to physical beating, and the rabbis' responses to it. And, we will see sanctions imposed by the rabbis ranging from social isolation to financial control to physical beating.

The overarching theme of the Torah, the earliest of all Jewish writing, is life. The foundation upon which all subsequent and relevant law is—or should be—grounded is that human beings are made by God in God's image (Gen. 1:27).[3] Therefore, by deliberately harming another person, one is committing *hillul HaShem*, or desecrating God's name. *Pikuah nefesh*, the saving of a life, is the converse of this, as it is the sanctification of God's name. *Pikuah nefesh* is probably the single most important principle in all of Jewish tradition. The Talmud, a compilation of biblical interpretation and codified law on the Torah, expands on it. There we find the statement, "If a person destroys a life, it is as if he destroyed an entire world. If a person saves a life, it is as if he saved an entire world."[4] Eleazar ben Azariah went so far as to rule, "Saving a life supersedes the Sabbath."[5] Centuries later, Rabbi Elliot Dorff, in his *responsum* on domestic violence, writes that saving a life takes precedence over all but four other negative commandments: adultery, incest, murder, and idolatry.[6] Hence the preponderance of Jewish doctors, the great Maimonides among them.

While the active saving of a life is of prime importance in Jewish tradition, so is that of indirect intervention. "Neither shalt thou stand idly by the blood of your neighbor," commands God in Leviticus (19:16).[7] As we saw in the Introduction, communal responsibility for the actions of the individual is reflected in the use of the collective "we" in repenting for sin. This blame taking occurs at great length during the Yom Kippur prayers, and in a much shortened form in the weekday service. In the communal declaration, "Our hands did not spill this blood, neither have our eyes seen it" (Deut. 21:7),[8] the Torah brings taking responsibility for one's neighbor one step further. Here the Torah says that the entire community is accountable for what happens to its members. Quite often only the first half of the verse is quoted. But, it is critical that, not only have the elders not actually committed the crime, they must not through negligence have allowed it to happen. In more recent times, we have read horrifying stories of the child sexual abuse that was ignored and covered up by organizations including the Roman Catholic Church and the Orthodox Jewish Youth Movement, NCSY.

When it comes to domestic violence, Twerski says that a community that does not provide shelter and support for those in need of protection is in violation of this precept of not standing idle.[9] We will see in Chapter 5 just how this mandate to provide for abuse victims is carried out in reality.

While the preservation of life is of primary concern in Judaism, Twerski states that the maintenance of dignity follows closely behind. "Love your neighbor as yourself" (Lev. 19:18)[10] is probably one of the most well known and often cited commandments among both Jews and gentiles. (That commandment, of course, assumes that one loves oneself, an assumption that may not be true. Abusers themselves may suffer from low self-esteem and hence lash out at those they perceive to be weaker.) However, there are other, later rulings that expand on that basic law. "Maintaining the dignity of a person is so great that it may override *halacha*," states the Talmudic admonition that emphasizes the need for respecting another person,[11] and, "One dare not demean any human being in the world."[12] More germane to our discussion, the Talmud says, "A husband should love his wife as much as he does himself and should respect her even more than he respects himself,"[13] and, "As with another person whom one is commanded not to beat . . . even more so with one's wife whom one is obliged to honor more than one's own self."[14]

Even in the case of a murderer condemned to die, his or her body must be accorded the dignity of a quick traditional burial. So, if that is the case for another person, even a murderer, how much more so would the law hold for a man's wife?

The Talmud contains many rabbinic rulings on the treatment of one's wife. Although the most succinct is, "A man dare not harm his wife,"[15] others include "A man must be especially careful not to hurt his wife's feelings since she is easily hurt and liable to cry,"[16] and "A man should always be careful about his wife's honor, for blessing is found in a man's house only on account of his wife."[17] The latter two smack of quaintness, if not outright condescension; however, these rabbis recognized that the husband in ancient times was dominant in all ways. He had total control of everything from the finances of the household to the sole right to give a *get* (still true today). So, the rabbis' explicit admonition to men to treat their wives well stands out, especially compared with the standards of the time and surrounding cultures.

As one outstanding example of the subservient position women held in biblical times, the book Numbers (5:11–31) devotes an astounding twenty-one verses to the ritual of *mei hamarim*, the waters of bitterness.[18] In this narrative, a husband can accuse his wife of infidelity based solely on a fit of jealousy. In the test of her loyalty, she is humiliated in two ways, first by having to uncover her head in public, then by having to drink a special potion that will cause her to become ill if she is guilty. Even if she were proved innocent, he would not be charged with the crime of false accusation. The Torah's proclamation, "This is the law of jealousy, *when a wife, being under her husband . . .* " testifies as to a woman's place—beneath her master/husband.

In his sixteenth-century commentary on the *Shulhan Aruch*, Rabbi Moses Isserles says, "It is a sin for a man to beat his wife, and if he does this habitually the court can punish him. Excommunicate him and whip him and apply all measures of force until he takes an oath never to do so again. If he violates this oath he may be compelled to divorce her."[19]

As for punishment of an abusive husband, Jewish law provides for that as well. According to Twerski's reading of the *Choshen Mishpat*, "A husband who injures his wife in any way is liable for damages, and even if there were no intent of harm. The principle that a person is always responsible for his actions and must pay for accidental injury, applies to the wife as well."[20]

Rabbi Nachman of Bratslav, founder of the Bratslaver *Hasidic* movement in the eighteenth century, wrote about the ultimate punishment of an abuser. Commenting on both physical and emotional abuse by a husband, he says, "If he spends all one's murderous anger upon her, shames her, raises one's hand to her, God forbid, the Almighty will demand recompense of him."[21] This is a wonderful sentiment, but maybe too late a punishment to help the wife.

On Friday evening in many Jewish households, the husband recites *Eshet Chayil,* or "A Woman of Valor." While only a portion of the chapter of proverbs is read, we can see that King Solomon describes the wonderful attributes of a wife, from her care and feeding of her husband, children, and household servants, to her kindness and wisdom. Solomon describes her value as "far above rubies" and says, "She doeth him good and not evil all the days of her life." Most important for the current discussion, it states, "Strength and dignity are her clothing."[22]

For a while in the 1970s many Jewish feminists decried the recital of the *Eshet Chayil,* saying that it denigrated women. But, as Twerski points out, nowhere in all the accolades is the woman lauded for accepting abuse.[23] In fact, we read, "She maketh linen garments and selleth them." This proverb makes a strong statement that a woman can contribute to the support of the household while her children and husband bless and praise her. "Her husband is known in the gates, when he sitteth among the elders of the land," more than suggests that he gains stature from his wife's wisdom and business acumen. Compare this stance with the abusive behavior of a husband who tries to keep his wife from working, with the attitude that it dishonors him. In some ways, the *Eshet Chayil* prayer may set up an unrealistic expectation of what the wife should be and do—not dissimilar to what those very same feminists did in telling women that they could be and should be superwomen, successfully having both families and careers.

Unfortunately, treatment of the woman as an *eshet chayil* is not consistent in the Bible. In the Book of Judges (11:1–33) we read the tragic story of Jephta's daughter. She died as a result of her father's ill-considered vow to sacrifice the first thing that came out of his house in return for victory in battle with the Ammonites.[24] Jephta treated his daughter as an object to be sacrificed. Aside from discussion over whether his vow was valid and how he should have responded to his situation when he realized it was a human being who exited the house (Judaism explicitly outlaws human sacrifice), Jephta's tragic behavior teaches us a story of abuse. The earlier part of his life is often left off in relating the story of his daughter's horrendous fate. Because his mother was not his father's wife, but a harlot, Jephta's family emotionally abused him and treated him as an embarrassment, throwing him out of the house, causing him great loss of dignity. It is no small wonder that he developed a chip on his shoulder and a reputation as a fighter.

When his brothers then came to him for leadership in battle against the enemy, they viewed him as nothing more than a means to an end. Treated as an object, Jephta exhibited some classic behaviors in the passing of abusive behavior from one generation to another. He lost dignity and therefore felt a need to abuse another person's dignity by objectifying her.

Dignity extends to the sexual relations between husband and wife as well. Although rape, both within and outside marriage, is not a modern phenomenon, Jewish law dealt with it hundreds of years before secular law even acknowledged that it existed. Maimonides, writing in the twelfth century, says regarding forced sexual relations, "He is not to have intercourse while drunk, nor in the midst of a quarrel; he is not to do so out of hate, nor may he take her by force with her in fear of him."[25] Aside from confronting sexual abuse, this passage belies the common myth that Jews don't drink.

Rabbi Jacob ben Asher went even further in protecting a woman from her husband. He wrote in the early fourteenth century, "If a woman claims that her husband does not lie with her in any way similar to the way husbands lie with their wives . . . this claim suffices for him to be compelled to divorce her."[26] In other words, if her husband forces her to perform sex acts that she finds repulsive, she is not obligated to remain with him.

I find it intriguing that women of that time period would discuss the intimate details of their conjugal relations, both with other women and with a male rabbi. This situation stands in stark contrast with what we know today about Jewish women's hesitance to tell anybody about their abusive situation. Of course, people did live in very close quarters in some parts of the ancient world, which made it hard to keep secrets.

In summary, upholding one's partner's dignity is of primary concern in a relationship. This holds true through verbal, sexual, and physical treatment of one another. As Twerski writes, "To assert that a wife may be treated with anything less than dignity is essentially considering her a non-person."[27]

While the Torah does come out forcefully against the commission of violence by one human being against another, Naomi Graetz, in her excellent book, *Silence Is Deadly: Jewish Tradition and Spousal Abuse,* prepared an argument demonstrating that the Torah, through its use of metaphorical language, actually sets the stage for tolerating abuse that has persisted for thousands of years.[28] As one example, she presents the metaphor of God as the angry, jealous husband of Israel who humiliates and abuses his wife.

She quotes from the prophet Hosea, drawing a parallel between Hosea's fickle, promiscuous wife, Gomer, and the wanton Israelites. God is the husband, who calls his wife/Israel demeaning names such as "harlot" until she comes crawling back to him, begging for forgiveness. Note that, despite the fact that the male Israelites are also sinning, they are lumped together with the women and drawn as a female harlot worthy of abuse. Graetz quotes the following portion of the book as proof of Hosea's humiliation of his wife:

Therefore will I take back My corn in the time thereof,
And My wine in the season thereof,
And will snatch away My wool and My flax
Given to cover her nakedness.
And now I will uncover her shame in the sight of her lovers,
And none shall deliver her out of My hand.
I will also cause all her mirth to cease . . . [29]

The following section is my own choice as an example of social isolation as abusive behavior. In it Hosea says, "Thou shalt sit solitary for me many days; thou shalt not be any man's wife; nor will I be thine . . . afterward shall the children of Israel return, and seek the Lord their God, and David their king; and shall come trembling unto the Lord and to His goodness in the end of days."[30] In other words, "If I can't have you, nobody will, and then you'll come crawling back to me, your lord and master." If ever there was an example of a controlling husband socially isolating his wife, this is it.

This metaphor of the vengeful, punishing husband, Graetz claims, even without the weight of law, has penetrated the conscience of the Jewish people over the centuries by its constant repetition in the weekly Torah readings and accompanying *Haftarot* (supplementary readings from the prophets).[31]

So, the problem is not so much the law prohibiting violence, which, Graetz admits, exists on the books. It is the interpretation of it and the consistency with which justice is meted out. Unfortunately, rabbis, who are relied upon to interpret the law and carry out justice, are not all as sympathetic as one would expect based on the central religious tenets as outlined in the Torah. Graetz places the opinions of rabbis through the ages into five categories, according to their attitudes toward spousal abuse.

The first category concerns rabbis who believe that it is permissible to punish a wife. While Graetz admits that "gratuitous wife-beating, striking a wife without reason, is unlawful and forbidden," physical abuse was allowed for one of two reasons: either to "teach her the right way," or to maintain *shalom bayit*, peace in the home.[32] Either reason is offensive to the modern reader, the former because it treats the wife as a pet dog, the latter because it assumes that violence can lead to peace. Graetz cites rabbis who permit husbands to beat their wives when they fail to do their housework, when they curse his or her parents, when they scream so loudly that the neighbors can hear them, or when they provoke an argument. As the sixteenth-century Rabbi Moses Isserles writes, "It is not customary or proper for Jews to beat their wives . . . But if she is the cause of it, for example, if she curses him or denigrates his father and mother and he scolds her calmly first and it does not help, then it is obvious that he is permitted to beat her and castigate her." Given that abusers often attempt to justify their battering by accusing their wives of provoking an argument, how do we protect these women? Rabbi Isserles's ruling continues: "And if it is not known who is the cause, the husband is not considered a reliable source when he says that she is the cause and portrays her as a harlot, for all women are assumed to be law-abiding."[33] We can see in Isserles's presumption of innocence a precursor to modern American jurisprudence, something that was certainly not rampant in the world in which he lived. And yet, there it is: Not just any plaintiff, but a female one, is presumed innocent until proven otherwise.

Not only is *shalom bayit* cited as a rationale for beating a wife, the principle is cited far too often as a reason to send an abused woman back to her husband, both in ancient times and today. The fantasy of the perfect Jewish family leads well-intentioned but ignorant rabbis to send a woman back to her abusive husband. Under the mistaken impression that it is better to keep the family together, they put her in harm's way *and* violate the commandment not to stand idly by the blood of one's neighbor.

Even Maimonides, who normally opposed violence, expresses the opinion, "A wife who refuses to perform any kind of work that she is obligated to do may be compelled to perform it, even by scourging her with a rod." However, his views are not consistent. He also writes, "A man should honor his wife more than his body and love her as his body."[34] How can we explain this inconsistency? It may help to recall that Maimonides lived in

Moslem Spain and Egypt, where society accepted the treatment of women as chattel. However, I find Maimonides's position on the rod more disturbing than other rabbis' because on top of all his other accomplishments, he was a physician. As such, he most likely treated women who had suffered at the hands, or rods, of their husbands.

An adage from the *Midrash*, sermonic interpretations of biblical text, that "a kosher woman is one who complies with her husband's will"[35] has been perverted by those who rationalize their right to beat their wives. The basis for this perversion comes from a gross misunderstanding of the passage in Genesis 3:16, wherein God tells Eve, "He [Adam] shall rule over you."[36] Twerski explains that one may not cause another person or oneself to violate Torah law. He uses the analogy in which a husband would not be allowed to ask his wife to cook for him on the *Shabbat* because that would be a violation of Torah law concerning the day of rest. Similarly, by abusing one's wife, either through physical beating or by humiliating her, the husband violates the Torah's express condemnation of hurting another person.

The second category is that of rabbis who unconditionally reject any form of spousal abuse. Theirs are the opinions that most resonate with us in the twenty-first-century Western world, although their remedies for abuse are just as violent as the batterers' actions. Three medieval rabbis, Rabbi Simha Ben Speyer, Rabbi Meir of Rotenburg, and Rabbi Perez ben Elijah of Corbeil stand out in their rulings, the last because he actually attempted to change *halacha* to deal with abuse.

The first of the three medieval rabbis in chronological order is Rabbi Simha. He said wife beating is worse than general assault because, beyond the basic obligations to respect other people because they are made in the image of God, a husband must honor his wife because of the obligations he assumes with the *ketubah*, the marriage contract. In other words, he is responsible for his wife's welfare and protection. "Therefore," Rabbi Simha writes, "penalize him severely, whether physically or financially, for what has happened. Great repentance is necessary, and deal severely with him in the future as you see fit."[37] In other words, the husband is bound both morally to God and by a legal document, the *ketubah*.

The second of these rabbis, Rabbi Meir of Rotenburg, writes, "If he persists in striking her, he should be excommunicated, lashed, and suffer the severest of punishments, even to the extent of amputating his arm. If his wife is willing to accept a divorce, he must divorce her and pay her the *ketubah*."[38] Note that the Jewish woman has the right to refuse to accept the *get*. It is fascinating that the wife may not want the divorce if her husband treats her so poorly, but we see that same reaction among women today, centuries later. Going out on one's own, particularly with children, was and is a difficult choice to make.

In another, somewhat less brutal *responsum*, Rabbi Meir echoes Rabbi Simha's opinion that a man must honor his wife more than another person. He writes, "Far be it from a Jew to do such a thing . . . We should hasten to excommunicate him. Thus, a husband who constantly quarrels with his wife must remove the causes of such quarrels, if possible, or divorce her and pay her the *ketubah;* how much more must a husband be punished, who not only quarrels but actually beats his wife?"[39] Here, too, we find a rabbi who would prefer a divorce to an abusive marriage.

As early as the end of the thirteenth century, Rabbi Perez ben Elijah of Corbeil, France, actually wrote a *takanah* on the subject of allowing a woman to divorce her abusive husband. According to Graetz,

> A *takanah* is an amendment to *halacha* that changes an existing law. It usually redresses an existing social problem whose source is the law as practiced. It is an agreed-upon procedure, often announced publicly, by a group of rabbis constituting a rabbinic court . . . A *takanah* overrides and abrogates accepted *halachic* rules that precede it. Thus, it is a radical revision of an existing practice.[40]

Rabbi Perez's words are poignant in their understanding of the horror that an abused wife experiences. Considering that they were written more than seven hundred years ago, they are surprisingly apropos today.

> The cry of the daughters of our people has been heard concerning the sons of Israel who raise their hands to strike their wives. Yet, who has given a husband the authority to beat his wife? Is he not rather forbidden to strike any person in Israel? . . . Nevertheless, we have heard of cases where Jewish women complained regarding their treatment before the Communities and no action was taken on their behalf . . . We

have therefore decreed that any Jew may be compelled on application of his wife or one of her near relatives to undertake by a *herem* not to beat his wife in anger or cruelty so as to disgrace her, for that is against Jewish practice.[41]

Rabbi Perez recognizes that abuse is not just physical; it is a "disgrace," a loss of her dignity, precisely what in the late twentieth century Twerski writes is anathema to Judaism.[42] He also acknowledges and reprimands the Jewish community for ignoring the cries for help of the "daughters of our people." He then outlines a process for obtaining justice and freedom for her. The first step involves granting a *herem*, or excommunication, of the abusive husband, a powerful incentive for him to behave. After all, the Jewish community then was smaller and more insular; Jews did not intermingle freely with gentiles. To oust from the community one of its members would have lasting repercussions. On the other hand, Rabbi Perez understood also the power of the community to bring its members into line. If the *herem* still did not encourage the husband to give the *get*, then the *beit din*, rabbinical court, would have the authority to provide alimony to the woman. Whether she was given an actual *get* in this case is not clear.

Also not clear is why this particular *takanah* was never accepted into mainstream usage, but we can surmise that it was not in the rabbinic mindset to give the woman an equal footing in her marriage. What is clear is that the mind-set is still unreceptive to this day. Graetz confronts the twentieth-century scholar Louis Finkelstein, who decided that Rabbi Perez's *takanah* probably did not enter the mainstream because it was not necessary—wife beating did not exist among Jews.[43]

When I asked one rabbi of a *beit din* how he felt about the use of civil law to address abuse as opposed to fixing *halacha*, he said, "I feel okay about it." He did not see any need to change *halacha* because civil law was available to achieve the same results. The rabbi repeated several times the religious tenet, *dina demalchuta dina*, the law of the land is the law, to provide support for this position. Since we live in a country with protections, he said, we should therefore use them. What he did not address was the fact that only 6 million Jews live in the United States, where these civil law protections exist. The world's Jewish population is 13 million. What are the 7 million Jews without American civil protections to do?

My own favorite opinion was written six hundred years after Rabbi Perez wrote the words above. Rabbi Abraham Paperna, a prominent Polish rabbi, pulls no punches when he rails against the status quo:

> These are our mothers, our sisters, our daughters, our flesh and blood. We must be concerned for their welfare and not let them be ridiculed and downtrodden by men of greed, who treat them like dust to trample on and allow decisions to be made against them. This failure is your fault, rabbis of Israel! Instead of getting on a soapbox to curse the Zionists, instead of debating in the "palace" business deals of the Colonial bank, instead of forbidding the new methods [of study], you should be sifting through the terrible confusion of rabbinic literature and working on ways to make *halachic* decisions to help.[44]

Rabbi Paperna expresses here the frustration that modern scholars and activists of many creeds experience in attempting to gain a sympathetic ear.

Finally, we arrive at our time in the history of Jewish law. Although I contacted every major movement's rabbinic association and seminary, only three had issued resolutions on the topic of spousal abuse, and only one had published a *responsum* on the subject. That one was written by Dorff on behalf of the Conservative movement.[45] He reviews the millennia of opinion on the topic of wife beating, and summarizes the Conservative movement's opinion on spousal abuse. Dorff writes that, beyond providing guidance on Jewish law on the issue of family violence in his *responsum*, "We certainly cannot interpret Jewish law to allow us to be less moral than what civil law requires."[46] Furthermore, he exhibits a deep understanding of abuse as more than simply physical assault. He recognizes verbal and psychological abuse as well.

> Most cases of abuse cannot be justified in any way as rooted in a concern for discipline. They are, instead, bald exercises of physical might for purposes of exerting power over someone and/or of expressing one's own aggressions on innocent victims. Judaism unequivocally sees these as forbidden. Jewish law specifies punishments for those who strike others and demands that the objects of such attacks do

everything in their power to escape such situations, even if it means defaming the assailant or embarrassing oneself. Judaism also prohibits verbal abuse of all kinds, claiming that in significant ways it is worse than monetary fraud.[47]

Denial is the third category of rabbinic response to domestic abuse in the Jewish home. In the thirteenth century Rabbi Tam said, "Wife beating is unheard of among the children of Israel."[48] Even in modern times, as a direct example of this attitude, Hertz[49] writes glowingly of the Jewish family that never experiences violence despite being surrounded by drunken and abusive revelers. He quotes Jewish and gentile sources alike to support his naive view of the Jewish family. As he quotes Zangwill, "But no Son of the Covenant was among the revelers or the wife beaters; the Jews remained a chosen race, a peculiar people, faulty enough, but redeemed at least from the grosser vices—a little human islet won from the waters of animalism by the genius of ancient engineers."

Even today, as the general media has focused a great deal of attention on the problem of domestic violence—from newspaper accounts to feature length movies—far too many rabbis remain in denial. Too many told me that they have never been approached by a congregant about abuse, so they assume it does not exist in their congregations. But, it is not just rabbis who deny the existence of abuse among Jews. Throughout the course of my research I was confronted with denial and evasion. The president of a synagogue sisterhood refused to speak with me because "we don't have that problem in our congregation." A leader of a national women's organization told me that domestic violence would not be considered an appropriate topic for an annual convention because "we want to depict the beauty of Jewish life, not that [seamy] side." I believe the message of denial is being transmitted from the top down, from the professional and lay leadership alike, nationally and locally, like a contagion.

In a slight variation on denial, apologists for the faith, Graetz's fourth category of rabbis, attempt to defend Judaism from criticism, both from within the clan and without. Their reaction is understandable in some ways. For thousands of years, the Jewish people were driven from their own land and from the lands of their dispersion. They lived in countries that may have tolerated them for the contributions they made to commerce, but loathed them and blamed them for a wide variety of social and medical ills. Too often the loathing turned to persecution, and worse. More often than not the blame was placed on Jews to deflect attention from the despots leading the country. Protecting the Jewish community from those who meant to do them harm was paramount. However, as Graetz asserts, by participating in apologetics, we assume that Judaism is too fragile to take criticism, whereas the opposite is true. The religion was built up through discussion and argument, as witnessed in its vast libraries of law and commentary.

Apologetics takes several forms. First is that of displacing the blame onto the surrounding culture. For example, Maimonides, considered one of Judaism's greatest thinkers, lived in twelfth-century Moslem Spain and Egypt. Apologists claim that Islam's belief in the superiority of the male and its condoning of wife beating explains Maimonides's acceptance of the practice. After all, Maimonides was surrounded by Moslems and Islamic culture. Apologists claim that the laws of Judaism were far ahead of their time in treating women better than other religions did. And, in fact, in considering the *ketubah,* the marriage contract, we can see that women were given protections that women in other contemporaneous cultures were not. However, the contract was not always honored, and there was a clear loophole. Among others, Rabbi Solomon ben Abraham Aderet writes in thirteenth-century Spain, "But if she is the cause of the beating—i.e., if she curses him for no reason—the law is with him, for the woman who curses her husband in front of him, leaves without her *ketubah*."[50] In this act we see the ultimate in financial control. The husband "purchases" his wife through the *kinyan*, acquisition, process, and signs the *ketubah*, the marriage contract that is supposed to guarantee her financial independence in the event of a divorce. If he claims that she cursed him, he can divorce her and send her away penniless, keeping the dowry money for himself. (Note how Rabbi Solomon's opinion is diametrically opposed to that of Isserles, who ruled that the wife should be presumed innocent for lack of witnesses to the alleged curse.) Today, the *kinyan* ritual remains a part of the betrothal. Although many apologists say that it is merely a symbolic ceremony at this point in history, I believe that the message of merchandise exchange is stronger than mere metaphor.

In early Talmudic rulings, Graetz writes, the rabbis forced the husband to pay damages if he beat his wife. However, the damages are paid to the "owner" of the injured. Since the wife is the husband's property, her money was actually his, so she would never see it. Here is a Catch-22 if ever there was one. While the rabbis did arrange for land to be purchased for the wife, the husband could take all the earnings that the land produced. The sole consolation for the wife would be that if she were eventually to divorce him, she would have the land and its produce to support herself.

The second form of apologetics is justifying physical abuse as being necessary to educate the wife and preserve *shalom bayit*. Aside from the offensive view of the wife as child or pet, the practice may have evolved in some times and places because girls were married off as children, and the husbands may have felt that they were taking the place of parents. However, beating children is also anathema to Jewish sensibilities, so the explanation still does not sit right. Finally, apologists attempt to marginalize the prevalence of spousal abuse by saying that even if it does occur, it does so at a much lower rate than among other groups. If experts' estimates are correct, then this argument fails as well.

The fifth and final category of rabbinic response to spousal abuse is what Graetz calls evasion of responsibility, or "wringing of hands," to use her words. This is the method of doing nothing because, as these rabbis claim, they are helpless to change *halacha*. They profess to be sympathetic, but, regardless of the misery and humiliation it causes, they say that they must follow the letter of the law. One Orthodox rabbi, for example, says that *halacha* doesn't need to change because it works fine just the way it is. Furthermore, in attempting to justify his position, he says that women can be just as recalcitrant by refusing to receive a *get*. What this rabbi fails to reconcile is his own admission that it is women who most often request the *get*, not the other way around. Despite the financial hardship they will suffer, and despite the recognition that they will suffer socially in their very insular communities, they are willing to undergo divorce because *they want to get way from their abusive husbands.*

It is interesting here to look at a concept related to *takanah*. *Tikkun olam*, or repair of the world, comes from the same Hebrew root word and is yet another important tenet of Judaism. Based on the *aleinu* prayer that Jews recite three times daily, *tikkun olam* aims to "perfect the world under the rule of God," according to Telushkin.[51] Human beings are set on earth to help in the repair work. In the second century Rabbi Tarfon taught, "You are not obliged to finish the task; neither are you free to neglect it" (*Pirkei Avot,* 2:21).[52] Graetz, among many others, asserts that those rabbis who have the ability to perform the task are showing little effort to rectify the problem.

As we learned earlier in the chapter, a *takanah* is legislation designed to alter *halacha*, often created to bring law up to the standards of the society in which the Jews were living and to the sensibilities of the times. The process can be likened to that of achieving an amendment to the U.S. Constitution but without a formal vote. These are radical changes, and they are not taken lightly. However, they have occurred and do continue to occur. Graetz cites several examples of *takanot* (plural of *takanah)* instituted over time, ranging from that of prescribing the schedule on which the Torah is read to enacting a ban on polygamy. This latter *takanah* was designed precisely because polygamy was not tolerated by the Jews' neighbors. Similarly, sensibilities of our times have changed regarding our views of women as chattel. When apologists claim that Jews' treatment of women is far superior to that of other groups, they are living in ancient times. By continuing to give the husband exclusive control of the divorce process, they deny dignity to the woman. And, as we learned previously, the denial of dignity leads to an abuse of power and control.

Related to the issue of the *get* is the *agunah,* or chained woman. This term applies in several situations, including those in which a husband is lost at sea or in battle, or through divorce. In the last case, because her husband refuses to give her a *get*, the woman may not remarry in a religious ceremony. Any children she has without a *get* will be considered *mamzerim*, or bastards. This is a particular problem for observant women. They are, in effect, held hostage, often with financial extortion as the bargaining chip the husband will use to give the *get*.

The Rabbinical Council of America, the association of Orthodox rabbis in the United States, has developed a two-part prenuptial and arbitration agreement. These two documents, each signed by the bride and groom and two witnesses, are in actuality a civil contract. The arbitration agreement commits both parties to submit to the *beit din,* rabbinical court, their dispute for judgment. The prenuptial agreement sets a specific amount of money that will be paid to the wife for her maintenance in the event of a separation. As one Orthodox rabbi explained to me, the sum entered into the contract is so "outlandish" that it is a great inducement to the husband to give his wife a *get*. Yet another Orthodox rabbi stated, "This is standard now in Orthodox circles." If either partner refuses to abide by the stipulations of the contact, the other can bring suit in a civil court of law to enforce it.

The two religious movements that have developed prenuptial contracts are on extreme ends of the observance spectrum. The Orthodox, while it cannot seem to make a change in the Jewish law it holds so dear, uses civil law to get in through the back door to give help to women. Rabbis of the Reform movement, on the other hand, bluntly told me that *halacha* does not figure in their decisions in more than an advisory capacity. The Conservative movement, according to Telushkin, has inserted a clause into its *ketubah* obliging the husband to give his wife a *get* in case of divorce, but, strangely, not one Conservative rabbi mentioned this change to me.[53]

One Orthodox rabbi asserted quite strongly that even though the husband must give the *get*, the wife must accept it. He presented the position of Rabbi Gershon of the ninth century, which states that one cannot make a woman take a *get* against her will. He then described a case in which a woman had holed herself up in a motel, refusing to accept a *get* from her husband. A group of rabbis drove three hours in an attempt to convince her to accept the *get*. She still refused, and there was nothing they could do to further the process. This incident may indeed have occurred, but even this rabbi admitted that the vast majority of women not only accept the *get*, they request it.

Graetz has assembled a formidable argument on the subject of granting the *get*.[54] The withholding of the *get* is symbolic of the abusive treatment women receive not only at the hands of their husbands, but at those of the rabbis who preside over her divorce. Moreover, it is symbolic of the basic inequality of the wife in marriage. Graetz proposes for the twenty-first century a *takanah* to end this millennia-long method of psychological abuse by providing a woman with the *halachic* means to divorce her husband. She proposes equal footing for both husband and wife, eliminating the husband's sole power to end the marriage. In the event that either wishes a divorce, the *beit din* will sit down with them and arbitrate mutually agreeable terms. If that is not possible, the *beit din* will then grant the *get*. I believe that Graetz's proposed solution would not only address the concerns expressed by the rabbi above regarding a woman's acceptance of the *get*, but would also provide a level playing field for both husband and wife.

The bottom line of the *get* issue is that it is based on the inequality of the marital parties (not partners), and inequality sets an atmosphere that allows for abuse of power. Power can lead to abuse, both psychological and physical, and from there to violence.

The relevance of the *beit din*, and any ruling it makes, is entirely dependent on the community's acceptance of it. For example, the *herem*, or excommunication, is almost exclusively relevant in the Orthodox community, where being deprived of religious honors, such as ascending the pulpit to bless the Torah, represents a real loss of prestige. The unwillingness of so many rabbis to participate in carrying out sanctions against a batterer make the institution of *herem* appear weak and would be laughable if the situation were not so serious.

A case in New York illustrates just how powerless the *herem* is if the community does not support it. An Orthodox man in one of the boroughs of New York was excommunicated from his congregation for spousal abuse, but he immediately went across the river to New Jersey, where he was welcomed into a Conservative synagogue. The reality is that the *beit din* is not all-powerful as it was in the days of insular Jewish *shtetls*, or villages, and ghettoes. American Jews live in modern society and, barring the building of a massive wall around an equally massive ghetto, they are going to abide by modern standards. This is the ironic converse of the *takanah*. If the majority of rabbis don't accept it, then it won't become *halacha*. If the community won't accept the *beit din*'s *herem*, it reduces the court's power. Consequently, the community itself is weakened. When I spoke with one rabbi, he claimed that he has only come across one case in all his years as a rabbi in which he "was set to go before the congregation on a *Shabbat* and denounce this man" before the man finally agreed to give his wife a *get*.

Three additional Jewish legal precepts are relevant to the discussion of spousal abuse and the law—specifically, what is a Jew's responsibility to report suspicions of abuse, or knowledge of it, to the civil authorities? The first is the prohibition against *lashon hara*, gossip or slander. From the earliest reference to talebearing in the book Leviticus, "Thou shalt not go up and down as a tale bearer among thy people"[55] (19:16), Judaism has frowned on gossip. Slandering an individual is considered as grave as murder because it harms a person's reputation. "Gossip is more hideous than capital crime," says the Talmud,[56] and "The penalty for slander is equal that for all the cardinal sins."[57]

Orthodox Rabbi Mark Dratsch discusses *lashon hara* as it relates to the reporting of a crime.[58] He begins by citing a ruling that one witness is not sufficient to testify against an accused person. Although he cites the late nineteenth-century rabbi known as the Hafetz Hayim, who ruled that any gossip must be substantiated enough to bring to a court of law, he states that the need to prevent further injury to the victim trumps concern for the presumed innocence of the accused. He then provides a talmudic ruling that condemns anybody who withholds evidence. This discussion's relevance to the topic at hand is obvious: Grave danger can come to the wife and children if nobody is willing to report that abuse is occurring. Unfortunately, relatives, neighbors, friends, and fellow congregants often fail to report their suspicions, either due to embarrassment or out of fear of intrusion or retribution.

This failure to intervene makes it all the harder for an abuse victim to get help, and the difficulty is exacerbated when one considers another facet of *halacha* that Dorff addresses in his *responsum:* the victim's responsibility to escape her situation.[59] He states emphatically that a woman must find her way out of danger. However, we have seen that all too often a woman is told to go home, keep quiet, and not endanger the husband's reputation or the children's marriage prospects by speaking out. She is made out to be the villain. Unfortunately, aside from quoting various rabbinic sources, Dorff's *responsum* does not provide guidance to his rabbinical audience.

The above discussion brings us to the relationship between Jewish law and state civil and criminal law. The second Jewish precept of community responsibility is that of *hillul HaShem*, desecration of God's name, and this particular tenet has been twisted in ways to make it almost unrecognizable. We saw earlier that harming another person is a grave violation of the principle that each person is created in God's image. To injure another person is to injure God and to desecrate His name. However, when it comes to reporting a crime to state authorities, the Jewish community has almost unanimously succeeded in sweeping dirty secrets under the rug for centuries. Rabbis have encouraged this because airing the crimes publicly would commit *hillul HaShem* by bringing shame on the community. This, despite the fact that the real damage was done to the victims, not to the perpetrators. One attorney who represents clients in divorce cases, both with and without abuse allegations, told me that Jews are among the most reticent about reporting—even to her, their legal counsel.

Related to the issue of *hillul HaShem* is the principle of the *mesirah*. For centuries, *mesirah* has forbidden Jews from reporting crimes to civil authorities. Maimonides writes, "Whoever adjudicates in a non-Jewish court . . . is wicked and it is as though he has reviled, blasphemed, and rebelled against the law of Moses."[60] Dratsch explains this severe ruling as a method to ensure that Jewish law would take priority over civil law, and bases it on the biblical verse in Exodus 21:1, "Now these are the ordinances which thou shalt set before them."[61] In other words, Torah law takes precedence over secular law.

One *Hasidic* rabbi's assertion, backed up by more than a few rabbis I spoke with, that "we take care of our own," is both wrongheaded and arrogant, yet an example of abiding by the *mesirah*. Unless these rabbis have been trained specifically and intensively to deal with domestic violence, they can do irreparable harm. For instance, by telling a violent husband where he could find his wife's shelter, a rabbi put a congregant in potential danger *and* placed a stumbling block in the husband's path by leading him into the temptation to abuse again.

One rabbi told me that the *beit din* arranges for women to stay in a safe home until one or both partners are in treatment. When I asked him how safe a woman would be in this underground apparatus, given the tiny, insular nature of the religious community, he said, "We don't have men who are pathologically seeking to really go after the wife. My experience has been that you have a husband who, when he's alone with his wife, strikes her, but he would not go to somebody else's house, break in, and go after her. That level of violence I've never seen." He may never have seen it, but the police have, when it is too late to help.

On the other hand is the Jewish principle of *dina demalchuta dina,*[62] the law of the land is the law, which supports adherence to secular law. The main purpose of the *dina* principle was to try to ensure that the Jews of the Diaspora host countries would be welcome and less likely to be considered a threat, even if not accepted as full citizens. By living according to their own laws and ignoring their host countries' statutes, the Jews would be perceived as thumbing their collective nose at their hosts. Dorff put the tradition into historical perspective by pointing out that rabbis developed *dina* mostly to deal with commercial law.[63] However, as the Enlightenment allowed Jews to acquire rights and privileges they had previously been denied, and as the *batei din* became progressively weaker, it became obvious that a higher authority was needed to control criminal activity.

In more modern times the *dina* principle has come to be applied to all issues of obedience to civil law. Nevertheless, while spousal abuse can rightfully be considered a *hillul HaShem*, too many rabbis take it on themselves to ignore the law of the land. According to Twerski, "*Torah* law requires recourse to a *beit din* and not to secular courts or police. The exception to this is when one is threatened by violence, when it is permissible to call for police protection if one has no other way of protecting oneself."[64] What Twerski fails to recognize is that domestic violence is progressive. According to experts, "It is rare that no other power and control tactics exist besides physical ones. By failing to intervene early on, the community puts the victim in danger."[65]

Given so many rabbis' blindness to the serious threats faced by the women in their congregations, we must be concerned with the attitude that rabbis can judge on their own what is dangerous. When rabbis believe that they can "take care of their own," they may put their congregants in potentially life-threatening situations. When they tell women to go back to their husbands, with the mistaken notion that the abusers will change and that the wives can "make things right," they may be guilty of the sin *"Ya'atznu ra,"*[66] "We have given bad advice."

In the end, both the Orthodox Dratsch and the Conservative Dorff say that the overriding principle of "neither shalt thou stand idly by the blood of your neighbor" must prevail. *Dina demalchuta dina* requires reporting the crime to the civil authorities.

I believe that it is not only a moral and ethical obligation to report abuse. It is a practical matter. Regarding the embarrassment of the Jewish community that so concerns many rabbis, I believe that those who fail to report abuse cause greater shame later on. We have only to look at the child sex abuse calamity that has befallen the Catholic Church to get more than a hint of the horror that religious leaders can inflict on the very faith to which they have pledged their lives.

A few medieval sages, well ahead of modern times, do comment on the possibility of using civil law to help wives escape their abusive husbands. Rabbi Meir of Rotenburg, writing in the thirteenth century, says, "If the husband does not observe the peace [imposed by the *beit din*], and continues to beat her and verbally abuse her, we agree that he should be excommunicated [the *herem*] by the upper and lower courts and be forced by the non-Jews to issue a divorce."[67] A contemporary of Rabbi Meir, Rabbi Simha of Speyer, writes, "If the husband . . . continues to beat her and denigrate her, we agree that he should be excommunicated and forced by Gentile authorities to grant her a divorce [in accordance with] what Israel [authorities] tell you to do."[68] This latter rabbi recognized that denigration was also a form of abuse worthy of serious attention.

Twerski also discusses the modern-day responsibility of the community in relation to the above declarations. He states, "A society that demands such self-effacement and does not provide a woman with the resources and abilities to defend her dignity is an accomplice to the abuser . . . Then the community is tacitly encouraging the abusive behavior and is an accomplice to the sin."[69] I see an inconsistency between Twerski's call for communal responsibility and his hesitancy to use the civil authorities to impose sanctions on the abuser.

Many of the rabbis I spoke with claimed never to have had a case come before them in all their years in the pulpit. Graetz cites the case of a prominent Conservative rabbi who stood before the convention of the Rabbinical Assembly and stated that he had never seen a case of domestic violence in his congregation.[70] This is not surprising, if we judge by the women I spoke with. Fully half of them did not consult their rabbis, and gave as their overwhelming reason that they did not consider their rabbis approachable on the subject. Since most of the rabbis had never given a sermon on the topic of abuse, it is no wonder that the women viewed them this way. We are caught in a vicious cycle of ignorance and denial, resulting in pain and injury.

It may be helpful to step back for a moment and look at how decisions regarding Jewish law and daily practice are actually made in the present day. The *beit din* is a court of justice whose jurisprudence is based on *halacha*. It executes all legal transactions for the Jewish community that require its expertise, including divorce, financial claims, and sensitive congregational issues. When it comes to the marital situation, the court involves itself not only in divorce, but also in intervention during the course of the marriage and postdivorce.

The *beit din* in Boston uses the services of between fifteen and twenty rabbis and works with cases anywhere between Boston and New Haven, Connecticut, although not the Berkshires. Between three and five rabbis will sit at any given court meeting. All the rabbis who serve on the *beit din* are educated in the United States at the Rabbi Isaac Elchanan Theological Seminary (RIETS) at Yeshiva University in New York, and are therefore Orthodox. According to their spokesman, these rabbis helped develop the Orthodox prenuptial contract, which was referred to above.

First, let us take a look at how the *beit din* deals with a divorce. According to a rabbi associated with the court,

> Somebody will call the *beit din* and say, "I need a *get*." The *beit din* will then contact both parties, the husband and the wife and say, "Your partner wants a *get*." They will verify that the civil divorce is in place, that it is far enough along that it's not going to stop. Ninety-nine percent of the time the *get* comes at the end of the civil divorce. The only time we do it beforehand is if we're terrified of the recalcitrant husband or wife situation, because that person can trap the other person into [never] getting married again. When we smell that we'll do it beforehand. And then, in fact, we won't give the actual document until the civil divorce is complete. We are on very high moral ground on the "law of the land is the law."

The rabbi reported that more women request divorces than do men, and that between 5 and 10 percent of partners are considered recalcitrant. "We generally define recalcitrance as if in three years after the civil separation one of the partners still refuses to give or take a *get*." It is important to note here that lawyers report that divorce cases involving abuse can take up to six years to adjudicate.

As for intervention, I was quite surprised when one rabbi told me that women in abusive marriages not only come to him for help, but that friends, relatives, and neighbors will call to report abusive marital situations. No other rabbi I spoke with had conveyed that experience. Of course, this rabbi worked with the *beit din*, whereas the others were pulpit rabbis. In fact, most of the rabbis in this study had not had any experience with reports of abuse among their congregants. This rabbi described the following scenario:

> I observed that a marriage was floundering. The husband was a real control freak. I went in for early intervention. I spoke to him and spoke to her. He was starting to tie up telephone lines, so she couldn't make long distance calls to her parents. I saw that the marriage wasn't going to last. I saw that it was going to take three or four years [for her to get out]. I saw to it that he paid for her to get a graduate degree. When she got out, she was ready for the world.

In this case the rabbi wisely determined that social isolation, manifested by cutting off the wife from her parents, was a form of abuse. He intervened early enough to make a difference in the outcome of this woman's life.

Sometimes a domestic situation becomes violent. At this point, the *beit din* becomes involved again. As the rabbi explains, "We get calls. The *beit din* will get her out of there. We will get her a safe place to be. There is an underground of safe homes and shelters, not in Massachusetts, but certainly in New York and other places. We will get somebody to take this woman in and put her in a safe environment. Then we call in a whole group of psychologists and social workers . . . that work with rabbis."

So, we now come to the question of whether rabbis actually make use of the American criminal justice system in helping victims of spousal abuse. (We will leave the question of other types of help to Chapter Five.) According to the police chiefs, domestic violence unit heads, and department spokespeople with whom I spoke, the answer is a resounding "no." Almost all of them told me that Jews, whether clergy or laypersons, rarely, if ever, call for help. They explain that, in general, middle- and upper-middle-class abuse victims don't call the police at nearly the same rate as lower income people. Certain ethnic groups rarely call. The police point to several groups, mostly new immigrants, who have fled lands with oppressive regimes and corrupt police. They do not trust the police here, despite having fled to this country for freedom. Jews, despite having lived here for a long time, have long memories of their people's oppression. The new dependence on civil law for ensuring the *get* makes this hesitance to use the criminal legal system quite the paradox.

A lawyer who works in family law spoke with me about the various legal issues involved with Jewish divorce, particularly as it relates to those that involve domestic violence.

> These divorces are different, yes, especially in religious cases. The husband has to give the *get*, and many abusers use the *get* as a negotiating tactic so he will withhold his consent to the religious divorce unless the wife meets his demands. In nonreligious families it's not a problem. In religious cases, it becomes an issue. I have seen men use it to ask for ridiculous terms: waiving alimony, agreeing that the women will get less than 50 percent of the marital estate, negotiating down child support. This is usually not played out by the attorney. If an attorney does this, he or she can be called to task. It's usually done behind the scenes. Usually I'll get a call from the wife, saying, "He knows I want this, and he's going to go to the rabbi next week." He wants to negotiate down what he's paying. The women want it over and they are willing to make concessions. I send the "CYA" [cover your ass] letter telling them that they are selling themselves short. I recommend that they don't settle and they can get so much more. Once, I had a Jewish judge, and the husband wanted a waive of alimony. It was a long-term marriage, the children would be emancipated soon, and the wife had been out of the workforce many years. The judge did a lot of questioning, asking, "Do you understand that you are giving up your right to alimony? I don't think this is fair. You need to understand that if there is any side agreement, if you are holding anything over her head, I need to know." We ended up putting in a provision for alimony. But, the client said she wasn't going to enforce it. "I want the divorce," she said. There are a lot of issues that come up when there's domestic violence. First of all, there's getting the truth to come out. Many times, more in Jewish divorces, I don't even know about the domestic violence until we are well into the case, because the woman is so embarrassed, so uncomfortable and afraid. I see this more among Jews. The repercussions they are met with, such guilt from the sidelines. The husband's family will refuse to

provide for the grandchildren. They will refuse to believe that it could happen. There are serious issues that need to be considered even if they weren't abused. If there is a restraining order against him he cannot be considered for custody. Often in Jewish divorces it's verbal and emotional manipulation. If you can get a restraining order and then another instance of abuse starts, then the financial starts. I do see that a lot more in domestic violence cases.

One Orthodox rabbi with whom I spoke described the difference between the situation in Israel, where family law is adjudicated through the religious courts, and the United States. A relatively new law on the books in Israel states that a man does not have to give a *get* but when he does not, and the court requires it, he may be "taken off the books; he can't get a bank account; he can't get a credit card . . . a driver's license . . . a passport." This is all well and good, but it still does not address the problem of divorce for those living outside of Israel.

The biblical injunction "Justice, justice shall you pursue" opened this chapter. While Judaism began its long history with the Torah and its many laws revering life and dignity, the interpretation of those laws has not been consistent.

The prophetic verse, "The righteous shall live by his faith,"[71] implies that anybody obeying the rules of Torah could not possibly commit abuse of any kind. However, simply maintaining the minutiae of ritual practice does not make a "righteous person," as Twerski pointed out. In my synagogue we sing the words, "The world stands on three things: study of *Torah*, ritual practice, and acts of loving-kindness" while marching with the Torah. If the last is missing, abuse can result.

Related to the religious behaviors practiced outwardly, in *Pirkei Avot*, the Sayings of the Fathers, we read, "When a person's fellow creatures are pleased with him, God is pleased with him."[72] Unfortunately, it is precisely the population of men who behave with strict adherence to Jewish ritual outside the home that provides perhaps the greatest challenge for the community to confront. It is the image of the saintly man that surprises so many when the truth comes out. In fact, the community often blames the woman for the failure of the marriage while continuing to hold the man in a place of honor.

The great strength of Judaism is its ability to debate and discuss issues, and to help *halacha* evolve with the times and places of Jewish living. Its weakness is based on that same fact, that there is no single authority whose word is law. As we saw in the case of Rabbi Elijah of Corbeil, not enough rabbis accepted his *takanah* aimed at righting a grievous wrong. The seeming inability to find a well-respected rabbi who is willing to take on the problem of the *agunah* and the *get* is a disgrace to Judaism. It is in itself a *hillul haShem*. We are no longer living in the Middle Ages. *Takanot* have been written and adopted to help Jews live in the lands of their dispersion. While the Orthodox movement has developed a civil law solution to the problem by using a prenuptial agreement, its rabbis continue to "wring their hands," to use Graetz's phrase, regarding a *halachic* one.

People expect their religious and communal leaders to lead by behaving morally. We have seen that disastrous consequences can result when they attempt to keep secrets for the purpose of protecting their own reputations or in the mistaken notion that they are defending the collective whole. The Jewish community must pay attention and learn a lesson before it suffers its own explosion.

4

"THE ERRORS
OF THE SAGES"

THE RABBIS AND WILLFUL NEGLECT

> The errors of the sages are regarded as willful sins; the sins of the ig-
> norant are accounted as unwitting errors.
>
> —*Talmud: Bava Metzia*[1]

WHETHER A CROCHETED *KIPPAH* OR A TRADITIONAL FEDORA, THE
rabbis all wore head coverings, and that was about the only consistent char-
acteristic among them. Of the thirty-three men and women with whom I
met, the vast majority was affiliated with the Reform and Conservative
movements. They graduated from seminary or received private ordination
anywhere between the 1940s and the very year the interview took place.
There was one cantor in my sample, and, as a member of the clergy, I included her with the rabbis rather than with the Jewish professionals, such
as social workers and Jewish Federation executives.

Only one rabbi refused outright to meet with me, and with several others
I could not get past the secretaries who guarded the men with great zeal.
These rabbis were uniformly Orthodox. In the Boston area, several small
congregations have answering machines rather than full-time secretarial staff.
I received no return calls from messages left on these, which was unfortunate,

because most of these congregations, too, were Orthodox. Obviously it would have been preferable to have had more representatives from that movement. With several other rabbis, scheduling difficulties and winter weather precluded setting a meeting date. Although the winter of 2001–2002 in New England turned out to be one of the mildest in meteorological history, there were still the inevitable glitches. After one particularly difficult time in scheduling, I did conduct one interview by telephone, having obtained the rabbi's signature on the consent form prior to asking any questions. Only one rabbi refused to have his interview recorded on tape.

As with the survivors of abuse, I asked a series of questions of a wide cross section of rabbis across Massachusetts. I had originally aimed for the somewhat unrealistic goal of meeting with every rabbi in the three focus federation umbrella areas in Massachusetts, but I discovered after a couple dozen interviews that I had reached the point of diminishing returns. I continued on until I had met thirty-three rabbis in the three areas on which I focused. This number comprised almost half of the total number of rabbis in the state.

And, again, as happened with the survivors, what I found most interesting was not the "yes" or "no" responses to particular questions, but the narratives that resulted from the questions. Questions led to new topics, and responses provided me with new avenues to explore beyond those I had originally intended. As with a musical composition, it is not necessarily the notes, but the spaces between them that provide the interest.

Did your rabbinical seminary formally address the subject of spousal abuse in its curriculum?

The overwhelming majority (twenty-five out of thirty-three) of rabbis reported that their seminaries did not address the subject in a formal way. Three responded that the subject was touched on in a minimal or informal way only, and in one of these cases only because the professor had a particular interest in the subject.

If so, did it teach the subject from the perspective of law?

Only two of the entire sample stated that their seminary curriculum taught Judaism's response to spousal abuse from the perspective of law. One of these rabbis was Orthodox, one Conservative. One Reform rabbi explained to me that seminary students are trained to read code, they are not trained to apply it to specific subjects. Another stated, "Jewish law informs what we do but we are not restricted by it." However, several Reform rabbis referred to the late

Rabbi Julie Ringold Spitzer as having been the catalyst for that movement's consciousness-raising about the subject of domestic violence.

Were you trained in pastoral [spiritual] counseling to deal with the abuse of a congregant?

A slightly greater number of rabbis were trained in pastoral counseling than in Jewish law, but not specifically in relation to spousal abuse. A few rabbis indicated that there "might have been" a one-time mention of the subject in class, or, in some cases, an entire class period may have been dedicated to crisis counseling in general, but not to spousal abuse specifically.

One Reform rabbi said, "There was a voluntary course when I was in school called Clinical Pastoral Education, for all crisis types. I'm afraid spousal abuse was only one lecture, but it was covered."

In your perception, has the preparation changed since you graduated?

More than half the rabbis interviewed either did not know if the preparation had changed since their own graduation or said that it had not. One rabbi believed that consciousness about the problem had risen in his Orthodox movement. Of the rabbis who did feel that there had been a change in the curriculum, Reform outnumbered Conservative by a margin of more than two to one.

The Hebrew Union College (HUC), the seminary of the Reform movement, has added a new layer of pastoral counseling requirements, according to several of the more knowledgeable rabbis I spoke with. "The whole approach to pastoral counseling has changed," one told me. A course called Clinical Pastoral Education is now required of all seminarians at HUC. Although the course does not necessarily address spousal abuse per se, it does deal with crisis intervention.

Do you feel prepared to deal with spousal abuse in your own congregation?

Less than one-third of the rabbis in my sample felt prepared to deal with a congregant victimized by abuse, whereas almost one-half responded anywhere from "no" to a resounding "absolutely not." One Conservative rabbi was adamant that "this not be viewed as a women's issue, but that it be viewed as a community problem." Here are some sample responses from both Conservative and Reform rabbis.

No, I didn't feel prepared when I came out of seminary and I still don't, although some of the education I have gotten since has been

helpful. There was a seminar for clergy run by the district attorney
and that helped me; it certainly sensitized me . . . So the answer is I
feel woefully unprepared to do it, but as long as I have phone numbers
of people who can do it and can be supportive, I think that's my role.
[My job is] to let the person know that I care and to follow up. I have
not found a comfortable way to deal with it.

This next rabbi was even more unsure of his ability to deal with a congregant.

Prepared? Absolutely not. That's one of the good things that Professor [XX] taught us. He said, "Know what you know and know what
you don't know." The best thing a rabbi can do in his community is to
know the resources. As a congregational rabbi . . . there are many
times that I was out of my league. You can meet with someone once
over an issue and hear them out . . . If they want to meet with you a
second, and you're not a licensed counselor, then the second time is to
help hook them up with a professional and there's no third meeting.

In contrast, a few rabbis did feel prepared, in large part due to training
they had received outside the seminary walls. The first rabbi is not affiliated
with a particular movement, which, at first blush, I thought would put him
at a disadvantage. However, as we can see from his words, this seems not to
have been the case.

Yes, for a couple of reasons. First there is a very vast and strong infrastructure in this area. I feel prepared personally because three years
out of seminary is three lifetimes . . . you have so many experiences;
people talk to you. Whether you actually get involved in the treatment
per se or not, you're a part of it.

The following Orthodox rabbi expressed the greatest amount of self-
confidence of all the rabbis I met. He said,

I was trained in New York to address social issues [family, relationships, etc.], then I trained other rabbis in Boston. When I was young I

thought it [spousal abuse] was a function of poverty, but it wasn't, or a lack of education, but it wasn't. It had nothing to do with either.

Within the Jewish community there exists a certain amount of competitiveness and mythology surrounding the members of other movements. Virtually every person with whom I spoke, whether survivor, layperson, or member of the clergy, thought that the problem of spousal abuse was more serious in movements of Judaism other than his or her own. In relation to the subject at hand, several Orthodox rabbis expressed the opinion that liberal movements produce family violence due to lack of ritual observance. On the other hand, more than a few Reform and Conservative rabbis stated with certainty that abuse was more rampant among the Orthodox, particularly the ultra-Orthodox *Hasidic* sects. Witness this quote from a Reform rabbi:

> There is a dramatic difference in dealing with this kind of stuff in a liberal Jewish community and in dealing with it in the Orthodox, or especially ultra-Orthodox community, because the way that they deal with Jewish law and deal with these kinds of issues is so different. It's a very different, a much more closed culture. We're part of American society and we are fundamentally liberal in approach. For sure we should be doing more to talk about this, but I don't think that there is anything in the religious institutions or in the particular society that we're part of that hides this more than anyone else does—which is a lot. People hide it.

Safe Havens is a Boston-based program that trains clergy of all faiths and teams from congregations in dealing with domestic violence. Of those rabbis who did feel somewhat prepared to handle a crisis of spousal abuse, virtually all had attended the Safe Havens training. However, one rabbi who did attend still did not feel adequately prepared to deal with a crisis of this magnitude.

What do you do when a congregant comes to you with an account of spousal abuse?

Rabbis here reported a host of impediments to giving the proper attention to a congregant. These obstacles range from lack of knowledge to an abuse victim's fear of her husband's revenge to the rabbi's hesitance to risk the wrath of an abusive husband. The Conservative rabbi quoted here expresses the difficulty of dealing with allegations of domestic violence within his congregation:

> To disclose these things is a very difficult piece. I can only imagine it . . . but knowing how hard it is on the one hand but also the lack of opportunity to disclose on the other really traps a person, handcuffs a person actually. So, the question is, what are we doing or how can we improve ourselves in terms of being open for disclosure? More has to be done, but what I think it comes down to is that a person is very lost. Talk about being in the wilderness, this person is absolutely without support while he or she is going through it.
>
> I would find that person a place [to go] . . . and I would recommend calling the authorities that need to be called, recognizing that people are extremely afraid and that there is a social stigma that goes along with that. But as things get written in the paper . . . people won't want to call the authorities right away.
>
> There's a tendency for caregivers, especially if it's people in my congregation where I know both of the folks, to rationalize away the risk because, let's face it, there is some political and emotional risk to the discomfort of confronting someone who is part of my community. And on the other hand is perhaps a somewhat serious risk of overreacting; you see somebody who is in pain and difficulty. Clearly some intervention is warranted, but is it right every time to call the police just because there has been some abuse? Part of me would say "yes" and part of me would say "there needs to be some intervention," but that may be an extreme intervention, especially given what I understand about the inconsistencies of the system sometimes, and how it depends on who's called and how they respond. My first sense is that what may be needed is help and support for the family and not retribution and punishment. Again, that depends a lot on the nature of the abuse and the nature of the other circumstances.
>
> It depends on the nature of the report. How severe was the abuse, how long had it been going on? A read on the person's resources for taking action on their own behalf. The presence of children in the

family or not. And then, like most counseling situations, a range of interventions depending on how serious it is and . . . if the person's life
is at risk, that's a very different kind of an intervention than if for the
very first time in a marriage somebody has lost his temper and become
physically abusive in a way that's not life threatening but is obviously
cause for serious concern. To me those seem like somewhat different
circumstances, with a slightly different response, all of which would
require an intervention of some sort. There are several different tasks,
it seems to me. One is to provide support to the person sitting in my
office and to give them a safe place to bring these concerns, and to
some extent give them what I know from popular culture and some of
the limited reading I have done on the subject to deal with their own
denial about and rationalization about this behavior. [Including] that
it's never okay to hurt somebody you love. To either encourage this
person to notify authorities or to notify authorities myself, or certainly
getting them into a program like Safe Havens *(Author's note: Safe
Havens is not a shelter to which to refer people),* again a lot depending
on the specifics of the situation. It becomes equally important not to
overreact or underreact, which is easy to say and hard to calibrate.

One Reform rabbi outlined some steps he would take.

I would put her in touch with resources [shelter, notifying law en-
forcement] immediately. It is most important to reassure them that the
community is there for them and that they are not alone.

This Orthodox rabbi also felt that referral to others was appropriate.

If I feel that, once having discussed the matter with the aggrieved
party, this is an issue that I am not equipped to handle, I would make
appropriate referrals to those who are trained far better than I am.

The following narrative illustrates the most extreme of the rabbis' views
in keeping the secret of spousal abuse within the Jewish community. In this
case, the *Hasidic* rabbi did not trust even the local Jewish social services
agency.

I don't send them anywhere. There are times when I would direct her to the Jewish Family Service, even though I don't have such extreme faith in it . . . what happens when people have problems at 8:45 [P.M.]? What do you do? You have a whole night to contend with. But if a person comes to me, I ask them right away did they speak to anybody before, did you speak to JFS. They may feel more comfortable with me, so I will listen to them and then I would see whether I could speak to the husband as well as the wife. There are wives who are also abusive, sometimes quite abusive.[2]

If I'm going to help them I have to listen to them, and I would ask the woman if the husband knows that she came to me and does she think the husband would want to talk to me, and I would make an effort to call the husband. Naturally, if it's a person that I know I would feel comfortable calling and asking him to speak to me.

This rabbi continues:

The business of hot lines is like this: There are emergency situations, life and death situations, where there's no question that any hot line would be good for that. On the other hand, if it's a problematic husband and wife situation, I wouldn't consider a hot line the place to call. If it's a matter of an extreme nature, I certainly wouldn't ask her to call a hot line. I wouldn't call police, but I would call her right away and try to advise her as to what to do. I certainly would make it my business to speak to one of the partners.

At this point, I asked the rabbi if the women were punished when their husbands found out that they had spoken with him.

There are times when the husband is angry that she did it behind his back. I would explain to the husband when I speak to him that he shouldn't blame her, and I wouldn't tell the husband the kinds of things she said about him anyway. But I would tell him that she's very upset—you have to really play it by ear in each particular situation . . . there are no two cases [alike].

This rabbi struck me as both dangerously naive as to the nature of abusers and overly protective of the image of the Jewish community. He assumes that his advice to the husband not to take out his anger on his wife will suffice.

This next rabbi does recognize that marriage counseling is not likely to help in a situation of abuse. According to experts with whom I spoke in the field of abuser rehabilitation, even those men who participate in specialized long-term programs demonstrate 50–60% recidivism rates.

> If I have reason to believe that it's really impacting on the individual, then at that point I would see to it that they see someone else. At times I'll even suggest marriage counseling, even though I understand that probably at this point it's irrelevant. If it's physical it has to be dealt with immediately. I would immediately get them to a shelter.

On the other hand, here this same rabbi put the wife at grave risk by confronting the husband. Did he know that she had told the rabbi? Who was protecting her while the rabbi was accusing the husband?

> At one point I tried to confront a husband whose wife said he was abusive. I said to him outright, "Are you physically abusive of your wife?" He denied it, which of course I expected him to. As we talked there was absolutely no acknowledgment whatsoever, and at that point I realized, I'm not the one to do this. Sometimes you try to be that savior and it just turns out that you're not. I realized that I had to advise her to get out of that relationship but to seek help in terms of the abuse.

In the following narrative, we see an Orthodox rabbi begin by trying to gather information from the victim. Recall that experts such as Twerski recommend strongly against putting a couple together in a counseling situation when abuse is involved.

> I try to learn as much as I can about the situation. Depending upon circumstances and the background and what the person is telling me, if I feel that it would be helpful to have the accused individual meet with me jointly or privately, I would make that recommendation.

But here, the same rabbi displays a practical knowledge of just how long and torturous the process of leaving is.

> I'll ask her if she spoke with anybody else. Has she called the police? Who did she speak with—a counselor, a therapist? Is she prepared to do anything about it? Depending on the answer to those questions [we] will determine what the next step is. If the abuse has not been happening over a long period of time, my experience has been that they are not prepared to do much about it. Coming to me may be the first step in a longer process before they're ready to talk to anybody else, do anything, move out.

Contrast the above with the following Conservative rabbi's statement.

> I don't believe that the first place that people will go is the rabbi. First, I'm a man. My sense is that for most of the people who come to me, [I'm] the last person they come to. For what I represent, who I represent, the issue of shame and silence—all those things. Once they talk to the rabbi, there's nobody left to tell. If I'm going to tell the rabbi whom I know in all these other arenas and all these other contexts, then it's not going to be the first place I'm going. First I'm going to go to a therapist or, in a violent situation, to the police. If I'm talking to my rabbi, I'm coming out fully.

Remember that only half of the twenty women affiliated with synagogues ever sought out their rabbis' help. The Conservative rabbi here mentioned that sometimes he sees women from other congregations. He stated that, even in large congregations, there is not enough room for both members of a couple to feel comfortable in the case of a divorce. Abuse exacerbates the problem. He said, "Sometimes the abuser is in a leadership position. So it makes it impossible to be able to see the rabbi as a real disinterested party." Recall how Chaya described her experience with the rabbi of her Orthodox synagogue as biased toward her husband and against her.

In the following example, an Orthodox rabbi stated that he had received training on domestic violence fifty years ago, an amazing forty years ahead of the curve for society. However, when we look at his response to the problem, we see that he operated under the false assumptions and myths that untrained people do.

> I never tried to act as if I have a Ph.D. in psychology or psychiatry. I've never tried to play that role and I don't think that is my role. I try to make myself available as the first point of contact if people don't know what to do about their problem, so people can feel free to call me. I don't try to treat them or deal with it. What I try to do is to get them into the hands of people who are professionally trained to do so.
>
> My principal role is to be a resource that people feel comfortable to go to without being judged.
>
> A congregant once came to me and indicated that he was having great difficulty with his wife . . . The number of hours that he needed of me was something I felt I couldn't handle and told him that he should see somebody who could help him. But I wasn't sure. Then, . . . I simply called his wife. She stopped me and [told me] she was the one that was being abused. Anyway, because I had this relationship with him I continued it and called [some people]. I asked if they were aware if there was a problem. I learned to my shock and dismay that several of the neighbors of this man were [rotating shifts] walking by the house at night to make sure that there was nothing terrible going on. When I called his wife, he stopped calling me. I realized that could happen, but I was very glad I did it. I kept in very close touch with her friends who essentially were guarding her. She ultimately simply left the house.
>
> I saw my role as trying to expedite getting help for him and I did. But then after I contacted his wife, I realized that I was at risk, and he just ceased to see me anymore.

Note here an important point. The rabbi observed that he was putting himself at risk by contacting the wife, but never did he consider the fact that he was putting the wife at risk by letting a violent man know of this contact. This rabbi claimed to have had training in domestic violence, but the action steps he took were the direct opposite of what is considered by experts in the field to be appropriate behavior.

I then asked this same rabbi if he felt the victims wanted him to intervene. At this point, he admitted,

> Not all the time. Because they're afraid of them [the abusers]. They feel that they have no one to protect them in context, so that if in fact he were to become aware either directly from me or indirectly that she had come to see me, he may take it out on her in a circumstance in which she would not be able to defend herself and [yet] she is not ready to move out. There are also issues relative to whether there are children or not, and how much they are aware depending on their age and whether or not it [the abuse] has rippled over into the kind of interaction she may have with them. These are all the variables I have found that will feed into her decision into what she needs to do. I really can't do much without her consent and her willingness for me to be involved in that manner.

The question of whether or not Judaism matters came up in several conversations with rabbis. I asked them if they felt that victims of abuse were looking for protection under Jewish law. Did they feel that their husbands would be more likely to listen to their rabbis than to someone who doesn't care about Jewish life? This Conservative rabbi answered firmly:

> No. The reason that playing the Jewish card doesn't work is that it [abuse] is in the family. If my grandfather abused my grandmother, then it's part of the history there. There's a sense that that kind of verbal play could have been very abusive . . . Grandma was stuck in the kitchen, Grandpa didn't allow her any access to the money.

One *Hasidic* rabbi told me of a particular woman who came to him for advice. Her husband was abusing her severely.

> I called the husband in and told him that Judaism absolutely forbade abuse. If he has a mind to divorce her . . . so be it, but to hurt her feelings, even a stranger, you don't hurt a stranger's feelings, and especially when there are children. Why should children be exposed to

this? It had an effect for a while; for a few months it worked. But as time went on he went back to hurting her.

"Were these religious people?" I asked him. "I question the sincerity of their religiosity," he replied.

Have you ever addressed the subject of spousal abuse in sermons?

"We have so many important things to worry about. If I thought this was a real problem, then I would do something about it. Show me some statistics." You may remember this quote from Chapter 3, but it bears repeating. It seems to summarize a rabbinical attitude toward spousal abuse.

The majority of rabbis (nineteen out of thirty-three) had never addressed the subject of spousal abuse in even one sermon. Only a third had ever spoken about the abuse in the context of other themes, such as social ills (alcoholism, drug abuse, gambling) or in discussing ethical Jewish behavior in general. This Orthodox rabbi stated:

> No, I've been fortunate that this wasn't a problem of widespread consequence. When I was younger and a little more activist, I let it be known that I had this training and exposure and was sensitive by way of simply saying I'm a resource if you need me. Some people did come. That's as far as it went. I never saw this as a big enough problem to address it as such in the congregation.

In the above quotes we see a rather blatant example of denial. Whether from an innate repulsion by the idea of such behavior, or an unwillingness to believe that it could exist among Jews, denial is a powerful strategy. Apologetics is another strategy developed over generations of discrimination against, and persecution of, Jews. As we saw earlier, Jewish writers felt a need to defend Jews and Judaism from those who would harm them. Some romanticized the Jewish wife and family, saying that social ills such as abuse, alcoholism, gambling, and the like rarely, if ever, occurred among Jews. Others blamed any abuse that might happen on the cultural environment. The disintegration of society and its morals were the cause of abuse in the Jewish family. Another Orthodox rabbi asserted:

As far as Jewish law is concerned I have addressed this publicly in
synagogue on *Shabbes* mornings or in lectures over the years. Jewish
law has no tolerance for spousal abuse; it's grounds for divorce. At the
same time . . . it's against Jewish law to beat up your wife, with somebody who can't control himself that's not going to help, he's got other
problems. Just the cerebral awareness of what the law [says] doesn't
necessarily mean that you're going [to] have an individual ready to
take the step necessary to abide by that regulation.

I asked this particular rabbi about the women who complained to me
that their abusive ex-husbands continued to receive honors from the synagogue, ranging from sitting on the *bimah,* the pulpit, to getting *aliyot,* honors, to blowing the *shofar,* the ram's horn, at the High Holidays. He asked
me if these women had informed their rabbis that their husbands were beating them. In every instance the woman said "yes." The same Orthodox
rabbi then declared forcefully:

Then they are absolutely correct. They weren't given that additional
layer of communal protection; their claim against the leadership of
those communities has great validity. If there's agreement on the part
of the wife, I am prepared to get up on *Shabbes* morning and identify
him and say people shouldn't say "hello" to him, shouldn't say "*Gut
Shabbes*" ["A Good Sabbath"] to him, and if he's in business that
people shouldn't go to his store.

In all the conversations I had with rabbis, not one had actually ever
done this, and not one of the communal leaders or survivors had ever witnessed such an event.

One federation leader criticized rabbis' preparedness and willingness
to deal with domestic abuse. He took issue with his own rabbi's seeming
unwillingness to address the topic in even one sermon.

There are places that people would go where they would expect to be
able to open up, to [the rabbi] who will send them in the right direction. Wouldn't it be nice if the rabbi talked about something other
than his trip to [X]? There's something about sermons today that's ir-

relevant. The real social issues are not being attacked with the type of fire that they used to be attacked with.

Unfortunately, it is often the women and children who suffer greater consequences of abuse within the congregation. Recall Chaya, who was ostracized by the women in her Orthodox congregation when word of the abuse became known. Remember the persecution her son suffered at the hands of a "religious" teacher at his day school. She belonged to one of these very congregations whose rabbi, quoted above, displays his ignorance of this treatment. And consider Judith, who, despite a very supportive rabbi, was forced to leave her synagogue due to congregants' cruel behavior toward her. One Orthodox rabbi told me:

> One of the difficulties in the Orthodox community in particular is that it is hard to hide in a small town. In a place like New York or Chicago, where the Orthodox community is much larger, you can get lost. When you have children of school age and they're going to day school, it's even more difficult to get lost. It's hard to hide. We're aware of that, although this coalition has created a few safe houses in the general area, and we're also connected with an Orthodox body in New York which runs a twenty-four-hour hot line.

An Orthodox rabbi then addressed an issue related to the above-mentioned ostracizing of abuse victims. The behavior he described illustrates another aspect of social control, one I had never heard discussed before.

> I know that when a woman divorces because of abuse the husbands of her friends try to distance the wives from her. What bothers them is that they will raise the specter in the wife's mind that she is abused, because, "Maybe I behave in similar ways and I don't want somebody telling her that this is abuse because she is going to come to me and say 'You're an abuser.'" There's a real fear of having these women get together, and the husbands in subtle ways try to distance their wives.

Have you ever participated in a panel at your synagogue dedicated to spousal abuse?

Only four of the thirty-three rabbis I spoke with had ever participated in a panel on domestic violence at their own synagogues. Of course, it is remotely possible that a panel could have been held without a rabbi present, but, given other participants' responses to my question on this subject, I doubt it. The following Conservative rabbi appears to understand his own limitations in the area.

> My sense is people know who in the community are really good at this and who are not, and I'm sure that I don't give off the signals of being very adept at dealing with this, so it's possible that people see others or hold back. Maybe if I spoke about it more, maybe if I did more sermons; whatever you talk about extensively is what people think you're interested in. That's always an issue. On the one hand we talk about spiritual matters, we talk about education, we talk about Jewish tradition. All of these "social issues" we may talk about once or twice—we don't do eight sermons in a row on abuse or alcoholism. If we did we would probably get more people coming to us but, again, the role is so vast and varied and you have to make your choices of what you can do and how much you're going to give to each of these issues. And I'm not saying it's more important that someone comes to me to talk about *kashrut*, Jewish dietary laws, than about spousal abuse, but I probably talk more about *kashrut* than I do about spousal abuse. Maybe I'm more comfortable talking about it. I certainly know more about it. Maybe that's how it comes out to the congregation and the community, so while I may be sympathetic, it's not something they're going to run to me about.

Ironically, this rabbi who didn't see many cases of spousal abuse in his work probably had himself brought about the low turnout at his office door. Why would a woman even think to approach her rabbi when that rabbi had never before uttered a single word expressing the view that abuse is wrong? (Recall that not one woman I interviewed had ever heard her rabbi speak on the subject.) This finding jibes with that of the rabbis' revelation that they had never given a formal sermon on the topic. The best I could find was that one rabbi said he addressed the subject "indirectly," another "informally" at couples' club get-togethers. It is interesting to note that some of the women with whom I spoke happen to belong to these very rabbis' congregations. They had never heard those rabbis speak even indirectly about the subject.

In tremendous contrast, another Conservative rabbi was the most vocal and energetic of all the rabbis I interviewed for this study. He dedicates one sermon every year to the topic of spousal abuse, and participates in relevant panels in both the Jewish and secular communities. He told me that he has been approached by an average of one woman a year (not necessarily a congregant) who is seeking help in breaking free. I believe that this rabbi has seen more abuse victims than all the other rabbis in my study because he has made his position on abuse public. Abuse victims know that they can approach him because he has a visible record.

Yet another rabbi felt that the synagogue would not be the appropriate sponsor of a spousal abuse program. Instead, since domestic violence is a universal problem, he suggested the Jewish Family Service, or even the United Way, should sponsor an educational and outreach program.

Have you ever participated in a panel in your community dedicated to the subject of spousal abuse?

I had anticipated that, even if the rabbis had never directly dealt with abuse in a Sabbath or High Holiday sermon, then at least they would have been involved on a different level. However, only four rabbis had ever organized or participated in a panel discussion at their own synagogue, leaving twenty-nine rabbis who have never addressed spousal abuse in an adult education program.

Again, most (twenty-six out of thirty-three) rabbis had never participated in a panel sponsored within the general community. However, for some of those who had participated, their involvement was restricted to attending a rally or vigil.

Are you aware of whether the annual convention of your rabbinical association has ever addressed the topic of spousal abuse in Jewish families?

Two-thirds of rabbis responded that they were not aware of convention coverage. Some said that they "guessed" it would have been the topic of a breakout session, but not the subject of a plenary. Of the remaining one-third of the rabbis who were sure that spousal abuse had been addressed at a convention, most were affiliated with the Reform movement. This Orthodox rabbi claims here that his association is open to the subject:

We've [the Rabbinical Council of America] been very willing to deal
with this. While the anecdotal evidence seems to suggest that our
numbers and percentages are lower than the general community, our
conviction is that one case is one too many. So we're prepared to go
public on it.

Interestingly, this very rabbi acknowledged only moments later that the
incidence of abuse in the Jewish community is probably comparable to that
of the general population.

*Have you ever attended an education session on spousal abuse at one of
the rabbinical conventions?*

Over two-thirds of the rabbis I interviewed had never attended a session on spousal abuse at a rabbinical convention. Obviously, if two-thirds of
those rabbis were not aware whether a session had ever taken place, then
this result is not surprising. However, even among those who were sure that
one had taken place, only one-third had actually attended a session.

*Have you ever attended any other forum, workshop, or course focused on
spousal abuse within the Jewish community?*

Fewer than one-third of all the rabbis in the sample had attended a
course. The *Shalom* Task Force is a program specifically designed for Jewish clergy. This group has sponsored several workshops in the Greater
Boston area, but most of the rabbis I spoke with were either unaware of the
program or "did not have time" to attend. What is interesting is that, in answering both this question and the one above, several rabbis could not remember if they had been present for such a program, despite the serious
nature of the subject matter.

*Have you ever attended any other forum, workshop, or course focused on
spousal abuse outside the Jewish community?*

At this question, things began to look up for a while. Eighteen of the
thirty-three rabbis I met had indeed attended a workshop on spousal
abuse. Virtually all of those rabbis stated that they had participated in one
Boston-area program—Safe Havens, an interfaith program designed to
train clergy and teams of congregants. However, that organization's records
indicate that only ten synagogues have ever participated in their training
programs, so I will attribute the inconsistency to lapses of memory. The

nonrabbinical member of the clergy described her experience with the Safe
Havens training program to me.

> The purpose of Safe Havens is first to educate a core group of people,
> including at least one member of the clergy, as to the complexity of
> spousal abuse. It's so easy if you're not in an abusive situation to say,
> "Well, why don't you just leave?" I think very often people don't un-
> derstand. What are the different avenues available? Why it's some-
> times more dangerous than staying. What they hope is that, given all
> this information, you will then come back and create a plan realizing
> that every house of worship has a different structure, for disseminat-
> ing that information to the community and also making the commu-
> nity aware that there are people available to help them if they need that
> help. Information here has gone primarily through our monthly
> newsletter. Everybody here gets the newsletter, so it's not threatening
> to a woman who's in an abusive situation. It's not like there's some-
> thing [lying] around the house that she shouldn't have, from a doctor
> or a counselor.
>
> One of the things that Safe Havens pointed out . . . [o]ften you're
> more helpful than you know and you never know how helpful you've
> been. Because what you do is you start putting out information for
> people, so they won't necessarily come to me, but that doesn't mean
> that they're not reaching out to help that is available to them that they
> otherwise wouldn't know is available. Because of the Safe Havens pro-
> gram several lecturers came and spoke; publicity goes out in our
> monthly bulletin, I have some things out here on the bulletin board.
> Also some crisis [hot line] information . . . for students who are being
> abused by a boyfriend. We have had programs on abuse for our stu-
> dents. We had somebody come in and speak on abusive relationships
> to our high school students.

Several of the rabbis responded that they have been invited to attend this
training program but have not been able to take, or were unwilling to make,
the time to attend. Safe Havens does indeed require a time commitment,
both for training and implementation within the teams' own congregations.

One Conservative rabbi told me that he and several congregants had attended the Safe Havens program. They had intended to run an education session at the synagogue, but internal politics within committee had indefinitely postponed the event.

After repeatedly responding "no" to the seven questions above regarding whether they had spoken about or attended an educational program on abuse, some of the rabbis became somewhat sheepish. Two remarked to me that they were "embarrassed" that they had neither spoken about the topic nor managed to get any education on the issue. One told me that she would bring up the subject with the convention planning committee of her professional association. Three younger rabbis said, "Thank you for raising my consciousness." Unfortunately, rabbis outside the metropolitan Boston area claimed that they have not had access to a spousal abuse training program in their own communities.

Have you ever been asked to hang a poster in your synagogue that advertises a "hot line"? Did you agree to do so?

More than two-thirds of the rabbis had been asked to hang a poster in the synagogue, either in the women's rest rooms or on a bulletin board. Every one of them agreed to do so, except for one rabbi who presides over a congregation in rented facilities. Of the nine who had not been asked, five said that they would agree, and the remaining rabbis responded that they would consult with lay leaders to get their opinion before agreeing to do so. That some rabbis claimed not to have been asked prompted me to wonder if congregants simply hung them without bothering to ask. One Reform clergy member described her temple's experience with posters in her temple.

When you leave Safe Havens, you come back as a group and discuss what you can do within your community, and [hanging posters] was one of the steps that we had decided to take . . . There were posters, but I'm not sure they stayed for long. Nothing really became of that. It didn't really make it into the bathrooms like I was hoping. I think the committee, and this is really the committee's job, fell a little short in terms of implementing the action steps that they had outlined . . . We also had posters around the building, and other educational information. The challenge is putting it somewhere where people can find it, where the abuser wouldn't take it. I know it would be safe in my office, but would somebody feel safe coming in and getting that information from me?

Like the above participant, several others discussed the nuts-and-bolts problems of information dissemination. Most people come to the synagogue on *Shabbat* exclusively. The first obstacle is that the rest rooms where posters would most likely be located would be crowded on *Shabbat;* it would be difficult to take a card or flier with so many witnesses present. On top of that, observant women would not tear a form from a poster or carry a slip of paper home. They would have to make a special trip to the synagogue under one ruse or another during the workweek in order to get into the rest room. If they work, that would complicate matters. Such are the impediments faced by women struggling to get help.

The following rabbi invested so much energy into the process of decision making that it never became clear whether the congregation did anything regarding posters.

> I would agree to discuss that among our clergy, and then I would want to incorporate our lay leadership in that discussion. So, I would be predisposed to but I wouldn't say "yes" without any kind of process because I think that the people to whom others might turn have to be incorporated into that decision. I don't think those decisions are made unilaterally. That's a real forum for leadership. I think that it's important for requests like that for community resources to be a part of the social action, *tikkun olam* community of the congregation, and for the congregation to have a concept of how it deals with many issues of social concern. For example, on that same wall could go hot lines for drug abuse, for Habitat for Humanity, or a lot of worthy issues of *tikkun olam.*

The comment did come back, albeit a minority one, that people were uncomfortable with the posters in the women's room because children use those rooms as well, and they felt that this wasn't "appropriate . . . that it wasn't the right thing to do to have those kinds of posters and information suggesting such things occur when you have kids coming in and focusing their attention." This reaction was not restricted to rabbis. In asking for

permission to hang posters recruiting volunteers for this study, one Jewish
Community Center director refused to allow a poster in the main women's
dressing room for the same reason.

In the following narrative, an Orthodox rabbi discusses the issue of the
mikveh, the ritual bath that we discussed earlier.

> Another aspect of this is the *mikveh*. Here again we got a split opin-
> ion—some wanted it, and others felt that when women go to *mikveh*,
> that is not the kind of thing they want to look at . . . it's a spiritual time
> for them and it has very great meaning for them, and by having this
> kind of a poster making such a declaration [it would be disturbing].

Finally, one congregation's rabbi reported that the committee suffered
from such great infighting that no aspect of the Safe Havens program was
implemented.

Would you report suspected physical abuse to the police? Why or why not?

This question immediately provoked detailed Talmudic-like question-
ing. What kind of abuse? How long had the abuse been going on? Are there
children involved? Do you mean reporting with or without the victim's
knowledge? The only item on which almost all the rabbis agreed was that
in cases of life or death, they would call the police. But, even here, the response was not unanimous. The few who had studied with Safe Havens
worried that, given that the most dangerous time for a woman is immediately after she leaves her abuser, they would be putting her in danger. Some
rabbis were concerned about their legal obligation to keep confidential the
information the woman had revealed to them. They stated that they would
have to call on legal counsel to help them with the decision. One rabbi believed (falsely) that she was a mandated reporter (more on that later).

> That is a tough question. We have to balance the mandate against
> *lashon hara* [gossip, or literally, "evil tongue"] with the principle of
> "do not stand idly by the blood of your neighbor."
>
> I would probably call resources of mine to find out what (a) my
> legal obligation is and (b) what privilege is there; is it an option for me
> to make the phone call? Has child abuse come up?

There is a difficulty in taking a counseling situation and reporting. Without permission I would not report.

Part of my job is to protect the innocent and to allow for those who are infringing upon the rights of others to embark on *teshuvah* [repentance], the first step to taking responsibility.

So, what was this rabbi saying? If we were to wait for the abuser to repent, the wife could die.

Let's return for a moment to the subject of the *mikveh*. The woman about to enter the *mikveh* must be completely free of impediments to spiritual cleansing before immersing herself in the waters of the ritual bath. The female superintendent of the facility checks her naked body for stray hairs, fingernails, and so forth. The "*mikveh* lady" has the greatest access to the most secret nature of a woman's life. Does she have the obligation to report bruises, cuts, scrapes, or worse? This Orthodox rabbi didn't have an answer, although he was fairly certain that a poster should not hang in the *mikveh* to let women know that they could get help. He felt that "they don't want to have their focus disturbed."

There is a difference, though, between the *mikveh* lady seeing the evidence of physical abuse on the one hand and whether she should or shouldn't deal with it, and how she should deal with it is another host of questions.

On the other hand, this Reform rabbi was a bit more willing to report abuse, with some provisos:

In theory, I think I would [report]. If someone is being beat up, I think I would. There are always potential complications with anything that goes on, and I would probably want to make sure I knew what I was talking about. If someone came to me with this, I would probably refer them to JFS, so I don't know if my first thing would be to call the police, or if it would be to call JFS and consult with them about what's going on with this family and should we call the police.

A Conservative rabbi was more focused on gaining consent from the abuse victim.

> Only with the permission of the person who has been abused [would I report]. I would certainly go after that person to find out what had happened. If I got vague answers or answers that I intuitively didn't trust, I would try to get that person to make an appointment with me. I would be pretty explicit with that person in raising the question whether or not he/she had been physically abused. If they answer "yes" I would certainly encourage police intervention, but I wouldn't do it without the permission of that person. I would want to persuade the victim to . . . separate herself from the abuser.
>
> I would talk to the person before dragging police into a home. It's not clear where the problem lies. If somebody tells me about it, I have a very different posture. Unequivocally, yes. I try to do what I'm trained to do, not what I'm not. I don't want to shirk responsibilities, but I don't want to go . . . where I'm not trained.

In this next passage, we meet a rabbi who would welcome some clearer guidelines, both for the victims and for his own protection.

> The law is inconsistent. They're saying that we should report about child abuse but not about spousal abuse, [but] to me they are parallel issues. The advantage of having the law require it is that it makes it easier for us to make that decision so we're not open to lawsuits and other problems . . . it's hard enough to know when you raise an accusation that a family is going to go ballistic on you, and the likelihood in those circumstances is not that the person who is being abused is going to side with you. They're going to back their spouse who is the abuser in most cases. And knowing that and knowing that you could be accused of "you're attacking us, you're persecuting us," we can have lawsuits against us. But if we're required by law to do it, then . . . we have no choice, we have to do it.
>
> There are definitely things which are ambiguous, but you know that there are kinds of bruises, kinds of things that just don't happen. You don't get cigarette burns or you don't get marks behind your ears.

People who understand this stuff, they know. That's what the training would do, to tell you what the difference is. A law would make our lives easier, but we could also feel, "Well, there's a potential problem here I'm not sure [about] but I have to report it," and someone's life could be ruined. So there's always a downside to everything.

With an adult the situation is different. With a child you can take them out of that home and that child will be protected. An adult won't necessarily leave the home, they won't necessarily press charges, and it could put them in a much more dangerous situation if I were to report. It's more complicated.

The subject of mandated reporting came up in some interviews with the rabbis, and their responses varied. One Conservative rabbi erroneously thought that she was required by Massachusetts state law to report spousal abuse to the authorities. As of this writing, there is no such law in the Commonwealth, although several states do require certain professionals to report suspected abuse. Only in 2002 did the Massachusetts State Legislature pass a law to add clergy to the list of mandated reporters for child abuse.

Here is where spousal abuse comes in. If a child is abused in Massachusetts, *or is witness to spousal abuse,* a rabbi would be required to report that suspicion to the Department of Social Services. Because an adult victim is considered capable of caring for herself and reporting the abuse, there is no requirement to report. Ironically, it is precisely when she is being abused that the woman is most vulnerable and in need of help. This Conservative rabbi was very conservative when the subject of reporting came up.

I'm not sure I support it. I think there are so many gray areas. I think there should be some guidelines that require more reporting of some sort, that where there is evidence of abuse there ought to be a way to intervene or get someone to intervene to pull that person out of the situation. I'm even a little suspicious of mandatory [reporting] with children, not because I think it's wrong but because there are the cases of misrepresenting, misreading a situation, which [cause] tremendous anguish with the family. When you take a step like that, the net goes out and you catch a lot of dead fish and tuna and old shoes in the net that you sent out to catch cod. So the question is, does that mean we should stop putting the net out? Probably not, but you have to recognize that the people that get caught in the net may be innocent, there may be different situations, and we have really hurt the situation. I'm reluctant to throw these nets out there . . . It's not a problem of the system, it's how we abuse the system. We need some kind of check and balance in the system . . . to avoid the number of people who get caught in that net.

Another rabbi felt that the issue of confidentiality should be of overriding concern. It is obvious from this narrative that the rabbi mistakenly believed that he was a mandated reporter.

No. Please understand that I'm not trying to be difficult or confrontational. It would depend upon the way such information came to my attention. If I learned of abuse in the context of an otherwise pastoral encounter, I would not report it, and I would ignore the provisions of the state statute because I believe that the communication or the ability of the clergyman to confidentially communicate and receive communication as part of his/her pastoral responsibility is a stronger and overarching public policy than the provision of mandating reporting. If I felt that the woman was in serious danger of violent harm or death I might violate my own principle. If she were seen with a black eye or a broken arm or something like that—it depends on how that information came to me. I think we should encourage people to come to their clergymen.

I'm telling you that I value the confidentiality relationship very highly. It is an extremely important public policy objective so that it would take a lot for me to breach that. That doesn't mean I wouldn't take that seriously. I'm not convinced that calling the police . . . that they're the best agency to deal with these things. I do not look upon myself as a police agent.

Are you familiar with secular (Massachusetts) law on spousal abuse?
Only four rabbis felt that they were familiar with the state's law on spousal abuse. Three said they felt they had only a little knowledge of the

law. Surprisingly, one of the rabbis who felt he had little knowledge is the same rabbi with the most extensive experience in dealing with victims of abuse. Of those who were knowledgeable, all had taken training workshops from either Safe Havens or the *Shalom* Task Force. The following rabbi sums up for his colleagues, "I should be more familiar than I am. More important than the law is how it's enforced. From going to something that wasn't even on the map fifteen, twenty years ago [domestic violence law enforcement] has made a lot of strides."

How do you feel that Jewish law relates to secular law on the subject of spousal abuse?

Two-thirds of the rabbis I interviewed believed that Jewish law would support secular law, citing the precept of *dina demalchuta dina,* the law of the land is the law, which we discussed in Chapter 3. Six admitted they did not know the Jewish laws regarding spousal abuse, and one stated that Jewish law would not support secular law. Of course, having seen that virtually every rabbi stated in response to the question above that they had no knowledge of Massachusetts law, they had to operate on either their knowledge of what *halacha* would say about secular law, or simply by gut instinct.

Since Orthodox and Conservative rabbis operate under the constraints of *halacha,* it is logical that they would be more knowledgeable of it and see that it supports secular law. Consider the following two remarks. The first was made by an Orthodox rabbi:

> A husband may not take his wife against her will. He may not take his wife while she's sleeping. He can't put himself upon her to do his will. She has to consent and she has to participate. My understanding is that *halacha* has been way ahead of any contemporary legal setting that I'm familiar with. In *halacha,* spousal rape has been on the books for three and a half thousand years.

A Conservative rabbi added his perspective on the relationship between *halacha* and secular law:

> In American, Western, Oprah society, there's this sense that "I'm the victim." There's always this strong sense of "this has been done to me and therefore I did what I did." This is a very un-Jewish perspective.

A person, even when they're a victim, is still responsible for what they do next. It doesn't mean that they always know what to do next. A very big aspect of Judaism is personal responsibility. If it means that person just makes a phone call . . . she was responsible; she made the decision, she made the phone call . . . no matter how bad her situation was, she made the call. She took some action. I think that that is something that we need to teach more—that you have to always do what you can, you are still responsible to do what you can do. I do think this is one thing the Jewish perspective has to offer to the American, Western thing. We can teach people to be responsible . . . teach empowerment throughout your life. It's hard to take responsibility for your actions, but that's the Jewish way.

This rabbi's perspective is a direct reflection of that given by Dorff, cited in Chapter 3.[3] He stated that people must take responsibility for themselves, quoting rabbinic sources that assert saving one's own life is of primary importance. However, as much as I applaud people taking responsibility, I think it is naive and shortsighted to expect people who live in fear to be able to think rationally. Considering what we learned from the survivors about their experiences, I think it may be an enormous burden both this rabbi and Dorff place on them. For many of the abuse victims, the community just wasn't there to help them.

The following four statements were made by Reform rabbis who have little use for Jewish law: "I have very mixed emotions. I am not sure it does a good job." "I don't work in a *halachic* framework. It's almost irrelevant." "My knowledge of Jewish law says that [it] does not provide helpful remedies in the twenty-first century." "Jewish law only works for those constrained by it." (But, rabbi, wouldn't that also be true of secular law?)

Have you ever counseled engaged couples about violence in a relationship?

Virtually every rabbi I interviewed meets with an engaged couple prior to performing the marriage ceremony. In fact, most won't consider officiating without having met at least once with the couple. However, although four rabbis do mention conflict resolution in their premarital talk, only four rabbis have ever discussed violence in the marital relationship. A few rabbis said that they would consider adding a discussion of violence to their meetings, saying, "I probably should," "I really should," but another two rabbis said that they would do something only if they see a problem. But how do they see a problem if they only meet with the couple for an hour at most and do not truly know the bride and groom?

A few of the rabbis expressed a very negative reaction to the concept of discussing violence. They "didn't see the point." After all, they say, these couples are "in love" and violence is the furthest thing from their minds. Consider this Conservative rabbi's response.

> No, I would not consider it. I'm not sure how helpful that is. I don't think that education or preparation are the kinds of things that neces- sarily discourage violent things from happening. I really don't believe that by talking to a couple in terms of prevention that I'm really going to accomplish much . . . The couples I see are generally very much in love. If I were going to take five minutes to talk about domestic vio- lence, it would seem very remote, and, second, I don't think that abu- sive scenarios and abusive situations are going to be coached out of existence before they are even on the horizon. It is so far off the radar screen when they are the happiest and in love and planning to spend the rest of their lives together. It doesn't seem to me that the preven- tion is going to work.
>
> Of the six to ten people I've met with over the years and counseled, not for any of them, bar none, did they anticipate the problem or did the problem hit suddenly.

In a most paradoxical twist, the above statement came from the very rabbi who is among the most active in educating and advocating about spousal abuse. His position seems to be that we should educate only after a marriage is already made, rather than when some proactive, preventive work could head off problems before they start.

Contrast the above rabbis' negative responses regarding the efficacy of premarital education to the survivors' responses that, in hindsight, there were definite signs of trouble ahead. If somebody had pointed out to them the behavioral signs of abuse, these women acknowledged that they might have been more alert. Forewarned is forearmed. This next rabbi, affiliated with the Orthodox movement, has a diametrically opposed perspective on premarital counseling.

We have a responsibility to make people aware of the difficulties and pitfalls. They have to come to terms with reality quickly, with all kinds of issues. They have to learn how to deal with money, they have to learn how to deal with sex, they have to learn how to deal with religion. With their independent careers, dividing tasks.

This rabbi then continues, and, unfortunately, his account struck me as blatant victim blaming.

I must confess that at that point in people's lives [prior to the marriage ceremony], they're really not listening. In my experience of people who were victimized, they put themselves at risk, and all of them had a problem with self-esteem. They made the marriage because they felt some pressure to do so, without realizing that they had to take into consideration their own real needs and their own entitlements as an autonomous human being. Women are often raised to be passive and to accept patriarchal domination, still in this day. It's a recipe that they have to marry somebody . . . it's a recipe for disaster.

Here are the thoughts of a Conservative rabbi who seeks to head off abuse before it starts.

One of the things I ask couples who are getting married is to describe their family of origin. Because if there is any indication in their description that there is something to be concerned about in the family of origin—a nasty divorce or anything like that—then it's something that I point out to them. Whether you like it or not you are going to re-play the tapes that you learned at home. I can't stop you from doing that, but at least the two of you ought to be aware of it and maybe you can short circuit the tape somewhere along the line, and not get into the same patterns that you learned at home. Sometimes I miss it. I re-member when a couple [I married a few years ago] was sitting with me, several comments they made led me to think there might be prob-lems. We talked about them briefly and everybody said, "Oh yeah, I understand." I think he said, "I'm really afraid that she's going to take all my money." So we talked about it . . . and I really didn't pursue it aggressively, and it turns out four years later that [they divorced due to abuse]. It's hard to say to a couple that comes in to you that "you really shouldn't get married," but sometimes you want to just say, "Look guys, wake up, this is ridiculous." The attempt here is to figure out if there are things we need to deal with.

A Conservative rabbi who had become jaded by the number of divorces he has seen gave this account:

I used to be much more romantic about young couples getting married—they'll figure it out as they go along. I'm much more proactive in watching the dynamics of couples now. First of all, I will only agree to be part of the wedding if they meet with me several times. If I see a red flag, if there was a bitter divorce, if there was abuse, that's going to impact upon the marriage. I say, "I want you to start [attending] premarital counseling. I want that to be part of this process. If you don't want to, then you'll have to find another rabbi. In three months or six months if you are broken up as a result of the process, I'll consider that a good thing; if the relationship is stronger I'll consider that a good thing." If there hasn't been conflict at all in a relationship, I'll send them to a counselor!

If you could design a dream program to deal with the problem of spousal abuse in the Jewish community, how would it look?

This question was not among the original survey items, but the topic came up immediately, and so often, that I ultimately included it in every interview session. Since one of the goals of this research was to develop recommendations for dealing with domestic violence, I felt it would be helpful to ask the very people who are on the front line what they would need. The following quotes summarize the combined efforts of the rabbis' thoughts on developing a program.

Some rabbis set out lofty missions but gave no immediate strategies for achieving them.

I think the human condition is such that it's always been a struggle for human beings to control themselves. There is impulsive and evil behavior which is not deliberate. It's not thought through. It represents the human proceeding as an animal, not permitting the sense of control or shame or restraint or self regulation to prevail . . . If there's [only one thing] that Judaism has to teach, it is that when you control yourself, you celebrate our creation in God's image.

I think there's somewhat of a vicious cycle at work because the perception is that it's not a widespread issue in the Jewish community. It's hard to garner resources for it, which is not meant as a justification, but just as an explanation. By resources I mean financial and people resources. I think that if the initiative were taken, that people probably would come forward who either have experience with this or have concerns about it for some reason. On the surface, the perception is that it isn't much of an issue in the Jewish community. Therefore, in terms of the triage decisions all communities have to make about how they allocate limited . . . resources, I don't think it's high up on the agenda.

So, then, where do we go from here? Other rabbis outlined fairly specific curricula to address the problem at the educational level.

There's certainly the myth that it doesn't exist in the Jewish community, so I think the first thing . . . is just the information sharing. And sometimes simply statistics—people knowing that this is in fact contrary to the stereotype of Jewish communal life, just like we don't have any alcoholics, we don't have any abusive spouses. Probably first-person testimony . . . With sermons I find that people remember the stories . . . more than they remember the facts and the abstractions. [We should] make them aware of resources available in the community should they find themselves in need of them, [and] depending on the length of the program, to acquaint them with Jewish values, as they relate to spousal abuse. Something about anger management.

I'd like to see statistics to dispel the stereotype that this does not happen in the Jewish community. The more we become integrated into society, the more like the rest of society we become. It's important to realize that we're not as protected and as safe from what happens in general society as we think we are. So the statistics would be an important component.

Two rabbis seemed decidedly uncomfortable in focusing only on women as abuse victims.

I would want to talk with some people to know more about the nature of the problem. There seems to be more abuse of men by women than most public discussions of this issue are prepared to acknowledge.

I'd very much like to bring several speakers to such a program. Of course survivors, both male and female, to speak about the harm process—how they went into it, how they developed steps that they took to empower themselves. And also . . . someone who is still in the process. Of course, giving total protection or anonymity to that person . . . That would be such a slice of reality to realize that I might have something in common with that person. I think to see that whole thing . . . would help [the audience] to recognize signs of danger before they get worse. That would be one goal. Another would be to sensitize to the pitfalls in relationships. Thirdly, to empower the community to do something about this. If you know somebody who is somewhere within that process, what do you do? I would like to have a component of the law. On many things we're afraid . . . we [rabbis] don't know what our rights are . . . at what point we're afraid to be sued. We're endangering ourselves, whether legally or physically, so I think people need to feel that they're protected. That will help empower themselves to help someone.

The second of the two rabbis also wanted to include a discussion of the spiritual and psychological aspects of abuse.

There should be a medical/psychological component. People should know that abuse isn't merely physical; it's the fact that it's cyclical. When a person does something bad it lasts for four generations. When a person does something good the consequences last for a

thousand generations. And when we start to think about what that
means, it means that the consequences of the doer's lifetime. It means
that there are consequences that the next generation will display. It's
not just the consequences. Every action has a consequence. The consequence to the abuser is to make the abuser less human, less in the
image of God. Let's say the second generation continues to abuse.
And the third generation . . . In order for the abuse to stop, anywhere
in that cycle it has to stop. People have to understand that, and here is
where I would come in because my theology is that each of . . . us has
a choice . . . It is directed by our past to a large extent. If we . . . realize
that he or she is in a position that he might be a second generation, "I
might have it implanted in me. Maybe it hasn't come out yet; I'd better
start watching out for symptoms."

And, one rabbi felt unprepared to educate others due to his own state
of ignorance.

I think that for me to design an ideal program would be presumptu-
ous because I still don't think that I understand. Usually when I encounter information on this issue, I feel that it is a part of a larger
feminist agenda that may be skewing some of the relevant factors in
order to fit a desired critical perspective. Some say that it is such a
small percentage that it is irrelevant, but then I read *New York Times*
stories . . . suggesting that it isn't such a tiny peripheral factor. So I am
insecure as to my command as to the extent and the source of the
problem.

Ignorance, confusion, inconsistency, and fear. These four characteris-
tics can sum up the rabbis' responses regarding the topic of spousal abuse,
regardless of sect. Many are ignorant of the extent of the abuse problem
within the Jewish community, and as a consequence, do nothing to address
it. They are confused about their responsibilities vis-à-vis state law. They
are inconsistent among themselves regarding how Jewish law applies to the
problem of spousal abuse, or even if it does apply. Some rabbis even
demonstrate inconsistency within their own beliefs and behaviors. Finally,
they are fearful of their exposure, both to possible harm at the hands of an

abuser and legal liability if they report suspected abuse to the police. Some are clearly cynical toward police response.

What do the various rabbinical associations say about domestic violence? Once I had heard the pulpit rabbis reporting on their own experiences, I was curious as to what their membership organizations would have to say about abuse. Of all the various movements' rabbinical associations, only the Conservative, Reform, and Reconstructionist have issued any statement at all on the topic of domestic violence. The Rabbinical Council of America, the association of Orthodox rabbis in the United States, reported, "We have worked with various federations on Project Sarah [New Jersey] and spousal abuse, but never released any formal statements."

Habad, the Lubavitcher *Hasidic* sect, is organized somewhat differently than other movements. The leader of the worldwide movement, the late Rebbe Menachem Mendel Schneerson, was the "central policymaking body," according to their spokesman, so it doesn't have the rabbis' group traditionally associated with the other movements. It does have a group called the *Kinnus Shlichim*, convention of emissaries, which meets annually but does not issue policy statements or resolutions. The national representative with whom I spoke gave what is certainly a wonderful sound bite in explaining why the group does not have a policy statement on domestic violence. "The Torah is the best policy statement that anybody could have," he said. His declaration, although pithy, led me to ponder. Since the word *rabbi* comes from the Hebrew for "teacher," what is the need for rabbis at all if they do not actually *teach* about the issues of marital, indeed human, relations raised in the Torah? The Torah is a wonderful source of law and ethics, but if the rabbis do not come out and specifically say that abuse is wrong, too many people may either misinterpret the text or ignore it. Without proper guidance, they may choose to rely on the fringe commentaries that support wife beating rather than the majority that condemn it.

The resolutions passed by the rabbinic associations at their conventions were introduced in a chronological order that reflects the level of liberalism of each movement. The Central Conference of American Rabbis (CCAR), the Reform rabbinical association, adopted two resolutions called "Violence Against Women" and "Domestic Violence" in 1990.[4] However, although the CCAR was the first rabbinical association to do so, it came a full seven years after its movement's Women of Reform Judaism issued its own "Resolutions Addressing Spouse Abuse."[5] The Reconstructionist Rabbinical Association (RRA) issued its resolution on domestic violence in 1991,[6] and the Rabbinical Assembly (RA), the Conservative rabbis' association, declared its policy on abuse in 1995.[7] The Rabbinical Council of America, the Orthodox affiliated association, has never issued a statement.

All the resolutions are fairly similar in their approach. They begin by describing the scourge that is domestic abuse, citing statistics as to its prevalence. They discuss Judaism's perspective, although they vary in the amount of weight they give to *halacha*. For example, the Reform CCAR barely mentions Judaism at all, other than to say that "Judaism affirms the sanctity of life and the inherent right of each person to a life of dignity and respect, and to a home which embodies such values." The RRA cites one psalm and one proverb at the top of its resolution, and refers to the fact that over the millennia there has been some disagreement among the rabbis as to what type of behavior is permissible. Finally, the Conservative RA mentions briefly the behavioral ideals of *b'tzelem Elohim,* in the image of God, and *shalom bayit,* peace in the home. All of the resolutions end with a list of items that the respective association should endorse, including giving an annual sermon during Domestic Violence Awareness Month, increasing services to abuse victims, and urging the legal system to accept battered woman syndrome as a legal defense. The RA goes so far as to "encourage rabbis and congregations to form a shelter or support local shelters for victims of domestic violence in their communities, donate a meeting room for a support group for recovery from domestic violence, [and] organize hotels to provide rooms when shelters are full."

In addition, Conservative Rabbi Elliot Dorff wrote an entire *responsum* on behalf of the RA's Committee on Jewish Law and Standards, the only such treatise produced by any of the rabbinical associations. Many of his conclusions are discussed in Chapter 3.

Few of the rabbis with whom I spoke indicated that they were aware of either the resolution or the *responsum.* We know that fewer have actually followed through on the good intentions of the associations' resolutions. For the most part, I gathered from interviews with rabbis, survivors, and communal leaders that very few communities have tackled this difficult subject, even from the most basic educational standpoint.

How do the rabbinical seminaries rate in offering course work on the problem of domestic violence? The Conservative movement's Jewish Theological Seminary offers one course on issues in pastoral care, which includes a segment on counseling women. The topic of domestic violence is discussed in this context. The course is not required. However, the seminary does offer a two- or three-day intensive course between semesters. Rabbis, psychologists, agency representatives, and survivors of domestic violence all come together to address both the *halachic* and pastoral care perspectives of domestic violence. Although the course is supposedly required, due to scheduling conflicts, not every student attends.

The Rabbi Isaac Elchanan Theological Seminary at Yeshiva University is the premier Orthodox seminary in America. Although pastoral counseling has been offered for many years, the school has expanded its curriculum recently to include courses on family counseling and crisis intervention. These courses are not required, but the seminary's spokesman stated that they draw the largest enrollment of any in the seminary. In addition to the semester courses, the school offers special days focused on different kinds of abuse, addressed by various professionals, including rabbis, psychologists, and social workers.

RIETS has a "close working relationship" with the RCA, according to the spokesman, but whereas the seminary addresses family violence in its courses, the RCA has not issued a resolution or policy statement on the topic of domestic violence.

Hebrew Union College is the seminary of the Reform movement, with locations in three cities—Cincinnati, New York, and Los Angeles. HUC offers a basic course in counseling, which includes three hours focused specifically on domestic violence. The required course (HUC is the only one of the seminaries to require a counseling course) focuses on how to detect abuse, the rabbi's responsibility to respond to it, and legal obligations of the rabbi. The *halachic* perspective is covered elsewhere in a variety of different venues, their spokesman said. The seminary also has an occasional seminar on the topic. According to their spokesman, students have not requested a course on the topic. "They don't see it as a problem until it is brought up," he said. "The relevance of any topic is critical to whether it takes."

As elsewhere, the coverage of domestic violence is inconsistent in the rabbinical seminaries. In some, the curriculum may cover family violence, but it does not address it as a whole, keeping *halachic* and pastoral aspects separate. In others, the subject is either a small part of one course in a five- or six-year program, or it is not required, making exposure to the problem a hit-or-miss proposition. Virtually none of the thirty-three rabbis with whom I spoke recalled having studied anything about domestic violence while in seminary, even those who had graduated recently. So we are left with the reality that unless all current rabbinical students learn about domestic violence and its many aspects, congregations will not benefit at any time in the near future.

After spending anywhere from forty minutes to one-and-a-half hours with me, had any of the rabbis in the original study sample become more cognizant of and sensitive to the problem of spousal abuse? Had they come to the realization that it's not just another religion's problem, another movement's problem? Would the rabbi who, with his congregants, had attended the Safe Havens training programs now recommit himself to implementing that program, or would it fall yet again into a morass of political maneuvering? I am hopeful that the simple act of asking questions will have sparked an interest in the subject, and that the interest will lead to action. I will keep in my memory those few young, idealistic rabbis who thanked me for bringing this problem to their attention.

5

"DO NOT SEPARATE YOURSELF FROM THE COMMUNITY"

COMMUNAL LEADERS' RESPONSE TO ABUSE

Anyone who has the ability to correct a situation and is derelict in doing so bears the responsibility for whatever results therefrom.

—Talmud: Tractate Shabbos[1]

ON THE DAIS AT THE 82ND ANNUAL *HADASSAH* CONVENTION SAT TWO speakers: Leonard Fein, the quintessential liberal activist and writer; and Ruth Wisse, archconservative professor of Yiddish literature at Harvard University. The topic for the session was "Liberalism Versus Conservatism: Is It Good for the Jews?" Wisse, veins bulging from her forehead and neck, accused the organization of violating its own principles and that of Judaism, and shrieked, "We are bleeding. They [*Hadassah*] are spreading through their fact sheets[2] all kinds of lies about domestic violence. And, in fact, what is it that *Hadassah* has to do with domestic violence?" The cavernous hotel ballroom echoed with the boos and murmurs of thousands of convention delegates. Unfortunately, Leonard Fein had departed the session early to catch a plane, leaving a dazed moderator and nobody else on the dais to rebut Wisse's remarks. Luckily, a few informed women surrounded her after the program, confronting her with the ugly facts about domestic violence. Whether or not she chose to believe them, I do not know.

That moment was a seminal one for me. Why should we care what a professor of Yiddish literature says about domestic violence and *Hadassah*'s involvement in advocating for laws about it? We should care because, by virtue of her public persona and her Harvard affiliation, Wisse's opinions carry weight. Whether or not she has the legitimate expertise to discuss domestic abuse is almost irrelevant. She has a bully pulpit, and she has used it to further her own agenda. Her influence on those in attendance at this and other gatherings of Jewish leaders is incalculable.

In Chapter 3 we learned what Jewish law has had to say on the subject of domestic violence over the millennia. For all the words on the printed page, however, I had to wonder what actions the Jewish community was taking to prevent abuse and to deal with its consequences. Wisse was obviously ignorant of, or chose to ignore, centuries of Jewish law and tradition that give priority to life and respect for human beings. I knew that *Hadassah* had printed the fact sheets, referred to above, advocating a stop to domestic violence, but what was the group actually doing to accomplish that lofty goal? Did other Jewish communal organizations deal with domestic violence? Did they acknowledge the existence of this scourge? Did they educate only their members, or did they reach out to the general Jewish community? Did they lobby for legislation at the state and federal levels?

In order to begin to get answers to these questions, I needed to look at the communal organizational structure. The Jewish community is organized along three main lines: The religious movements, volunteer organizations, and social service provider agencies. The overarching umbrella in most communities is the Jewish Federation. According to the national office of the United Jewish Communities (UJC), 156 Jewish Federations operate in the United States.[3] Each federated community is responsible for raising funds for its own operation and for the budgets of its constituent agencies. In addition, moneys raised in the annual campaign are disbursed to the UJC for distribution to Israeli social service agencies and to Jewish communities in distress worldwide. Although each community in this study has as its umbrella agency a Jewish Federation responsible for raising moneys for its member organizations and agencies, no federation is capable of raising enough to meet all the budget's needs. Consequently, each agency must then conduct a campaign for its own operational budget as well as occasional endowment or capital campaigns.

Federations range in size and scope of services. For example, those in areas with small Jewish populations, such as the Berkshires, not only raise funds, but may provide social services, such as a kosher hot lunch program for the elderly. In larger cities federations tend to confine their work mainly to fund-raising and a minimal amount of educational programming.

Both a religious and a cultural people, the Jews share one language of liturgy, and dozens, if not hundreds, of languages of the street and marketplace around the world. In the United States, that language is predominantly English, but, due to immigration from many lands of repression, it can also be Farsi, Russian, Portuguese, Amharic, or Spanish. Where the Jewish religion relies on canon law, *halacha*, and formalized ritual, it is similar to the Catholic Church. But that is where the resemblance ends. Unlike the Church, which is headed by the Pope, whose inspiration is believed divine and whose word is law, there is no ultimate human authority to whom Jews pay allegiance. Even in Israel, which has a Chief Rabbinate, there are two Chief Rabbis, one for Jews of European, Ashkenazic, descent, and one for those of Middle Eastern, Sephardic, descent. Neither of them claims to be divinely inspired; their task is to interpret Jewish law for their constituents. The Talmud itself, the so-called "Oral Law," consists of the transcription of discussions, and disagreements, by prominent rabbis on everything from broad ethical issues to the most minute points of ritual practice. Entire schools of thought are based upon the teachings and writings of individual rabbis. As one example that relates to *shalom bayit*, the schools of Rabbis Hillel and Shammai disagreed on how to affix a *mezuzah* to a home's doorpost. One said that it should be vertical, the other horizontal. They compromised by having it hang at an angle, symbolic of the negotiation and flexibility that must abide to maintain a peaceful home. To be sure, in some insular *Hasidic* communities, the *rebbe*, or rabbi, is the ultimate authority, and in one fringe case, among some members of the *Habad* movement, is considered the Messiah. However, that example is highly specific to a particular group and not in any way representative of the entire Jewish people. As an old saying points out, for every two Jews, there are three opinions.

Each community is home to a variety of synagogues. Since the rabbis of these synagogues would be the members of their respective rabbinical associations, those groups are discussed in Chapter 4. Most synagogues and temples belong to their own organization (United Synagogue of Conservative Judaism [USCJ], Jewish Reconstructionist Federation [JRF], Union of American Hebrew Congregations [UAHC], etc.). These are supplemented by brotherhoods, sisterhoods, and even Zionist organizations, whose missions are to promote the way of Jewish life espoused by their respective movements. In addition, there are youth groups affiliated with each religious movement, summer camps that draw staff from the seminaries, and day school and religious school faculties that the movements support.

On the nonreligious side of the coin, so many organizations make up the modern American Jewish scene the mind reels. Various volunteer and membership organizations represent a variety of Zionist, social advocacy, and philanthropic missions. In some communities, people have remarked that they are "overorganized." What they mean is not that that there is a highly delineated allocation of tasks and the resources to accomplish them, but that there are too many organizations for the number of people in the community. In some places, in fact, there has been such duplication of service that communal leaders have had to engage in serious strategic planning in order to conserve dwindling financial resources. Unfortunately, the tough decisions involved in trimming waste sometimes produce hard feelings, reducing the number of volunteers and donors who can help to achieve the very goals they hold dear. Reduction of helping hands and money further cuts services, and the vicious cycle continues.

In the past two decades, with more and more women entering or returning to the workplace, what was traditionally a rich resource for the community to fill its social service and fund-raising needs has dwindled to the danger point. Many organizations have closed their doors due to the drastic decline in their memberships. For example, in the central Massachusetts area, the Brandeis Women's National Committee, Women's American ORT (Organization for Rehabilitation and Training), Pioneer Women (now called *Na'amat*), and Jewish Women International (formerly *B'nai Brith* Women) have all ceased operations. Those that remain (*Hadassah*, National Council of Jewish Women, Women of Reform Judaism, and the Women's League for Conservative Judaism) have suffered a decline in membership. What is now the Eastern Massachusetts Chapter of Women's American ORT used to consist of several chapters totaling 4,000 members, but now counts a mere 450. And, in the Berkshires, where one does not find an overabundance of organizations, even

the Conservative sisterhood is extinct. These volunteer organizations are usually not funded in any way by their respective federations and must produce
their own fund-raising quotas to support their many projects and programs,
from schools to hospitals to residential homes.

A relatively recent phenomenon has also cut into the Jewish community's
ability to raise funds for its agencies and programs. Historically, Jews were ostracized from mainline institutions, such as art museums, symphonies, and
country clubs. Today, Jews are not only invited to become members, but are
asked to serve as trustees. Consequently, the moneys that they might have
given to Jewish organizations in the past now are going into secular coffers,
making the funds to support Jewish agencies that much harder to raise. And,
not only has assimilation reduced fund-raising ability, it has also taken its toll
on the membership rosters of women's and other volunteer organizations.

The Jewish social service agencies (e.g., Family Services, nursing homes,
elder service agencies) have professional staffs as well as boards of directors
made up of volunteers. Not every community has a Jewish Family Service. In
fact, of the 156 federated communities, 145 Jewish communities have agencies.[4] This does not take into account the many rural towns and villages
across the country with Jewish populations too small to have either agency.

It would be neither practical nor helpful for this study to cover every
chapter of every Jewish organization in these pages, particularly since many
do not include family issues as part of their agendas. For example, the
"Friends of" major universities restrict their energies to raising money for
their particular institutions. However, there is logic in looking at the groups
whose missions intersect with the religious, spiritual, and health-related aspects of their members. What, after all, is the purpose of a religious faith if
not to provide for the spiritual welfare of its members? And what is the purpose of organizations whose mission is to ensure the physical security of
the Jewish people if not also to guard the internal safety of it?

It is helpful to put each Jewish community in the context of its geographic area. What resources are available locally, and do these resources
reach out to the Jewish community and take into consideration the special
needs of the religion's practitioners? Due to a variety of considerations,
mostly having to do with budget constraints, this study focused on three
Jewish communities of Massachusetts for interviews with survivors, rabbis,
and lay and professional leaders. Although Massachusetts is decidedly one

of the smallest states in the nation, its wide range of communities, from large city to midsize industrial city to tiny, rural village, allows us to view the variety that Jewish life takes. However, when it came time to look at actual services provided, I set out to learn what other Jewish communities of comparable size across the country were doing in regard to domestic violence. Appendix B provides a list of resources from those cities and towns that responded to my request for assistance.

During the course of collecting data for this study, I spoke with almost sixty current and past Jewish leaders of local volunteer organizations, community domestic violence advocates, Jewish social service professionals, and federation executives, some at great length, about their communities and their constituencies. From the westernmost edge of the state to the Boston metropolitan area, virtually all were willing to talk with me. Very few volunteer leaders refused, but of those that did, all did so with the same response: Domestic violence does not exist within their own community, so talking with me would be a waste of time. To put the Jewish community's experience in perspective, I also spoke with the directors of numerous secular agencies, including hospitals, battered women's shelters, and batterer intervention programs. Although there are several people who stand out for their tremendous efforts in advancing the cause of family violence reduction, and deserve accolades for that effort, I have kept all sources anonymous both to preserve confidentiality and to encourage their openness in speaking about the subject. In addition to the local organizations, the national offices of many major Jewish organizations provided literature about their groups' work and generously shared their opinions and attitudes about the topic.

I asked these communal leaders, both lay and professional, about their awareness of the incidence of domestic violence in the Jewish family. Further questions proved their knowledge of the availability of programs and services in their own communities, and about the umbrella organizations under which their groups operated.

THE RELIGIOUS MOVEMENTS

Virtually every synagogue in the United States is affiliated with one of the major movements of religious life. The movements provide a wide range of services and programs to help the synagogues further their respective missions, hold national and regional conventions, and publish magazines and religious texts. In addition, a variety of *Hasidic* communities dot the landscape, including *Habad-Lubavitch*, *Bratslaver*, and *Satmar*.

Habad-Lubavitch

Of all the *Hasidic* groups, *Habad-Lubavitch* is probably the best known due to its active outreach program to bring Jews back to ritual practice. Based in Brooklyn, New York, the *Habad* (an acronym standing for wisdom, understanding, and knowledge) movement was founded in the eighteenth century as a way for the uneducated people of eastern Europe to be able to worship without having to be scholars.[5] *Habad* has sent emissaries to places as far-flung as Shawnee Mission, Kansas, and Las Vegas, Nevada, within the United States, and Japan and the former Soviet Union outside. Having lost its spiritual leader upon the death of the childless Rebbe Menachem Mendel Schneerson, administrator rabbis now run its multiple operations, from their ubiquitous "Mitzvah Mobiles" to an aid program for victims of the Chernobyl nuclear disaster.

I have chosen to focus on *Habad* over the other *Hasidic* groups due to its size (more than 2,000 centers throughout the world) and accessibility (I was unable to reach a human representative at any of the other movements). However, because it is organized differently from the mainstream movements, all policy statements come from the governing body, not from the laity. *Habad* has never issued a resolution on the topic of domestic violence.

Jewish Reconstructionist Federation

The youngest of the religious movements in American Judaism, the Reconstructionist movement is also the smallest, with about one hundred affiliated congregations and *havurot*, groups that study and pray together. Although considered a mainstream American movement, it is organized a bit differently than the larger ones. The JRF's Web site[6] lists only three components to its structure: the rabbinical college, the rabbinical association, and the synagogue arm. Given the movement's decidedly progressive leanings, it is not surprising that there is no specifically men's or women's organization. However, the JRF does support Wellsprings, a women's spirituality discussion group that is open to all. In addition, the national outreach department does conduct training programs for its member synagogues; domestic violence is but one topic included in the many covered in the course of the two-day workshops. However, by the time this book went to press, only four congregations will have participated in that training. The good news is 40 to 50 members typically participate in a training session.

The Orthodox Union

The Orthodox movement is firmly positioned at the right end of the religious observance spectrum, although there are many different "brands" of Orthodoxy, from the small independent *shuls* in the "old" neighborhood, to the vibrant Young Israel. The Orthodox Union is their organization. At its 102nd anniversary convention in 2000, the Orthodox Union (OU) issued its resolution called "The Jewish Home." Calling on the principles of *shalom bayit* as a primary goal in Jewish life, the organization acknowledged that physical, sexual, and emotional abuse occur in the Jewish home. The OU resolved to take a series of steps to combat abuse, including supporting legislation; developing public and synagogue education campaigns, with an emphasis on *halacha;* and assisting in the development of more kosher facilities for Jewish victims of abuse. In addition, they determined to support the training of a wide range of religious, health, and social service, and criminal justice professionals, particularly Orthodox counselors.

Union of American Hebrew Congregations

If the Orthodox occupy the right of the religious spectrum, the Reform stand squarely on the left. Focused heavily on social action, almost to the total exclusion of ritual observance (although this has been changing over the past few years), Reform is the most liberal movement in America. The synagogue arm of the Reform movement, the UAHC, passed a resolution called "Violence Against Women" at its 61st General Assembly, held in 1991.[7] Within its text, the UAHC resolved to educate its member congregations and their religious schools and youth groups about violence and "to create and disseminate information dealing with this crisis." The group also determined to mobilize its resources to help victims of abuse and to advocate for legislation and funding to address domestic abuse as a crime. In addition, the organization resolved to "promote vigorous enforcement" of existing laws prohibiting violence, although it is unclear precisely of what this "promotion" would consist. Does this pledge mean that the member congregations will report abuse to the authorities rather than sweep it under the rug, or simply that they will pass more resolutions? Finally, the resolution urged law enforcement and criminal justice professionals to receive training on domestic violence.

United Synagogue of Conservative Judaism

The USCJ is the lay leadership arm of the Conservative movement. Conservative Judaism, like Orthodoxy, relies on *halacha* and ritual life, but, like the Reform movement, participates in social action. Therefore, the movement finds itself situated between Reform and Orthodox on the religious spectrum. The stated mission of the USCJ is "to keep Conservative Jews in Conservative Judaism." Although the organization passed a resolution on domestic violence in 1993, it has never offered a session at its biennial convention on the topic of domestic violence. When questioned further, the USCJ's spokeswoman said, "There is a whole variety of other agencies that deals with these issues . . . We recognize the issue. We do need to recognize that it exists in such numbers that it is a problem. The synagogue is the place where they should come for help in how to seek help." Her response then begs the question as to how synagogue members would know or feel comfortable to come to the synagogue for help if the subject is never addressed there.

As wonderful as all the resolutions are, one point stuck out prominently. Only women were portrayed as victims of abuse. For practical reasons, women were the focus of interviews in this study; I had to draw the line somewhere in terms of how many people I interviewed. Further, I felt that it would be easier to get women to open up to me as another woman, to say nothing of the relative ease of finding female as opposed to male survivors of abuse. However, government statistics have shown that approximately 7 percent of men also suffer from physical assault by their intimate partners at some time in their lives.[8] It is crucial that Jewish organizations' resolutions and programs acknowledge that, if *shalom bayit* is the goal, they must reflect the reality that men are also victims of spousal abuse.

LAY LEADERSHIP IN THE JEWISH COMMUNITY

"We don't have these problems in our congregation," said a Women's Branch president. "That's ridiculous. Jewish men don't beat their wives," stated a Women's League past president. One National Council of Jewish Women (NCJW) leader told me, "I am almost saturated by the topic . . . You can't go into a public bathroom anymore and not see one of those posters. I almost think it has gotten over the other side of the curve . . . You go into a doctor's office and they ask you." "It's not an appropriate topic; we want to portray the beauty of the Torah lifestyle, creating a different kind of mood," a *Neshei Habad* leader told me. A *Hadassah* past president said, "There is such a need to make people aware of this. If we could help even one person by doing this program, it was worth it." And finally, an NCJW leader stated, "If something gets started but there's nobody to pick it up and stay with it, nothing happens . . . Everybody says it [domestic violence] doesn't happen, and then somebody comes along and says it does. Then, hopefully, some people get interested and get involved."

The wide range of these initial responses to my study topic by people active in volunteer organizations indicates the equally wide range of perceptions, not only about the prevalence of domestic violence, particularly as it relates to the Jewish community, but about the effort of doing something about it. Beginning in the summer of 2001, I traveled the state to meet with current and past presidents as well as other leaders of volunteer organizations and agencies within the three focus Jewish communities. Given the nature of volunteerism today, it is not uncommon to find a chapter president who was not even a member of that group five years prior. Therefore, in order to get a feel for organizational history, I invited both current and past presidents to join together to give me their perspectives. In some cases, I was lucky to find a member with a long institutional memory, and in those instances I interviewed that person as the organizational representative.

It is interesting to note that, in almost every case, despite initial reluctance, once we began to discuss the subject of domestic violence, the interviewees knew of somebody who had been abused or suspected was being abused. In fact, on one particular evening, the session almost ran away from me as the women in the room began to discuss another member's abusive husband. All were aware of this man's behavior, but none knew how to approach it or thought it was their business to do so, despite their concern for the woman. One NCJW past president told me, "We tried to have a program on domestic violence. We went to [the Reform rabbi], but he said, 'There is no such thing as domestic violence in the Jewish community. I won't have a program like that in my temple.' So, we didn't have the program."

The Leadership Conference of National Jewish Women's Organizations

The Leadership Conference,[9] representing more than 1.5 million women, was a coalition formed for the express purpose of educating its members about a variety of "women's" issues. The first item on the Conference's agenda was domestic abuse (why this was considered a women's issue as opposed to a family or Jewish community issue is a topic I will address later). Convening at *Hadassah*'s national headquarters in New York, representatives of almost every major Jewish women's organization attended the first two meetings, and the Women of Reform Judaism brought a report of a U.S. Department of Justice briefing on domestic violence they had attended in Washington, D.C. Organizations made plans, and each one agreed to take on a task in helping to accomplish the mission of educating their members about and advocating for domestic violence laws. Unfortunately, that was where activity stopped. No other group took responsibility after that for hosting a meeting. As most organization representatives reported, all activity by the conference stopped after the first two meetings. Some organization representatives with whom I spoke weren't even aware of the conference's existence. However, some of the participating organizations did become active in educating their members and communities about domestic violence, as evidenced in the following organizational summaries. Their individual contributions to the fight to eradicate domestic abuse appear in alphabetical order below.

American Jewish Congress.   The stated mission of the American Jewish Congress (AJC) is

> to safeguard the welfare and security of Jews in the United States, in Israel, and throughout the world; to strengthen the basic principles of pluralism around the world, as the best defense against anti-Semitism and other forms of bigotry; *to enhance the quality of American Jewish life by helping to ensure Jewish continuity* [italics mine] and deepen ties between American and Israeli Jews.

The AJC's Commission on Women's Equality participated in the Leadership Conference at the national level. It was their responsibility to distribute informational pamphlets to Jewish Community Centers in the areas of its operations, and to affix stickers to women's rest rooms, printed in both Russian and English, informing women where to go for help. The organization has a regional office in Boston, but no other location in Massachusetts. The Boston office goes above and beyond their commitment to the Leadership Conference by providing administrative support to the Jewish Domestic Violence Coalition of Greater Boston.

AMIT Women.   AMIT Women participated in the Leadership Conference on a one-time-only basis. The organization's national representative said they "probably" mailed the jointly produced informational brochure once to its membership, but was not sure. She had no other literature on the subject.

Emunah Women.   The largest religious Zionist women's organization in Israel, Emunah supports 255 projects in that country. The organization has sister organizations in thirty-two countries throughout the world, including the United States, where it has 40,000 members. Most of the organization's efforts are aimed toward supporting the high schools, a technical college, nurseries, and residential homes for abused children in Israel. In America, Emunah cultivates programs and projects with the purpose of "developing special values of religious Zionism and building a nation guided by Torah."

To support the mission of living a Torah-inspired life, Emunah participated in the Leadership Conference. It sent out the "Domestic Abuse Does Not Discriminate" brochures to its members and sponsored or cosponsored programs "here and there" around the country. (Emunah has no chapters in Massachusetts.) Although the volunteer organization reports that it met with "great resistance" from Orthodox rabbis in New Jersey, its members were successful in developing two safe homes there for Jewish women. Project Rachel in the Metrowest area of New Jersey and Project Sarah in Clifton/Passaic offer secure places for abused Jewish women and their children, while providing for the special needs of the religious.

Hadassah, the Women's Zionist Organization of America.   *Hadassah*, despite its name indicating a solely Israel-centered agenda, expends a great deal of time, energy, and financial resources on health and Jewish education domestically. The largest Jewish women's organization in the United States with more than 300,000 members, its vast volunteer infrastructure is supported by professional education and public policy staffs at the national office. Together they work to develop the organization's multiple education and advocacy campaigns.

In addition to producing the fact sheets referred to above, *Hadassah* lobbied for passage of the Violence Against Women Act and published the "Domestic Abuse Does Not Discriminate" brochure used by the organizations participating in the Leadership Conference. The brochure was disseminated throughout Jewish communities nationwide—in rest rooms, lobbies, and health clubs of synagogues and community centers as well as *mikvehs*, ritual baths, discussed earlier.

Hadassah's Education/Public Policy Division published a study guide for use by its chapters.[10] The book includes *halachic* and historic background, guidelines for advocacy and activism, and a listing of shelters and hot lines for victims seeking help. Unfortunately, the majority of the agencies it lists are in New York, leaving a large proportion of its members without resources.

Despite National *Hadassah*'s vision in launching the publication of the study guide at the Leadership Conference, which led to the production of the brochure used by the other participating organizations and a chapter in yet another book,[11] surprisingly little has been done at the chapter level to address the issue, either educationally or through hands-on projects, outside of distributing cards at Lilith Fairs (all-female summer concert festivals) across the country. Only one former chapter president interviewed could recall having had a program on domestic violence. In fact, although the study guide was published in 2000, most of the presidents I spoke with did not know it existed. One region secretary did "vaguely recall" one chapter in the Southern New England Region having sponsored a program at one time, and a past president of the Northern New England Region reported on a region-level program held in the mid–1990s. A few chapters and one region do collect toiletries or knitted caps for local shelters on a sporadic basis. The sampling of Massachusetts *Hadassah* chapters seems to mirror the experiences of those elsewhere, if orders for the study guides are any indication.[12] Considering its size and reach, one would have expected a greater response.

Jewish Women International.   Founded as *B'nai Brith* Women in 1897, JWI has set as its mission "to champion the rights of women, safeguard the emotional well-being of children, and perpetuate Jewish life and values." By narrowing its agenda, this organization has taken the lead in educating about and advocating for domestic violence issues. JWI has published two excellent resource guides on domestic violence, one for rabbis (now in its fourth edition), and one for its chapters' use in programming.[13] The rabbis' resource book is a compendium of Jewish law about abuse, sample sermons for each of four American religious movements, and guidelines on how to set up a congregational system to help victims of abuse. While visiting with rabbis across the state, I would surreptitiously look along their bookshelves to see how many actually possessed the volume. I saw one. In the course of conversation, only two rabbis mentioned possessing the book, although JWI reports that "orders are pouring in" for the new editions and that some Jewish agencies are placing bulk orders.[14] The lack I witnessed could very well be due to the absence of JWI chapters in the communities I visited.

JWI convened the first national conference on domestic violence in the Jewish community at Brandeis University in 1997 and is planning another one for an international audience in 2003. In addition to studying the issue and educating professionals in the field, JWI recently launched the Women's Economic Security Fund, which supports several different programs in the United States, Israel, and the former Soviet Union. In the United States, funds will go to life-skills programs in battered women's shelters and to Esther's Place, a model short-term readiness program for survivors of abuse. Despite the latter's name, neither it nor the former is specifically Jewish. It is unclear from the organization's materials how many Jewish women will benefit from these programs.

In addition to its work with volunteers, JWI maintains an e-mail listserve for about one hundred professionals who work in the area of domestic violence. A most exciting development in JWI's pace-setting work is their anticipated study in 2003 on the prevalence of domestic abuse in the Jewish home, to be designed and directed by professional researchers. Up until now, we have had to depend mostly on extrapolations from general population figures and anecdotal information. This kind of data is notoriously unreliable and lends an air of illegitimacy and amateurishness to what is a critical area of inquiry. Some studies that have used mass-mailed surveys (for example, those by the Columbus and Cleveland, Ohio, Jewish communities) had very low response rates of between 6 and 7 percent.[15] There is no way of knowing how valid a sample the researchers got from this endeavor, since it may very well be that the respondents were self-selected.

For all the excellent outreach, literature, and programming that JWI has accomplished, it is truly unfortunate that this organization's membership roster has been shrinking year by year. Few communities in Massachusetts have chapters that could disseminate JWI's work. The Boston area has one small group that runs a support group for survivors of abuse and sends out speakers to local synagogues that request a program on the subject. JWI participates in the Jewish Domestic Violence Coalition of Greater Boston, and it did provide volunteers for the Safe Transitions program at the Beth Israel Deaconess Hospital until financial woes caused the hospital to lose its volunteer coordinator.

Na'amat USA.   Na'amat is well known in Israel for its work in domestic abuse. In the United States, the group is organized into councils, and in Massachusetts, only one dwindling council remains open, and its member-

ship list is made up mostly of elderly women. Although the national organization, through its partnership with Israel, has domestic violence on its
agenda, the Boston chapter has "neither the means nor the people," according to one source, to hold a program on the subject. The local Boston office
does not even keep the national organization's literature on hand.

Other chapters around the nation, however, are participating in special
projects, including the Teddy Bear Patrol and the Back Pack Project. The
former provides stuffed animals for child victims of abuse and neglect. The
stuffed animals are used as a therapeutic tool for children removed from
their homes for their own protection. The Los Angeles Council has distrib-
uted more than 10,000 stuffed animals to children in the greater metropolitan area. The Back Pack Project furnishes area police departments with
backpacks for children who are removed from their homes with such sud-
denness that they must leave their own belongings behind. These backpacks are filled with necessary items such as pajamas, socks, toiletries,
school supplies, games, books, and stuffed toys. In Brooklyn, New York,
the *Na'amat* Council also has refurbished the playrooms at the district attorney's office "in order to make the environment more comfortable for
children when someone in their family is seeking counsel."[16]

National Ladies Auxiliary, Jewish War Veterans of the USA.   The auxiliary, like other organizations, has an aging population; most of its members
have been involved since World War II. Coupled with the age factor is the
dwindling activity at the chapter level. Even though Massachusetts, for example, has ten chapters listed, most do not hold active meetings. Some have
trouble finding leadership. However, having said that, the auxiliary has dis-
tributed press releases in its advocacy efforts, and some chapters do collect
items for donations to shelters.

National Council of Jewish Women.   The National Council of Jewish
Women's mission statement says that the organization "focuses heavily on
social justice issues involving women, children, and families." It lobbies leg-
islators and advises its member sections on how to write everything from
press releases to op-ed articles for local newspapers. In addition, the organization emphasizes hands-on projects in its local communities. The national organization participated in the Leadership Conference of National

Jewish Women's Organizations, and has produced materials on the topic of domestic violence, including a regular newsletter and advocacy guidelines for use by its sections.[17] The newsletter keeps the issue of domestic violence in front of every member on a regular basis.

As with the situation in the rest of the country, NCJW's presence is not consistent throughout Massachusetts, with no section at all in the Berkshires, one of about five hundred members in Worcester, and two smaller sections in the Greater Boston and south suburban areas. Both eastern area sections have held educational programs on the topic of domestic violence. The Greater Boston Section of NCJW was instrumental in financing the kosher sections of the kitchens at both facilities of the Second Step transitional shelter. In addition, they collect toiletries for women's shelters at their annual end-of-year luncheon. The South Suburban Section participated in a signature drive to help gain passage of the Violence Against Women Act. South Suburban also prepares a twice-yearly luncheon with entertainment for the women and children at a local shelter.

Women of Reform Judaism.   The Women of Reform Judaism is the women's lay arm of the Union of American Hebrew Congregations, the central body of Reform Judaism in North America. In 1983 it was one of the earliest groups to adopt a resolution on domestic violence, a full seven years before the Central Conference of American Rabbis, the Reform rabbinical association, and eight years before the UAHC in 1991 (the WRJ passed a second resolution that year at its convention simultaneously with the UAHC). WRJ also advocated on and lobbied for passage of the Violence Against Women Act. In addition, the organization prepared social action packets to send to rabbis, social action chairs, sisterhood presidents, and critical issues chairs in each of their affiliated congregations. Among the items in their resolution were provisions for education of teens and college students, education of law enforcement personnel and judges, recognition of battered woman syndrome as a legal defense, and funding for shelters and services. Finally, the WRJ reissued *When Love Is Not Enough*, the book based on Rabbi Julie Ringold Spitzer's thesis on Judaism's response to spousal abuse.

However, as I found with other organizations, few sisterhoods have even held basic education programs or occasional toiletry collections. Given that the affiliated groups within the Reform movement (the synagogue arm and the rabbis' association) have also adopted resolutions about domestic violence, this finding is surprising.

Women's American ORT.   Organization for Rehabilitation and Training (ORT) is a national Jewish fund-raising organization whose mission is to advance economic self-sufficiency through technological and vocational education. They accomplish this by providing financial support to both the ORT network of schools and programs throughout the world and to their postsecondary technical schools and technical resource centers for Jewish students, teachers, and community groups nationwide. Consequently, their participation in the Leadership Conference was not particularly within the sphere of their normal activities. However, since ORT is a women's organization, its leadership signed on to the list of participating groups. However, the national representative with whom I spoke was not aware of whether ORT had sent out brochures to its members and did not believe that ORT had ever passed a public policy resolution or developed a national initiative about domestic violence.

Women's Branch of the Orthodox Union.   Women's Branch is the organization of Orthodox synagogue sisterhoods and individual members throughout the United States and Canada. Their mission is "to organize, advise and serve sisterhood; to imbue Jewish women and youth with the spirit of Torah Judaism; to reach out to combat intermarriage through information and education."

According to the national office, Women's Branch works actively with the *Shalom* Task Force in New York and uses its literature for education and outreach purposes. After being rebuffed by the rabbis they approached for help in convening a conference on domestic abuse, they report having organized a program with other sisterhoods in the early 1990s in New York City. I found it fascinating to compare this with the response of the feminist NCJW quoted earlier, which accepted the Reform rabbi's decision without dissent. ORT's spokeswoman said, "We were absolutely overwhelmed" by the large attendance at the event. "Many of the women, maybe two hundred, were abused women." She said that following the event, programming and publicity went out, but then the subject became dormant. That dormancy coincided with the demise of the Leadership Conference.

The seriousness with which the national organization approached the subject and the energy and determination with which it overcame the rabbis' rejection are inspiring. However, it became apparent that this enthusiasm did not trickle down to the outlying areas of the organization's reach, at least in Massachusetts. That state has only five active Orthodox sisterhoods, two of which sit in the focus area of this study. Only one sisterhood president agreed to speak with me (a second agreed and then reneged after saying, "We do not have these problems in our congregation.")

Women's League for Conservative Judaism.   Women's League claims to be the largest synagogue-based women's organization in the world. It has a presence in most, but not all, Massachusetts Conservative synagogues. Its mission to promote education, religious observance, and Israel is accomplished through volunteer programs and projects, public policy and advocacy. Although Women's League was a participating organization in the Leadership Conference, it has not developed a program on domestic violence targeted at adults. What it has done is to construct a program on teen dating violence for use in the movement's afternoon religious schools, day schools, and youth group, United Synagogue Youth. The program's packet includes a long list of abusive behaviors, representing social, economic, and psychological control as well as physical battering. Unfortunately, this curriculum fails to address either the need of parents to have resources to deal with their children's questions, or worse, the problem of teens recognizing that their parents may be in an abusive marriage. One activist reported that the Jewish Domestic Violence Coalition of Greater Boston's suggestions for additions to the Women's League's resource guide were completely ignored.

It is ironic that, for all the legendary stereotypes about the Orthodox, it was two Orthodox groups, Women's Branch and Emunah, that overcame rabbinical resistance, the former to develop a conference on domestic violence in New York, the latter to establish two safe houses in New Jersey. It was the nonreligious National Council of Jewish Women that accepted a Reform rabbi's rejection of a program at his temple. Further, this very feminist organization did not seem to consider going to another rabbi's synagogue, or to another venue entirely, to accomplish its mission.

In summary, the news about national Jewish women's organizations is mixed. The work of some groups at the national level is admirable. JWI has taken the lead by devoting virtually all its domestic energies to educating its members and their host communities' rabbis about domestic violence, lobbying, and advocating for changes in laws. Due to the organization's absence in many communities, however, they are limited in the number of people the materials can reach. Of the others that have domestic violence as just one of many agenda items, NCJW, *Na'amat*, and *Emunah* have taken their commitment to the Leadership Conference seriously by participating in hands-on projects to help victims and their children. *Hadassah* has lobbied Congress and published brochures, fact sheets, study guides, and book chapters for use by its chapters around the country.

Women's organizations have responded to the problem of domestic violence where many other organizations have not. Unfortunately, although these organizations formed the Leadership Conference, not all have followed through on their tasks to bring awareness to their communities and help to victims of abuse. Some have completely dropped the ball, having signed on to the conference without going any further. Even for those groups whose mission statements do not specifically deal with family violence, one would have expected that, since their members are for the most part women with families, then they would have taken on this cause as one of their own. The contrast between the work done by national organizations and the comments by local leaders within the same organizations is stark. In many cases, the message obviously is not reaching the grass roots. It appears that something as basic as an educational program will not happen without one member's taking the initiative to get started.

On the other hand, since when is family safety and welfare exclusively a women's issue? Why were only women's organizations included in the Leadership Conference? Why weren't other organizations invited to participate? Several organizational representatives told me that family violence is not on their agenda (the Conference of Presidents of Major American Jewish Organizations, for example). However, family violence is not on the agenda of most of the women's organizations either. Jewish continuity, Jewish education, and synagogue support are among their primary areas of interest, but this did not stop these organizations from signing on to show support for the cause.

Non-Conference Members

Although these next organizations did not affiliate with the Leadership Conference, and do not have as their mission the fight against domestic violence, they do have one thing in common: the fight for the physical and spiritual survival of the Jewish people. Whether religious or secular in nature, the following organizations have a stake in the physical and emotional well-being of their constituents.

American Jewish Committee.   "Helping to ensure Jewish continuity" is part and parcel of the mission statement of the American Jewish Committee. However, its Web site has no mention of its interest in preserving the integrity of the Jewish family so that it will have a future. Calls to the committee's national office went unanswered, so there may be an entire treasure chest of programming of which I am not aware.

Anti-Defamation League.   Although not a member of the Leadership Conference, the Anti-Defamation League's (ADL's) mission is to fight prejudice, hatred, and violence against Jews. It does this by building bridges between Jews and other minority groups in communities across the country as well as by holding ongoing discussions with various religious groups to promote tolerance and understanding. The ADL is renowned for its efforts at educating the public on the negative impact of prejudice and racism, and recently formed an alliance with Barnes & Noble Bookstores called "Close the Book on Hate." The purpose of the program is to disseminate literature to help parents, teachers, caregivers, and so forth teach tolerance to children, and to hold events at Barnes & Noble bookstores around the country. The ADL has, ironically, never confronted the issue of violence perpetrated within the very community whose mission it is to protect, and the representative with whom I spoke seemed surprised by my questions about the group's stand on abuse within the home, as if he had never considered that there might be a threat to Jewish survival from within.

Conference of Presidents of Major American Jewish Organizations.   The conference represents fifty-two distinct Jewish organizations in America covering a wide range of religious and cultural interests. The role of the

conference is to present a unified front for the Jewish community when it lobbies Congress and the administration in Washington on a variety of subjects,
from church-state separation to policy in the Middle East. Its members are
high-powered men and women who in turn represent their own large constituencies, almost one-quarter of which are members of the Leadership Conference. The Conference of Presidents has never issued a policy statement on
family violence, nor does it plan to, according to its New York office.

Federation of Jewish Men's Clubs.   Known alternatively as the "Brotherhood," the Federation of Jewish Men's Clubs is the men's lay arm of the
Conservative movement. The group's spokesman told me that the federation had never sponsored an educational campaign nor issued a resolution
or policy statement on domestic violence because the group "didn't want to
step on the toes" of either the United Synagogue or the Women's League
for Conservative Judaism. He also told me that he did not believe that the
subject would be of interest to members.

Neshei Habad.   *Neshei Habad,* the Lubavitch women's organization, was
not a signatory to the Leadership Conference. The national representative
with whom I spoke said that the group had never had a session at its annual
convention on the topic of domestic violence, nor had it provided educational programming. She said, "I would think that these women would not
want to deal with the problem in a group setting with such a sensitive topic.
I don't know if they would attend. Maybe professionals who work with this
would go, but not like, you know, [other women]."

     She did feel, however, since *rebbetzins,* or rabbis' wives, are prime lead-
ers within their local communities, they should be trained at their own annual convention. She said, "Then they are being told, 'If someone
approaches you, then this is how you should act. We are sure they will approach you.' They [the *rebbetzins*] should have some training."

     One thing that the Orthodox community (not just *Habad*) provides
is a premarital course required for every man or woman wishing to be
married in the Orthodox community. Unlike the one hour that an engaged Conservative or Reform couple may spend with their rabbi prior to
a wedding, Orthodox brides attend between six and eight classes run by a
loose network of paid and nonpaid *kallah,* or bride, teachers. Every law

and tradition regarding marriage and family purity is covered, so that the couple is prepared for the marriage, at least as far as the law is concerned. According to the *Shalom* Task Force, however, the classes are inconsistent in their curriculum. At the very least, *kallah* teachers train brides on the laws of marriage and family purity. They may also teach about their own philosophy of marriage, but not on issues of how a relationship works. The Task Force spokeswoman said there simply is not enough time given the enormous amount of law involved and the small number of classes. Some teachers, she said, do look out for potential problems among the young brides, but they are able to do so more effectively in a one-on-one tutorial session rather than in a large class. Some teachers also present to their students warning signs to look out for, but she said that brides often ignore them, caught up instead in the excitement of wedding preparations.

Orthodox grooms-to-be spend one to two weeks studying Jewish law as it relates to marriage. According to a leading national educator at the Bureau of Jewish Education in New York, these classes are even more loosely organized than those for brides. "They're arbitrary and haphazard," he said. "A lot of the premarital training is better in the female sector. This is unfortunate in that marriage is a partnership and only one of the partners is getting trained."

In addition to the classes, both the Jewish Board of Family and Children's Services of New York and the *Shalom* Task Force offer consultation and training in local *yeshivas* for both boys and girls on conflict resolution within the relationship.

The combined efforts should theoretically result in a decrease in violence. However, given the high incidence of domestic abuse cases seen in New York, one must ask whether the lessons "took." The *Shalom* Task Force spokeswoman whom I questioned about this seeming paradox stated that the classes offered could barely cover the law in the time allowed. Behavioral aspects pertaining to the actual relationship are not addressed.

North American Federation of Temple Brotherhoods.   The North American Federation of Temple Brotherhoods is the men's lay arm of the Reform movement. According to their spokeswoman, the group has "never even considered [domestic violence] as a topic to pursue." She added, "There is

no reason why the brotherhood is not doing it. The sisterhood has a program, the Jewish Family Services have programs."

In sum, for the organizations that are not part of the Leadership Conference, I
have found no evidence to indicate that these groups have taken any public
stand on family violence. Again, although they may not have as their specific
mission the health and welfare of Jewish families, if they claim to care for Jewish continuity, then they should not only take a stand, but take it loudly.

Let's do some arithmetic. I will use *Hadassah* as an example here, although the numbers could and should be generalized to other organizations.
Between 1,500 and 3,000 members attend the organization's annual convention, depending on its location. If every one of the organization's 703 chapters were to send delegates, that would average out to between two and four
members per chapter in attendance. If domestic violence were addressed in a
plenary session (not a small workshop), then these chapters' representatives
would at least have the opportunity to hear about the problem. If even one of
the women who hears the message decides to bring the program back to her
chapter, and each chapter were to draw an average of forty people to an event,
then over 28,000 members would have been educated. Each one of those
may then discuss her experience with her friends and relatives. Multiply this
number by the various volunteer organizations in the United States, and we
would automatically have an educational infrastructure in place.

THE PROFESSIONAL JEWISH COMMUNITY:
AGENCIES FOR CHANGE OR THE STATUS QUO?

> If the lack of community services and cultural support deprives a
> woman of the ability to maintain her dignity, then the community is
> tacitly encouraging the abusive behavior and is an accomplice to the
> sin . . . A community that essentially compels a wife to accept physical
> or emotional abuse in silence is being an accessory and accomplice to
> her husband's transgressions.[18]

As hard as it is for Jews to believe it about themselves, we saw in Chapter 2 that the rate of abuse among Jewish women is comparable to that in

the general community. According to the U.S. Department of Justice, approximately 22 percent of women are physically assaulted by an intimate partner annually.[19] That leaves us with the mind-boggling figures of about three hundred women being abused in the Berkshire area,[20] another four hundred in the Worcester area,[21] and the astonishing sum of approximately 7,500 Jewish female abuse victims in Greater Boston.[22] The Boston statistics are too much for the mind to comprehend, and yet, the government reports data only for physical abuse. It does not include the untold numbers of incidents of psychological and economic abuse.

We have seen how the lay arm of the Jewish community has responded, or failed to respond, to the scourge of domestic violence. What has the professional segment done to confront what seems to be a spreading epidemic of family violence? Many Jewish cities and towns throughout the nation employ communal professionals, mostly from the ranks of social work, to run the agencies that provide hands-on service to their constituents . . . to families, children, and the elderly. Guided by the principles of *tikkun olam*, repairing the world, these professionals labor in agencies that often vie with each other for funding from both the federation under whose umbrella they stand and from the communities on which they depend for donations.

The smallest Jewish communities tend not to have family service agencies and must rely either on the secular programs available or on volunteers within the Jewish community. I did come across one community in this study that had a highly unusual method of dealing with domestic violence cases. The federation's executive director kept a list of counselors who agreed to see clients on a sliding-fee scale. She insisted that all calls come to her from rabbis for triage to counselors. This policy smacked not only of hypercontrol on the part of the director, but of a level of intrusiveness into what is already an intensely personal and private matter. Victims of domestic violence have been through a gauntlet of physical and emotional obstacles already, and they are extremely vulnerable when taking the first step out the door on the way to safety. To present yet another hurdle for them to overcome is both cruel and unnecessary. I found it hard to believe that professional counselors would insist, as the director claimed, that she screen the clients for them in order to keep them from being inundated. Even if the counselors were doing the work at a reduced rate, that should not affect the need for confidentiality. This federation executive could easily have given the names of the cooperating counselors to the rabbis whom abuse victims approached for help.

When it comes to the problem of domestic violence, Jewish communities vary widely in their responses, from providing no service at all to offering a full menu, from shelter and legal aid to career guidance and mortgage assistance.

Some of this variation can be attributed to volunteer support. As one federation professional stated, "We are a volunteer-driven organization so we work on issues they bring to the table. As a group they vote on what they want to address each year. Now it's breast cancer awareness . . . We don't have the manpower to do more than one social action issue at a time. We started and stopped [on domestic violence], which is probably not all that uncommon." In other words, community response is a hit-or-miss proposition, depending on the interests of the people at the helm at any given time. If the community's leaders don't see domestic violence on the agenda, then they do not allocate funds to deal with it.

More often the disparity can be ascribed to ignorance and denial. Recall one of the more disturbing interactions I had during the course of my research: the rabbi who claimed that he had never heard of a case in which a Jewish man stalked or assaulted his wife.

The most organized response to domestic violence I found came from the Jewish Family Services agencies. The next section will discuss what these agencies do.

Jewish Family and Children's Services

Only 145 of the 156 federated Jewish communities in the United States have a JFS; some communities have neither a federation nor a family service agency. (In my study area of three Massachusetts communities, all three had federations, but only two had a JFS.) The agencies that do exist receive only a fraction of their funding from their local Jewish Federations, forcing them to seek grants from government and private foundations, United Way, and their own annual fund-raising campaigns. And we can see an enormous range of domestic violence services offered by the agencies, from simple referral, in Syracuse, New York, to a full menu of programs, including vocational training and kosher apartment shelters for families in the New York metropolitan area.

The communities' array of domestic violence services does not necessarily correlate with the size of their Jewish populations. For example, Worcester, Massachusetts, with a population of about 15,000 Jews,[23] is comparable in size to Columbus, Ohio.[24] Although Worcester's JFS has expressed interest in developing services, it as yet has no program dealing with domestic violence. Columbus, on the other hand, has a full-time staff person working exclusively on domestic violence, with both American and foreign-born clients. (Columbus did have two staff people but recently let one go due to funding problems.) In addition to community education and outreach, the Columbus JFS provides direct services, including case management, safety planning, court advocacy, legal referral (immigration issues can be handled in-house), emergency funds, counseling, and career assistance. After attending a seminar on the topic of abuse within Jewish families, the director of one Massachusetts social service agency had his eyes opened to the fact that the problem of spousal abuse was much more widespread than generally believed. He sees the issue as one primarily of ignorance and denial and wants to tackle it from both educational and clinical perspectives. He told me:

> This really is an issue that several other [communities] are trying to address. Especially since the rabbis [and] synagogues are not necessarily addressing this within their congregations. And, in fact, some of the values within Judaism can discourage people from addressing this. So I thought this [domestic violence counseling and referral] would be a service to the community. We're not addressing it in any educational way now. I would like to start in the next year . . . Within the context of divorce there's often abuse that's occurred. I would say that in terms of people that are coming here specifically for domestic violence, we're only scratching the surface.

It is heartening that Jewish social service professionals are becoming more educated about the prevalence and severity of domestic violence and are developing programs to deal with it. The Association of Jewish Family and Children's Agencies, the national umbrella agency for JFCS, offers referrals to the member agency nearest the caller. The association also hosts a Web site that lists all member agencies and the services they offer. These services range from kosher meals-on-wheels and refugee resettlement assistance to a Hebrew free loan society and infertility counseling. However, domestic violence counseling is not included under any of the member agencies' listings, even those known to offer these services. Nor does a search of the terms *domestic violence, domestic abuse, abuse,* or *violence* bring up anything. The average person will not be able to determine whether the agency they choose can help them with the host of problems associated with domestic violence. To its enduring credit, my request for assistance from the association was met with an Internet "all points bulletin" to its members. Unfortunately, of the 145 affiliated family service agencies, I received only sixteen responses over and above the nine agencies I had already contacted prior to the association's call for assistance. The agencies that did respond are listed in Appendix B, with complete descriptions of the services they offer. Between the JFS-affiliated programs and the independently operated ones, it became apparent that Massachusetts is fairly representative of the rest of the country in the services it provides, ranging from no services at one end of the state to some services at the other.

As would be expected, Boston offers the greatest variety of programs and agencies in the state for Jewish victims of domestic violence. However, this superiority is only in comparison with the rest of the state.

Kol Isha.   *Kol Isha* was developed to provide a culturally and religiously sensitive system of care to Jewish victims of abuse in the Boston area. Housed at the Jewish Family and Children's Service in the suburb of Newton, it gets a small portion of its budget from the Combined Jewish Philanthropies, the local Jewish Federation. Despite Boston's enormous population of 233,000 Jews living in 97,000 households,[25] it supports only a part-time program that has a waiting list for its services. *Kol Isha* provides individual counseling, support groups, referral services, safety planning, court advocacy, and a limited amount of funding to assist with housing. In addition, the program employs one part-time Russian advocate and a part-time housing advocate. There are no funds to help women get legal assistance, leaving them to rely on pro bono services if their abusers have taken the family assets. Community education is available to Jewish communal professionals, volunteer groups, and youth groups. There is a small safety fund for providing transportation to a secure place as well as child care so that a woman can attend a support group.

As more people have become aware of the availability of the service, requests for information and help have increased. In less than two years of operation, *Kol Isha* received more than 1,300 information and referral calls and performed 645 client interventions. In the first nine months of fiscal year 2002, only its second year of operation, the agency took 875 calls for information and referral. This was an increase of more than 400 percent from the same time period the previous year. As word has spread about the program, more and more people are calling. That's the good news. The bad news is that there is such a strong need for *Kol Isha*'s services that, as mentioned, the agency has had to establish a waiting list.

The numbers seen at *Kol Isha* would probably be even higher than they are if (1) the staff were full-time and (2) the service were more accessible. Survivors living in the CJP area, which covers Boston and substantial areas north, south, and west of the city, cited several obstacles to using the services of *Kol Isha*. For example, one woman told me, "After working all day, taking care of the kids, and dealing with the ongoing stress of [postdivorce] abuse—he still won't stop—I just don't have the energy to *schlep* to Newton."

Compare Boston's JFS program with that of Philadelphia (Jewish population of 254,000),[26] whose clinicians in any of the seven branch offices are able to work with domestic violence cases. Philadelphia offers counseling and case management services, individual therapy, help with rent, mortgage, court costs, or utility payments. However, unlike Boston, Philadelphia has no support groups for survivors of abuse. In addition to providing referrals to lawyers and shelters, the Philadelphia JFS maintains an active file of other important contacts, from dentists to gynecologists to locksmiths. A thrift store sells everything from cars to clothes to household goods at discounted prices. A small pool of lawyers does pro bono work.

Philadelphia also provides funds for college education and housing "to help [survivors] achieve a level of self-sufficiency that they wouldn't achieve without this."[27] The Jewish Education and Vocational Services offers computer training. In addition to all these direct services, the JFS does outreach to the community, going to secular and Hebrew schools; among the topics presented are dating violence and conflict resolution. The *Koach* program involves a group of synagogues that each sponsor a client by paying for day care, food scrip, and so forth.

And, in a truly unique partnership with the federation's Women's Division, Miriam's Project sponsors Camp *Shalom*, a getaway in the Pocono Mountains for mothers and children who have survived abuse. A kosher environment with both fun and spiritual activities, the camp is a springboard for a year-round program of events for families who attend the camp.

Compare Boston also with Chicago (Jewish population 248,000),[28] whose groundbreaking SHALVA program, now sixteen years old, provides a twenty-four-hour information and referral hot line for Jewish women, crisis intervention, case management, counseling service, support groups, legal aid, financial assistance, rabbinical advocacy, community education, and prevention programs. SHALVA, which serves anybody defining herself as a member of the Jewish community, is not affiliated with the area's Jewish Family and Community Service. A completely independent agency that employs seven part-time staff and one full-time director, SHALVA receives only a tiny percentage of its $406,000 budget (half of what is needed, they state) from the Chicago Jewish Federation. Nonetheless, it handles three hundred cases every year, including one-time only calls, whereas the Jewish Family and Community Service was serving sixty-three domestic-violence related cases at the time this book went to press. In addition, yet another independent agency, the Jewish Children's Bureau, treats children who are either abused or living in abusive homes. Despite the Chicago program's size, Boston's *Kol Isha*, with its tiny budget of approximately $75,000 and three part-time staffers, handled 875 information and referral calls in only nine months of its most recent fiscal year and did 397 client interventions.

The District of Columbia metropolitan area has a total of about 165,000 Jews,[29] roughly 68,000 fewer than in the Boston area, but it, too, provides a higher level of domestic violence services. The JFS of Central Maryland staffs a hot line and provides community education as well as counseling and legal services for abuse victims, both male and female. The agency coordinates many of its services with Project CHANA, a program of Associated: The Community Federation of Baltimore. A grant allows clients to use staff attorneys at the House of Ruth general shelter and pays for private investigators to find where abusers may have hidden the family's financial assets. The community also supports a small, kosher safe apartment, and if that is occupied, will send people to a hotel. The agency is currently investigating the establishment of a batterers' intervention program.

The Jewish Domestic Violence Coalition of Greater Boston.   Founded in 1994, the Jewish Domestic Violence Coalition of Greater Boston is a group of agencies and individuals who meet together on a regular basis. Although many of its organizational supporters are local affiliates of national Leadership Conference members, it also includes other organizations and agencies. The focus of the coalition is education and providing a forum for sharing information, as well as outreach and education in the community. According to their literature, "The Coalition is based on the conviction that people have the right of *shalom bayit*, peace in the home, and that the community has an obligation to help protect its members." The American Jewish Congress provides administrative support, including office space and mailing and duplicating services. Project *Tikva* is the local affiliate of the *Shalom* Task Force, a national toll-free hot line based in New York. Its hotline personnel can refer callers to counseling and other resources either in their own communities or elsewhere. This group also sponsors training programs for rabbis. The *Kol Isha* partnership consists of three pieces: the *Kol Isha* Jewish Domestic Violence program, housed at the Jewish Family and Children's Service; Safe Transitions, the Domestic Violence Intervention Program at the Beth Israel Deaconess Medical Center; and the Jewish Women International volunteer program. Safe Havens is the interfaith partnership that provides training to congregational teams to provide education and support to victims of domestic violence. Individuals, including survivors and mental health professionals, make up another box on the organizational chart. Additional agencies, such as synagogues, shelters, and Jewish organizations, comprise the last element of the partnership. In other words, the coalition has a broad reach through the Greater Boston Jewish community.

Project *Tikva* and the *Shalom* Task Force.   "It hurts to call a domestic abuse hotline. It hurts more not to," reads the *Shalom* Task Force poster that hangs on synagogue bulletin boards and in women's rest rooms across the country. The *Shalom* Task Force is a hot line based in Brooklyn, New York. It was founded in 1992 by a group of Orthodox women after a physician approached them with reports of women's and children's injuries he believed to be from battering. The founders originally believed that non-Orthodox women would be more likely to use the resources of the general community, whereas Orthodox women had very specific requirements that could only be met within. However, over the years, the task force's audience has expanded to include women from all movements within Judaism. The response to the hot line was enormous, and as word spread of their successes, domestic violence advocates from Jewish communities around the country began to call and ask for help in establishing their own domestic violence programs. It became apparent to all that most communities did not have the financial resources to run their own programs for abuse victims. More basic was the fact that most communities had no idea how to approach this very sensitive topic.

As a result of these two concerns, the *Shalom* Task Force began to take on affiliates. First, they instructed communities on the information they would need to assemble in order to support the task force, such as counselor referrals. They established a toll-free hot line, which any abuse victim could call from anywhere in the country to get information about places to find shelter, counseling, legal help, and rabbis sensitive to and knowledgeable of domestic violence. The posters that hang in women's rest rooms in Boston and St. Louis and Chicago publicize the same telephone number.

The advantage of the central telephone number is not only its cost-effectiveness. The hot line provides confidentiality, which is of primary concern to women in smaller towns and cities. It is extraordinarily difficult for any woman to acknowledge that she is being abused. Finally coming out and asking for help is difficult enough for women in a big city, where they can move with relative freedom. How much more difficult is it when the very distinct possibility exists that someone on the other end of the telephone line can recognize her voice, or that the secretary at the counseling center would be a comember of the PTA? Where could she go for counseling and not be recognized?

The poster that appears in women's rest rooms across the country does provide a confidential hot line for abuse victims to call. What it does not do is let women know that abuse is not necessarily physical; psychological, social, and economic abuse can be just as hurtful to live with. Although the poster says that the number is confidential, it does not emphasize that the task force is based in New York, where nobody will recognize the caller's voice. Finally, the poster does not mention that the hot-line staff can assist the caller in finding help in a place where she probably will not be known. These last two features may encourage more victims to call, given the great resistance of women, particularly in small communities, to seek help for fear of embarrassment.

The task force organizes programs in affiliated communities for rabbis representing all movements. The Jewish Domestic Violence Coalition of Greater Boston established Project *Tikva* as the program's Boston affiliate, and it is an independent member of the coalition. The relationship has enabled the Boston group to tap into the task force's hot line at a fraction of the cost it would be to run one independently, and it has garnered additional benefits from joining forces. Project *Tikva's* job is to advertise the task force's services throughout the area and to provide lists of local area resources to the staff at the national hot line referral center. Its budget pays for its affiliation with the task force and the hot line, advertising costs, and insurance. Project *Tikva* is then entitled to bring in task force personnel from New York to conduct training workshops for rabbis.

A rabbi and social worker train the participating rabbis in how to recognize spousal abuse and how to deal with it, confronting the issue both from a *halachic* frame of reference and a practical one. The major hurdle faced by the current arrangement is that only rabbis in close geographic proximity to the training programs attend the sessions, and even then in small numbers. Although a recent training program in Boston attracted a roomful of Orthodox rabbis, a separate event aimed at Conservative and Reform rabbis brought only five.

If large numbers of rabbis in Massachusetts are not attending educational workshops through the *Shalom* Task Force, are they attending other programs? Safe Havens is the interfaith organization that trains teams of clergy and congregants to develop a response for their own synagogue community. In the four years of its existence, Safe Havens has trained only ten Jewish teams from the 198 congregations that belong to the Synagogue Council of Massachusetts, and at least one of those teams has not followed through on its commitment to develop a program. One shelter director responded to that news by reflecting, "Doesn't that speak volumes? How pervasive is the denial." It appears that one can lead a horse to water, but one cannot make it drink.

Bet Tzedek.   *Bet Tzedek*, the House of Justice, was founded in 1992 to provide pro bono legal services to low-income populations, with an emphasis on the Jewish community of the Boston area. Although it began as an independent agency, it is now part of the Jewish Family and Children's Service. The group participates in the Jewish Domestic Violence Coalition of Greater Boston, of which *Kol Isha,* the Jewish Domestic Violence counseling program, is also a member. *Kol Isha* depends on volunteer lawyers to help its clients and calls on a variety of groups for help, including *Bet Tzedek* and the Boston Women's Bar Foundation. *Bet Tzedek*, with about sixty-five volunteer lawyers, admits that it has been unsuccessful in getting attorneys to take on domestic violence cases. In fact, the only lawyer to take on a domestic violence divorce case for *Kol Isha* was not even Jewish.

Various lawyers with whom I spoke cited two reasons for their resistance in taking on pro bono domestic violence cases. The first is that divorce cases involving domestic violence tend to take much longer to get resolved than do those with no violence alleged. And, since they are not being paid, these lawyers are in effect taking on more pro bono hours than they would normally assume. As one lawyer told me, "We're not paid at all for pro bono cases. I took this one case that I was told was a simple divorce. It was far from it. My firm has already run up more than $75,000 on this one case, and, if it goes to trial, it could go up to $100,000." Even if the victim does have some money, batterers' attorneys often advise their clients to "grind" the wife down until her money is depleted, leaving the lawyer again with no payment.

The second reason that lawyers hesitate to take domestic violence cases is the emotional baggage that comes with each client. The attorneys said that they don't mind the legal representation, but they are very uncomfortable with the psychological issues that are part and parcel of an abuse case. They expressed a desire that social workers and other counselors instruct their clients clearly on how to interact with their attorneys.

An additional problem is that lawyers often drop out of a case midway, leaving the client in the lurch, and a new lawyer having to scramble to catch up. Adding to the morass, most lawyers are not familiar with Jewish issues such as the *get,* making the already difficult process of divorce that much worse.

However, women of wealth have no money either when their husbands have absconded with their assets. So, they are left out in the cold—too rich to get pro bono legal help and too poor to pay themselves. Here we see a repeat of the indignity suffered by the women Weitzman tells of, in which an abuse victim was denied help by a hot line because she was perceived to be too wealthy to need it.[30]

SECULAR COMMUNITY DOMESTIC VIOLENCE SERVICES

Just about every city and town provides some level of help for victims of domestic violence. However, because Jewish agencies may not exist or provide a full array of programs, the Jewish population must depend on the availability of services from the secular community. Again, I will focus on the three Massachusetts communities as an example of the range of services.

The Berkshire area has no specifically Jewish program to address domestic violence. With only a part-time social worker volunteering at the local federation, it is obvious that the bulk of social service must be referred to the general community. In a small town, this solution may not be such a bad thing—for the short term. In crisis, having the ability to rely on a team of trained domestic violence professionals can mean the difference between, literally, life and death.

Berkshire County hosts the Elizabeth Freeman Center, a counseling and crisis center with one central location and two satellites in the northern and southern ends of the county. The Freeman Center fields 8,000 telephone calls every year, serves 2,000 clients, and also runs one shelter and one safe house for women and children. These numbers are astounding considering the relatively small population of the area. Although the center employs Jews on staff, they do not recall ever serving any self-identified Jewish woman. This is not, the center tells me, because there are no Jewish victims. Given the reluctance of middle-class women in general, and Jewish women in particular, to seek out help at a battered women's shelter, the available facility does not seem to be an option. Jewish women are known in their small towns. Despite the ethical obligation of mental health professionals to maintain confidentiality, abuse victims in small towns fear that the mere fact of their presence at a clinic would attract undue attention.

Nonuse of shelters is attributed to both a woman's embarrassment at having to admit that she is an abused woman and not wanting to feel uncomfortable with people who are not familiar. In fact, most women who do use shelter services are low-income. According to shelter directors with whom I spoke, low-income women feel much more comfortable admitting they are abused, and they discuss it among themselves more freely than do middle- and upper-middle-class women.

It took half a dozen phone calls to the Berkshire Medical Center to reach a staff person knowledgeable about domestic violence services. This ignorance by staff of the hospital's services was disturbing. If I had been a victim calling for referral, I would probably have given up hope after the first or second frustrating call. Having finally reached somebody knowledgeable, however, I was informed that social workers on staff see patients on the floor, and that all nurses are trained to ask about abuse when they suspect it has occurred. In fact, all medical center employees attend a mandatory annual full-day training on "competencies," including that on domestic, elder, and child abuse. When I asked one staff person about this, however, she did not recall having covered that material. In addition to the services for abuse victims, the center runs the Berkshire Batterers' Intervention Program. Most of the program's clients are male abusers, sent either by court order or referred by the Department of Social Services if a social worker has found that violence has affected children in the home.

In central Massachusetts several agencies have formed the Worcester Intervention Network (WIN). Established in 1996, WIN consists of a unique collaboration among the city police department's Domestic Violence Unit and Daybreak, the battered women's program; CHANGE, a batterer intervention program; and the district attorney's office. Daybreak, an agency of the YWCA, provides advocacy, short-term counseling and shelter, and a crisis hot line. (Daybreak reports seeing few Jewish women as counseling clients, and nowhere near the proportion they represent in the general population.) The WIN program has seen a dramatic decrease in domestic violence arrests, from almost 4,300 in 1996 to about 3,200 in 2002. The Worcester Police Department attributes this decrease to the proactive approach WIN takes in confronting domestic violence. Missing from the network are two major elements: the faith community and volunteer organizations. If these two were added, the decrease might drop even more significantly.

The University of Massachusetts/Memorial Medical Center employs only one staff person dedicated to domestic violence work. She provides clinical counseling and support groups to victims of abuse and also conducts training and certification programs for both the hospital and general community, including scout troop leaders, parent groups, and health care providers. At this point there is no relationship with the faith community because, as members report, "nobody has asked us." I wonder first when the center's staff person would find the time to do so, but also question why the chaplains at the medical center itself have not been invited to participate in healing. Although the medical center's program also refers to Daybreak for legal advocacy, shelter, and case management, the unit director says, "The vast majority of clients at UMass have major mental illness. If it was not the result of the abuse, then it's a small problem that becomes bigger with the abuse."

Saint Vincent Hospital, also in Worcester, has trained all emergency room nurses to recognize the signs of domestic violence, but has no outreach to the faith community. I found this odd since the hospital is affiliated with the Catholic Church.

Only one Greater Boston area hospital has developed any form of outreach to the Jewish faith community for help in dealing with the emotional, legal, and financial needs of Jewish victims of abuse. Boston's Beth Israel Deaconess Hospital, the only hospital in this study to have a formal and long-standing connection with the Jewish community, is home to Safe Transitions. Although one might expect most victims of abuse to come through the emergency room, in fact, since both primary care and obstetrics and gynecology staff are trained to be on the lookout for signs of abuse, most patients come by referral from those departments. Safe Transitions trains its volunteers to be sensitive to the religious needs of patients, and it has an active relationship with both *Kol Isha* and private counselors known to be cognizant of the specific needs of religious women.

Second Step is a transitional shelter in Newton, Massachusetts. It is for women who have been in a crisis shelter anywhere from two weeks to ninety days. Although not operated under the auspices of the Jewish community, it does have a pantry set off for kosher use, funded by the Greater Boston Section of the National Council of Jewish Women. However, over the ten years of its existence, only three Jewish women have ever used the services of Second Step, and, despite the kitchen's availability, it has never been used. This is not surprising in that the socioeconomic status of most residents in the environs of Newton is very high, allowing victims of abuse in this neighborhood to go elsewhere for safety. In addition, anonymity would be almost impossible to achieve in the area's small, close community of Jews. What is surprising is that Second Step is building a new facility, also in Newton, which will also have a more fully equipped kosher kitchen.

Unlike most shelters for domestic violence victims, Second Step's location is not kept secret since it is intended for women no longer considered to be in crisis. However, one volunteer told the story of an Orthodox Jewish woman who came to the shelter, only to be pursued by her abusive husband, who had been informed by his rabbi of her whereabouts. This rabbi was demonstrating what Twerski describes as a tragically misguided attempt to promote *shalom bayit* under the delusion that abuse will stop just because the rabbi tells the couple to work things out.[31] Given the common problem of abusers continuing to harass, stalk, and otherwise abuse their victims up to and even beyond divorce, the idea of a known shelter, transitional or not, seems to be a leap of faith. Another professional working in domestic violence expressed the opinion that it is "a huge mistake in letting people know where they are."

It Is Time for the Community to Hold a Mirror Up to Itself

In summary, it is clear that, at least at the national level, some portions of the organized Jewish community have made a concerted effort to educate their constituencies about domestic violence. A few communities around the country have established programs to shelter, counsel, and provide legal aid to victims of domestic abuse, all in large cities. This leaves us with a nagging question: For all the energy expended by many Jewish communal organizations at the national level, why have so few communities translated that knowledge into action? Why is there only one underfunded counseling program for Jewish victims of domestic violence in all of Massachusetts, and no shelter or safe house, despite estimates of more than 8,000 Jewish female victims? Why is the counseling program underfunded? Why is no Jewish attorney with domestic violence experience serving that program, either in a paid or unpaid capacity?

Although Massachusetts is one of the smallest states in the nation, it has a reputation as both an educational mecca and bastion of liberal social and human services. All this is true, up to a point. The Jewish community of Massachusetts, when it comes to confronting domestic abuse, is lazy. And, it is not alone.

Jewish communities are dependent on *batei din* for help in resolving divorce. However, they have often found that these panels have their collective heads buried in the sand regarding the extent of domestic violence and the danger level of its perpetrators. In Massachusetts the *beit din,* without ever having spoken with the professional staff of *Kol Isha* about its services, refuses to send Orthodox women there for help because they claim the professionals are "ignorant of Jewish law," an accusation that even Orthodox therapists I spoke with say is false.

Add to this mix a sometimes competitive, if not downright obstructionist, mode of operating among groups and the situation is exacerbated. If the organizations that have taken it upon themselves to confront the problem of violence cannot work together with communication and honesty, then the community has little hope of providing a safe and secure family atmosphere for its members.

Given the decline in membership among volunteer organizations in general, and a total absence in some communities of a number of the more active ones on the domestic violence front, it makes sense to collaborate. For example, in Worcester, *Hadassah*, NCJW, and those sisterhoods that do still exist could gather their materials and plan a program together, pooling their dollars to publicize it to a wider audience than any could reach individually. The members of the extinct JWI chapter could be brought in to purchase new resource guides for distribution to the community's rabbis. Activist rabbis could then be invited to help educate their colleagues. A variety of programs and project ideas used by other communal organizations that don't exist in central Massachusetts could be easily found on the Internet and instituted locally.

Despite the drop in membership rosters, there is tremendous overlap in the people who do choose to affiliate. Many Jews tend to be members in other organizations in their community. For example, almost 60 percent of one sisterhood's members also belong to their local *Hadassah* chapter. And, synagogue-affiliated Jews tend to support their local federations. There is opportunity for collaboration in programming here if the leaders choose to take advantage of it.

The federation raises some money, but certainly not the bulk of that needed to support a family service, if there even is one in the community. If there is a program at the local JFS, one or more lay organizations may support it, actively volunteer for it, or do something as random and simple as collect toiletries for the local non-Jewish shelter once a year. If there is no program at the JFS, then there may be some educational activity by a local chapter of a national women's organization. However, these programs tend to be few and far between, the most prevalent being the simple hanging of posters in women's rest rooms.

In sum, the Jewish community's approach to domestic violence ranges from excellent in a few rare communities, to unsystematic in most, to nonexistent in many. Whether the problem is one of territoriality, absence of strong leadership, lack of communication, ignorance, or denial, it undermines efforts to achieve a serious mission: that of reducing, if not eliminating, domestic abuse.

THE JEWISH MEDIA AND DOMESTIC ABUSE: SHEDDING LIGHT OR COVERING UP?

For such a relatively tiny group, comprising only 2 percent of the total U.S. population,[32] the Jews produce an inordinate number of periodicals. According to the American Jewish Periodical Center, forty-seven English-language Jewish magazines and newspapers are currently published in the United States and Israel.[33] Some are general interest papers, such as the *Forward,* while others are published by particular organizations, such as *Hadassah* or B'nai Brith, for their members. Also included on this list is the Jewish Telegraphic Agency (JTA), a news wire service that feeds stories of national and international interest to many Jewish newspapers, particularly in small communities that do not have large staffs of writers. Some periodicals with which I am familiar were not listed in the catalogue, including *Na'amat Women* and *Tikkun*. I did not count in this tally academic and professional journals due to the narrow audience they serve.

The University of Minnesota has posted on its Web site a bibliography of articles, reports, and books on the topic of domestic violence in the Jewish community, published in both the professional and general press.[34] Although there is no dearth of publications from which to choose in the Jewish world, between the years 1980 and 2000, only 132 discrete articles on domestic violence appeared. Of these, only a few were printed before 1985. A few more emerged in the late 1980s, but it was not until the 1990s that more attention began to be paid to the issue. Even then, the overall paucity of articles shows a surprising lack of attention to what is without doubt a serious problem. Paradoxically, the general Jewish press out-published the Jewish women's media on the subject of domestic violence by a margin of approximately three to one. The JTA itself only published three articles with the words *domestic, violence, spousal, spouse,* or *abuse* in the title, according to its online search.

In the Introduction to this book I referred to *Shalom Bayit,* a conference sponsored by Jewish Women International and held at Brandeis University in 1997. What amazed, and frankly disturbed me in attending the meeting of psychologists, social workers, shelter directors, and other professionals was that I was the only media representative present, writing for the *Jewish Chronicle*. And I was only there because the chair of the conference had called to invite me. I had to convince my editor to send me, because, as she said, "We've already done that." In searching databases for articles on the subject of domestic violence in the Jewish community, it becomes apparent that one article may be considered enough to have "done that."

THE FUNDING CONUNDRUM

Funding is indeed a dilemma for Jewish communities struggling to raise money for what seems to be an unending need within their areas of service. Day care, day schools, adult education, elder programming, and nursing homes are just a few of the pressing needs of a population. Many smaller communities do not have Jewish social service agencies, and of those that do, many do not have the ability to deal with more than referrals to a clinic or shelter that specializes in domestic violence issues. Whether or not this is ideal is not the issue here. Whereas some of the largest Jewish communities have rallied together to provide outstanding services, most simply do not have the financial resources to support a full-service domestic violence program. They must, therefore, rely on the programs offered by the secular community. Whether those agencies in turn have sensitivity to Jewish issues is a hit-or-miss proposition. If the Jewish religious and lay leadership keeps a hands-off attitude toward domestic violence, then the secular programs are on their own in reaching out to potential Jewish clients and in providing services sensitive to Jewish needs.

However, when family health and safety are key to the future of a society, the choice not to fund education and treatment programs on domestic abuse is a shortsighted one. Ignoring a problem will not make it go away. And the quandary becomes more complicated when we attempt to reconcile the need for services with the very real hesitance on the part of Jewish women to use them.

In the long run, it is apparent from the survivors in this study that a general battered women's shelter is not going to attract Jewish women, no matter what the class of the neighborhood. (This absence is not restricted to Jewish women; middle- and upper-middle-class women, in general, tend not to go to shelters, according to the shelter directors with whom I spoke.) In the Boston area, having two transitional shelters with kosher facilities in an upper-middle-class suburb has not attracted Jewish women in any significant numbers. The survivors felt that the area was not large enough to protect their anonymity, and they simply did not feel comfortable there. In New York, Los Angeles, and Baltimore, on the other hand, shelters and safe houses operated under Jewish auspices have brought in large numbers of clients. So, we must come to the conclusion that there is more at work here than the availability of services per se. The potential client base is out there. Jewish abuse victims need a place in which they can not only feel safe with their children, but can feel comfortable with the culture of the other residents.

There is not one Jewish shelter or safe house in the Commonwealth of Massachusetts. In a small handful of communities, some private homes have served as part of an informal underground railroad for women seeking refuge, but a New York–based domestic violence activist told me that her group discourages the underground route to helping victims. She stated that, although well intentioned, the people who harbor abuse victims expose themselves and their families to potential reprisal at the hands of the batterers.

The use of the word *shelter* is in itself off-putting to many and a psychological obstacle to getting help. Every woman with whom I spoke almost physically recoiled on hearing the word, its connotation of noisy, chaotic, dormitory-style living overwhelming. The term *safe house,* on the other hand, seemed to convey a feeling of warmth and privacy for them and their families. Many of the women I spoke with felt that a *mezuzah* on the doorpost further suggested that a Jewish spiritual perspective on the violence would help in the families' healing. Whether or not the woman observed *kashrut* was irrelevant to her desire to be among her "own" people. Recall that all but one of the women interviewed for this study did state that, although they had never gone to a shelter and would not consider a non-Jewish shelter, they would have considered a Jewish-sponsored safe house had one existed at the time of their need.

When it comes to counseling services, women for the most part prefer to have a Jewish perspective and would probably take advantage of them if they felt confident that their anonymity would be ensured. However, some of the survivors in this study did not trust their local Jewish Family Service to be discreet, and they were in any event afraid of being seen entering and leaving the building. Despite the large numbers of Jewish women seeking counseling services from Jewish agencies (recall that Boston's *Kol Isha* received an average of one hundred calls a month in only its second year of existence), we can safely assume that there are many more who need help. If government statistics are correct, thousands of Jewish women who are suffering from abuse are not using the domestic violence services, Jewish or non-Jewish, that are available. If they are not appearing at secular shelters and counseling services, they may be using private therapists, many of whom are not trained in dealing with domestic violence. Or, worse, they may not be getting any aid. Jewish women in small communities essentially have no choices in where to turn for help. Quite often they do not want to use the services in their own communities, Jewish or not, for fear of being recognized.

One federation president told me, "No matter how hard JFS works at upgrading its profile, they [abuse victims] don't know somebody there." This leader's perception contradicts what survivors told me—that they prefer not to go for help where they are known—and underscores the level of misunderstanding that exists in both the leadership and grass roots of the Jewish community.

So, we are still left with another dilemma—how to provide Jewish services to Jewish women so that they will use them. And, equally important, how do we make this endeavor economically feasible?

This is where the *Shalom* Task Force can be enormously helpful. While it can provide referrals to shelters and safe houses, the reality is that most women do not leave their abusers immediately. The Task Force is a wonderful answer to the problem of finding counseling and support as the first step to escaping an abusive relationship. Its anonymous hot line based in New York virtually eliminates the likelihood of having one's voice recognized by the telephone staffer. A caller can be referred to a resource in either her own community, if she is comfortable there, or to one where she is less likely to be known. As a cost-effective approach to providing referral services, it is ideal.

When it comes to safe haven, we face two additional concerns. Given what we know about abuse victims' anxiety regarding confidentiality, along with the financial realities of nonprofit organizations today, it is not going to be cost-effective for any one community, outside of wealthy large cities, to build and maintain a safe house. I recommend that the Jewish communal leaders within delineated geographic areas collaborate to develop a regional strategic plan. This coalition of communities should explore building a safe house that meets several criteria. First, like other shelters, it must be located where it would not attract attention to itself. For example, a four-season vacation destination would provide the cover that a family needs. Families moving in and out of a resort condominium, for example, would not attract undue attention. Second, the safe house must be within reasonable distance of a city that has both Orthodox and non-Orthodox day schools. Third, counseling by trained domestic violence counselors must be part and parcel of the "package" that families undergo while living at the safe house.

One of the major hurdles that Jewish women face is a financial one. According to the Combined Jewish Philanthropies, 29 percent of single-parent households in Greater Boston have an annual income of less than $35,000, as compared to 3 percent of dual-parent households.[35] Survivors, social workers, and attorneys have all reported that abusive husbands often hide their assets and throw legal roadblocks in the way of a woman seeking a divorce, so that she either never has enough money to hire an attorney, or she runs out of money before the case is resolved. In effect, by not funding domestic violence programs, the victim suffers twice—once at the hands of her abuser and once again by the community that denies her services.

Discussing the lack of Jewish shelters in New England, one rabbi told me, "I think that the idea of moving out of one's home is anathema to the Jewish woman. The Jewish religion is all around the home. It's not around the *shul*. So the woman has to redefine her whole relationship to Judaism . . . it's dissonance."

But, even this rabbi has sent numerous women to shelters and safe houses in New York and elsewhere when there was no choice, because there was no place closer to the home in which these women would rather be.

Summary

To summarize our findings:

1. The national offices of several organizations, religious and nonreligious, have produced resolutions and policy statements on the topic of domestic violence, some going back to the early 1990s. Some have lobbied Congress for passage of the Violence Against Women Act, and a few have gone so far as to publish books and study guides for use by their members.
2. The message of the above resolutions and policy statements is not getting from the national level to the grassroots leaders, much less rank-and-file members, of most of these organizations. Furthermore, it is apparent from speaking with community leaders, both lay and professional, that they are more often than not completely unaware of the programs available to them from their own organizations. This finding confirms the rabbis' experiences noted earlier.

3. The availability of specifically Jewish services for victims of domestic violence does not seem to be related to the size of the Jewish community. However, although the network of services tends to be wider in bigger communities, the depth is not consistent throughout the country.

4. Media coverage on domestic violence in the Jewish community has been sparse. Moreover, despite repeated tragedies, such as the murders of Laura Jane Rosenthal, Elana Steinberg, Carol Neulander, and Blima Zitrenbaum, community response to these calamities has brought little introspection outside of an initial flutter of voyeuristic articles.

That JWI has done an extraordinary job of producing its rabbis' resource guide on domestic violence only to see it sit on a handful of rabbis' shelves, mostly unread, is distressing. That *Hadassah* has published a professional study guide for its members' education, never to see the light of day in most chapter education programs, is indicative of the trepidation with which the Jewish community views the subject of abuse. One rabbi's denial that Jewish men would ever violate a restraining order to stalk their wives or beat them outside of their homes is mere delusion. The following federation president's take on the problem of translating national policy to on-the-ground action is startling.

This is part of the indirect financial blackmail that occurs. In a congregation usually . . . the male is the one who is providing most of the funding and is making the decisions about rabbinical jobs. And the [victim] may have the contact with a rabbi. If one [rabbi] gets [him or herself involved] in a marital dispute, they are going to piss off somebody, and they don't want to piss off their salary. But there has to be some sort of contact, some safe point within a community that's confidential, too.

By burying its collective head in the sand, too many local Jewish communal leaders have failed to do their duty to their constituents. There must be a Jewish component to confronting abuse. Simply having a woman with a Jewish surname write an article talking about her experience with abuse does not address the serious spiritual aspects of the problem. Psychological abuse steals a piece of a woman's soul each and every time it happens, and that is against Jewish law. Beating a wife is against Jewish law. Raping a wife is against Jewish law. Withholding the finances to run a home is against Jewish law. When there is no Jewish component to an abuse program, an important part of the woman's identity is ignored in treatment of the problem.

From a tactical point of view, the Jewish community must do a better job in communicating. It is critical to spell out the realities of domestic violence—what it is, where to find help. Posters should be more informative. The *Shalom* Task Force has a toll-free telephone number, but do women realize that this wonderful service is based in New York, where their voices from places as diverse as Denver and Dubuque, Boston and Bar Harbor will not be recognized? Do they know that the highly trained staff at the task force can help them locate shelter, counseling, and legal services in their own or nearby communities so that they can maintain their anonymity? Do they know that they can be referred to Jewish agencies and to rabbis who are cognizant of and sensitive to the needs of abuse victims?

Due to the high discomfort level evident in discussing the subject of domestic violence, we really have little idea how many women are affected by the various outreach efforts by the organizations producing materials and running programs. How many women who see the ubiquitous *Shalom* Task Force posters in women's rest rooms call the toll-free hot-line number? If there is a specifically Jewish resource in town, do Jewish women use it or do they go elsewhere?

When recruiting volunteer participants for this study, I left piles of discreet, white mini-fliers in rest rooms and health clubs across the Commonwealth; I also placed paid ads and press releases in newspapers. The fliers disappeared fairly quickly, but I didn't receive the hundreds of telephone calls that matched the number of fliers. Are women still walking around with them tucked into a hidden compartment of their purses, as one woman did for months before she finally called?

These are questions to which we may never know the answers, but one thing is clear. Even if only a fraction of abuse victims take advantage of the information offered, we may have saved the lives of that fraction. The more education and resources we offer, the more victims we will rescue.

The idea of the Leadership Conference of National Jewish Women's Organizations was a wonderful one. Collaborating to confront the issue of domestic violence head-on was efficient and cost-effective. Given the overlap of membership rolls, many women got the message more than once, in multiple venues and through a variety of media. That the conference has gone dormant is not acceptable. That the message that did get through was aimed almost exclusively at women is unacceptable. Communities and the organizations in them need to work together, joining forces to share the resources developed at the national level. Letting those materials gather dust on shelves and in cardboard boxes cycled from president to president is a waste of time and energy. Worse, it sends the message that abuse is tolerated in the community and betrays the very families that these organizations purport to represent. The organizations need to challenge the rabbis who continue to show resistance to addressing the issue of violence from the pulpit and demand that communal leaders confront it.

It is critical that the Jewish communal structure end its generations-long division when it comes to matters of mutual interest and survival. I do not think it is histrionic to state that the very survival of the Jewish people depends on the community as a whole coming together to combat violence in the home. The Leadership Conference of National Jewish Women's Organizations was a good start, but even that is considered dead or dormant by many of its participating organizations, many of which have never done anything beyond distributing the slim informational brochure to its members. Collaboration is the key in developing both educational programming and hands-on services. The financial realities that most communities face require that they also begin to lose their generations-old territoriality.

Coalition building must not be confined to Jewish organizations. The Jewish community can learn a lot by studying the collaborative models used by Boston and Worcester to confront the problems of youth violence and domestic violence, respectively. When every member of Boston's Ten Point Coalition on youth violence was on board and active, youth crime statistics went down.[36] The Worcester Intervention Network has been successful in decreasing the number of domestic violence incidents by 30 percent through its proactive outreach program.[37] It can, I believe, achieve even greater heights by including the religious communities in its work. The Jewish community does not have to reinvent the wheel. Its leaders must take the step to initiate and participate in a collaborative confrontation against violence. This is true in both smaller communities that have no Jewish facility at all for social service and in larger cities that have general programs. One federation president summed up the situation nicely.

> So the wife doesn't want to uproot [the kids] from their school support system and their other support systems right there in their relatively affluent suburban communities. The wife can survive in an apartment on the other side of town, but it disconnects [the children] not only from their Jewish community, which doesn't live on the other side of town, but from their school friends. So the wife takes the abuse for longer and longer and becomes further immobilized because [her] strength is sapped away . . . At least when you are holding on to a thread, what you have is your sense of social status. It's mythical, it's smoke and mirrors to a large degree, but it's something that you're holding on to . . . Providing services probably would help. I don't think it would cost us that much, either.

In the end, the Jewish community has to decide if it is worth its while to provide the psychological, legal, and financial resources to help victims of spousal abuse. It has to decide what constitutes "continuity."

6

CONCLUSIONS
AND RECOMMENDATIONS

And for the sin which we have committed before Thee wittingly or
unwittingly; for all these, O God of forgiveness, forgive us, pardon us,
grant us atonement.

—From the Yom Kippur liturgy[1]

JEWISH VICTIMS OF DOMESTIC ABUSE ARE SUFFERING THROUGHOUT
the United States, but only some of the very largest Jewish communities have
addressed the problem in a systematic and comprehensive manner. Other
communities with both large and small Jewish populations have either not
done anything at all or provide only the most rudimentary of referral services.
After talking with dozens and dozens of rabbis and community leaders, I have
concluded that this vacuum does not stem from malice. It does result from ignorance, denial, and neglect. Ignorance exists because up until recently the
Jewish community did not place domestic abuse on the communal agenda.
The omission occurred, in part, because rabbinical and communal workers'
professional training lacked curriculum on the subject. It also happened due
to denial. Denial occurs because acknowledging abuse in the Jewish home is
too painful to accept, particularly given the standard of *shalom bayit* and the
myth of the perfect Jewish husband. Neglect happens because, as one rabbi
told me, "there are so many other important issues to deal with."

Below I list the problems I have found (with the very generous assistance
of the many people who agreed to talk with me) and some recommendations

for addressing them. These recommendations are not carved in stone. Rather, because each community is different, the solution for each will vary. Although there are plenty of problems associated with addressing domestic violence, I have focused only on those that pertain specifically to the Jewish community.

PROBLEM: RABBINICAL TRAINING

Judaism is a religion of great ethical values. However, the moral precepts regarding human beings' behavior toward one another, handed down through the millennia, mean nothing if they are not translated into action on the ground. Too many rabbis continue to operate in a state of blissful ignorance regarding social ills in general within the Jewish community, and domestic violence in particular. Although seminaries have recently begun to address domestic violence as a reality, the attention devoted to the issue is minimal in most of them. In addition, if the subject is addressed, separate courses cover the *halachic* material and the pastoral. The current method of a single lecture or nonrequired course is not sufficient to sensitize rabbis to the serious nature of domestic violence and to educate them regarding the steps to take when approached by a congregant in need. By giving short shrift to the topic, seminaries are sending the not-so-subtle message that domestic abuse is still a topic to be kept secret. Finally, it will take years before a critical mass of new rabbis learned in the ways of domestic violence are out in the field and able to teach their congregations.

As for rabbis already out of seminary, their rabbinical associations have touched on the subject of domestic violence only briefly at conventions, and never in the context of a full plenary session. Too many members of these rabbinical associations have never had the opportunity to be exposed to the issue because their seminaries never addressed it.

RECOMMENDATION: RABBINICAL TRAINING

All rabbinical seminaries should institute a full, required course to focus on the problems of modern society, including, but not limited to, abuse. The course should address the *halachic*, psychological, social, and secular legal issues. In addition, domestic violence, including all of the same topics, should be the subject of a plenary session at rabbinical association conventions. The latter would ensure that a maximum number of attendees would hear the message.

PROBLEM: THE ROOT OF VIOLENCE

When God was about to give the Torah to Israel, God asked them, "Will you accept My Torah?" and they answered, "We will." God said, "Give Me surety that you will fulfill its ordinances." They said, "Let Abraham, Isaac and Jacob be our surety." God answered, "Those are not adequate sureties." Then Israel said, "Let our prophets be our sureties." Again God replied, "Those are not adequate sureties." Then Israel said, "Let our children be our sureties." God said, "Such pledges will I indeed accept."[2]

For a people that professes to care so much for its children, as exemplified by the midrash cited above, there seems to be a "disconnect" between book learning and the behavioral repertoire needed to fulfill the *mitzvah*, "And ye shall teach it to your children" (Deut. 11:19).[3] Although it was not within the scope of this book to address the effect that spousal abuse has on the children of such a relationship, suffice it to say that children learn from the behavior that their parents model. What we have is a situation in which abuse can grow exponentially through the generations, as expressed in Exodus 34:7, "Visiting the iniquity of the fathers upon the children, and upon the children's children, unto the third and fourth generation."[4]

Violence is learned at an early age, both in the home and in the schoolyard. For example, bullying—which has long been considered nothing more serious than a youthful rite of passage—has recently been recognized as one of the most disturbing crimes among young students. And, although the majority of bullies are still boys, more and more girls are participating. The National Association of School Psychologists states that bullying victims face serious self-esteem issues, depression, anxiety, loneliness, and physical and mental disorders.[5] Whereas some victims may become suicidal, other victims, because they have been bullied, become bullies themselves. In fact, two-thirds of all school shooters between 1974 and the time of this writing were at one time victims of bullying. The shooters at Columbine High School endured years of bullying with no help from the teachers and coaches who were supposed to be their guardians. It takes no stretch of the imagination to posit that bullies learn their behavior at home. After all, we already know that child abuse victims and witnesses of spousal abuse often grow up to become abusers themselves.

Fagan and Wilkinson write,[6] "Bullying is a precursor to stable antisocial and aggressive behavior that may endure into later adolescence and adulthood." According to Russell Skiba of the National Association of School Psychologists, "They learn from their experience and turn it around and bully others. In fact, longitudinal studies have found that the consequences of being bullied can be long-term and often persist well into adulthood."[7] Bullies struggle with serious emotional issues such as very poor self-esteem; consequently, they lash out at weaker peers.

RECOMMENDATION: YOUTH EDUCATION

Jewish educators should take advantage of the time they have students in day school, afternoon school, Hebrew high school, and Jewish summer camps. National educational organizations should organize a blue-ribbon panel to develop a curriculum that includes the social, behavioral, emotional, and Jewish aspects of both healthy relationships and relationship abuse, whether a relationship is that of schoolyard playmate, teenage girlfriend, or potential spouse. However, the framers of this curriculum must be aware of the very real possibility that their students may well be living in abusive homes. Since bullies' similarity to adult abusers is startling, it opens the very real possibility that bullies are simply acting out what they learn at home. Therefore, the community needs a coordinated approach to deal with violence before it escalates. If the community fails to get involved and intervene early on, children will have a greater chance to grow up behaving in the only way they know how.

PROBLEM: LOVE IS BLIND

So many of the women I spoke with told me that, looking back with "twenty-twenty hindsight," they could and did recognize disturbing behaviors in their fiancés. However, they ignored the clues because they were so much in love and caught up in the excitement of wedding preparations. "Love is blind and I was naive," one woman told me. She did not notice the red flags of future abusive behavior. When asked if the officiating rabbis said anything about conflict or abuse in their meeting before the wedding, all the women said there had been no mention.

The various Orthodox communities do require classes for their engaged couples. However, it appears from the reports of huge numbers of spousal abuse cases seen in New York that either the lessons do not "take" or that the wrong subjects are being taught.

RECOMMENDATION: PREMARITAL EDUCATION

I urge rabbis to insist that couples wishing to be married in a synagogue should be required to take a series of premarital education classes. These sessions could be coordinated by the Jewish Family Service, if the community has one, and include a rabbi and a psychologist or social worker trained in domestic violence work. The curriculum must not only address the typical "conflict resolution" piece, it must also include a segment on recognizing the signs of potential abuse and ways to get help.

PROBLEM: IT'S NOT IN THE MAIL

Jewish Women International's excellent *Embracing Justice: A Resource Guide for Rabbis* had reached only a tiny fraction of the pulpit rabbis whom I interviewed.[8] Although many communities do not have a JWI chapter, the majority of the thirty-three rabbis I met with were in a JWI service area.

RECOMMENDATION: MAKE A GIFT

JWI should make a point of getting its rabbis' resource guide to every rabbi in the nation. By teaming up with the seminaries of the major movements, JWI's efforts would reap benefits far beyond the cost associated with the distribution. If needed, special grants to cover the cost should be obtained. The present system of depending on orders from individual members or rabbis will not ensure that a resource guide finds its way to every rabbi's study. In Washington, D.C., the Jewish Coalition on Domestic Violence recently received a grant from the Jewish Federation of Montgomery County to distribute resource guides to rabbis throughout the metropolitan area. This model should be copied in other communities. In addition to distributing the resource guides, I would recommend that JWI, either by itself or in coalition with local Jewish organizations, follow up to ensure that rabbis read, and use, the guides.

PROBLEM: HEAR NO EVIL

If the results of this study are any indication, the percentage of survivors who had ever heard their rabbi give a sermon on the topic of domestic violence is infinitesimal. The percentage of rabbis who have even mentioned it in a sermon is small. This is unacceptable.

RECOMMENDATION: SPEAK UP

Every rabbi should take advantage of a "captive audience" on the High Holidays to address the issue of domestic violence in the Jewish community. This would be a particularly appropriate topic when talking about *teshuvah*, or repentance. In addition, every rabbi in the nation should commit to giving a *Shabbat* sermon or other program for Domestic Violence Awareness Month every year.

PROBLEM: I CAN'T HEAR YOU

Although some Jewish women's organizations have instituted programs to educate their membership about domestic abuse, many of their members have not gotten the message. As just one example, even the current and past presidents of several Jewish women's organizations with whom I met were not aware of their own groups' education, programming, and advocacy efforts at the national level.

RECOMMENDATION: PACK THE HOUSE

Every Jewish organization—male, female, and mixed gender—should make sure that a plenary session at its annual or biennial convention addresses domestic violence. The topic should not be relegated to workshop or breakout session status. This approach will ensure that the maximum number of convention delegates will hear the message and perhaps bring it back to their communities.

PROBLEM: WOMEN ONLY

Although a good start at confronting the issue of domestic abuse, the Leadership Conference of National Jewish Women's Organizations had one major flaw. Inviting only women's organizations sent the not-so-subtle message to the Jewish community that abuse is a women-only issue. The Conference of Presidents of Major American Jewish Organization's claim that domestic abuse is not on its agenda is disappointing as they were one of the leaders of the "Jewish continuity" mantra.

Since Jewish continuity has become a rallying cry for federations, rabbinical associations, and educators across the nation, communities and individual philanthropists have earmarked money for day schools, summer camps, singles groups, and blitz-trips to Israel. Is domestic violence not a threat to the very continuity of the Jewish people?

RECOMMENDATION: BLUE-RIBBON PANEL

Convene a national blue-ribbon panel of organizational representatives and experts in the field to address the issue of domestic violence as a specifically Jewish community concern. The mission statement of this panel should make clear that, above and beyond the illegality of domestic abuse (both civilly and *halachically*), it is a threat to Jewish continuity.

PROBLEM: TRICKLE-DOWN THEORY

The national organizations that have taken on domestic violence as a cause have produced a variety of materials and hands-on projects. However, much of this information is lost when the organization does not have a presence at the local level, or if no volunteer takes on the project at the grass roots. Further, given the precipitous decline in volunteer organization membership, the Jewish community finds itself at a critical stage.

RECOMMENDATION: YOU GET WHAT YOU PAY FOR

The organizations represented on the panel should ensure that a paid staff is dedicated to getting the message to the grassroots level, and to providing support in producing programs. Given the financial constraints that non-profit organizations often experience, the participating organizations could share the cost of the staff's salary if that were deemed necessary. Territoriality on the issue of domestic violence is not appropriate.

PROBLEM: NO PLACE TO GO

Many communities, particularly among the Orthodox, believe that they can "take care of their own" by sending abuse victims along an informal underground railroad of private houses, without reporting assaults to the authorities. Domestic violence professionals with whom I spoke told me that, given the insular nature of these same communities, the process puts many people in danger, including the host family. Consequently, they strongly discourage the practice.

As we have seen, Jewish women tend not to go to general battered women's shelters. Even general shelters with kosher facilities attract so few abuse victims that one must question the cost-effectiveness of the venture. The concept of a *shelter* is foreign to middle- and upper-middle-class women, and frightening. Recall that every woman with whom I spoke was visibly disturbed by the thought of living in a shelter, devoid of privacy and dignity.

Among the hurdles in getting battered Jewish women into shelters are embarrassment and shame about their situation and discomfort in being with people perceived as being very different from them. Granted, most women who use battered women's shelters are of a low economic status, and not Jewish. These two factors alone cause particular difficulty around holiday times, both Jewish and Christian. However, whether a class issue or simply one of wanting to be with their "own kind," the lack of utilization is real.

RECOMMENDATION: *BEIT SHALOM*, HOUSE OF PEACE

Only one woman with whom I spoke went to a shelter, and she only did so because she was trapped on an island with no way off and no place else to go. However, the overwhelming majority of the women did express support for the idea of a Jewish safe house. The term *safe house*, as opposed to *shelter*, seemed to convey a feeling of warmth and privacy for families, according to the women with whom I spoke. These women's desire for a *mezuzah* on the doorpost and wine and *challah* on the table on *Shabbat* further suggests that a Jewish spiritual perspective on violence would help in the families' healing. As I mentioned earlier, whether or not the woman observed *kashrut* was irrelevant to her desire to be among her "own" people. Many, or even most, of these women may not care about these features normally, but I believe that having them would ensure that all Jewish women from all walks of Jewish life would feel welcome. I also believe that the traditions and ritual objects of their faith would promote a stable and calming atmosphere that they might otherwise not feel in a shelter environment. Even if only for a little while, such an environment can serve as a warm and welcoming bridge to guide them from their abusive marriages to a life free from fear, hurt, and danger.

As for a possible location for the safe house, I have learned from my talks with shelter directors that their facilities are usually deliberately situated in neighborhoods where frequent moves are normal. The sight of a family moving out after a few weeks or months is not unusual, and would raise no eyebrows. Not only would the neighbors not suspect who was living in the house, but it would make it that much more difficult for abusers to hunt down their victims.

A Jewish safe house, too, must be located in a place that would not attract undue attention, that has year-round traffic, and that sees families move in and out on a regular basis. It also has to be situated within commuting distance of a city or town that has a choice of Jewish educational opportunities, from day schools and *yeshivas* to afternoon religious schools. In Massachusetts that place is the Berkshire Hills. A tourist destination all four seasons of the year, the Berkshires are rural enough that a house could sit out of the view of others, or, alternatively, even stand within an established neighborhood of vacation homes or condominiums. Jewish communities in other areas of the country can adapt this model for their own geography.

At this juncture the community is faced with a challenge. The financial realities of Jewish communal life are such that building a safe house for individual small communities would be fiscally irresponsible. Having chaired more than a few annual fund-raising campaigns myself, I am well aware of the constraints that the Jewish federations of these communities face. Most Jewish domestic violence programs across the country receive only a tiny fraction of their budgets from federation allocations. Currently, however, the majority of the Jewish communities in the United States offer the bare minimum of services, if anything. Even Boston, with its enormous Jewish population, only supports a part-time program. Therefore, I recommend that Jewish communities pool their resources to make a safe house for abuse victims a reality.

There are many needs and little money to fund the programs and agencies already in place, so finding the money to build a safe house seems impossible. However, the family has always been the foundation of the Jewish people's strength, and the community must find a way to support it. One of Judaism's highest precepts is that of redeeming the captive. That tenet would most certainly apply here, where women and children are being held captive in their own homes through fear and intimidation.

PROBLEM: FUNDING SERVICES

Funding for Jewish community programs is a continuing problem through-out the country. Federation funding for battered women's programs, or even more generally, Jewish Family Services, is very limited, if it exists at all. In Massachusetts, only Boston's Combined Jewish Philanthropies allocates any money to the *Kol Isha* program at the Jewish Family and Children's Service, which has only a part-time staff, leaving a waiting list of people in need. An unknown number of people in need of services reside elsewhere in the state, and the central and western Massachusetts federations allocate no money at all for domestic violence services.

RECOMMENDATION: THE FUNDING COLLABORATION

Communities should collaborate by region to fund a network of services to victims and then share them. Social workers, psychologists, private investigators, and other professionals with expertise in domestic vio-lence work can rotate throughout the geographic area. This system would, first, solve the financial problems of individual communities, par-ticularly the smaller ones in an area. Second, by referring a client to a fa-cility away from her hometown, this arrangement could also address the problem of confidentiality by offering branch offices accessible to each other's residents.

PROBLEM: DEPENDING ON THE KINDNESS OF STRANGERS

Depending on pro bono attorneys to help with the myriad problems associ-ated with abuse, divorce, and the *get* is not fair to the numerous families who need full attention to their cases. Most of these lawyers are not trained to deal with domestic violence cases, which can last up to five years. One shelter director said, "The private attorneys who do this work as part of their community service are great. They spend time on the case. The court-appointed pro bono lawyers are awful." On the other hand, lawyers, too, need to earn a living. Representing a spousal abuse victim in court is not a two-hour volunteer commitment to sell cupcakes at a bake sale, but a heavy, and unrealistic, commitment upon professionals.

RECOMMENDATION: COMMUNITY LAWYERS

Along the same lines as the network of social workers and psychologists, communities should join together to engage attorneys to serve exclusively the needs of families facing the problems associated with abuse and divorce. Although many clients will choose their own attorneys, those who cannot afford to retain one can use these legal services and then pay the community back when their divorce settlements are finalized. This solution would help women whose husbands abscond with the financial assets. These lawyers would likely have no lack of work, given the larger geographic area of operation, and would have the expertise necessary so that they would not have to waste time "catching up." An added attraction to this solution is that lawyers from one community would not necessarily know the families involved in another, making the situation more comfortable for every party. Finally, and most important from the client's perspective, these lawyers would be working for them during work hours, not on their volunteer time.

PROBLEM: THE ABSENTEE CONGREGANT

Virtually every battered women's shelter I spoke with reported having Jews among the professional staff. One reported, "We have eighty active volunteers, and at least 10 percent of them are Jewish." If the proportion of Jews working in this field is five times that in the general population, why are so few bringing the topic to their synagogues? Can it be that these workers are not affiliated with synagogues, or have they been rebuffed in their attempts to broach the topic?

RECOMMENDATION: SPREAD THE WORD

Congregants who are active as domestic violence advocates should make a point of volunteering their services to assemble a panel of speakers on the topic for an adult or youth education program. If they meet with resistance, they should form a committee to confront the board and the rabbi.

PROBLEM: THE DECLINE OF THE COMMUNITY

A majority of synagogues have not reached out to local domestic violence experts for help in educating themselves about the issue and how it is impacting their congregations. And, only a few local chapters of national organizations have held scattered programs or undertaken projects (e.g., collecting toiletries at their annual donor luncheons).

The Jewish communal world is territorial, almost to the point of self-destruction. Years of decline in both membership and donations, drifting of Jews toward historically gentile organizations such as museums and symphonies, and an increasing tendency to rely on major philanthropists for support of agencies and programs to the exclusion of smaller givers, have all brought the community to the point at which it no longer knows how to use its grassroots supporters.

Too many communities currently operate in an unsystematic fashion to address the issue of domestic violence. Lay organizations may or may not adopt their national offices' initiatives, may or may not collaborate with other groups, and may or may not interact with their communities' rabbis.

RECOMMENDATION: COLLABORATION

Jewish communities must make a concerted effort to educate themselves on the issue of domestic violence. Under the leadership of the federations, which must make much more of an effort to recognize and include volunteer groups under their umbrella, communities must educate and provide services. Synagogues and local chapters of national organizations should band together to form a Jewish community response to domestic violence, beginning with education of rabbis and professional and lay communal leaders. The next step is to educate the constituents of each of these groups.

Although each organization has its own mission and its own strength, the community as a whole must recognize and acknowledge the plague that is domestic violence. Acknowledging each other's particular strengths is a good foundation for strategic planning and a way to break down the walls of suspicion and distrust that have kept them from accomplishing their goals.

So, where should the community begin its educational campaign? How will it identify the people to educate? Statistics vary widely among Jewish population counters. According to the *American Jewish Year Book,* approximately 6 million Jews live in the United States.[9] In contrast, the United Jewish Communities' National Jewish Population Survey reports 2.9 million households with 6.7 million members, but only 5.2 million Jews among them.[10] However, the American Jewish Identity Survey reports that only a fraction of households affiliate with synagogues.[11] It is essential that an educational campaign start with that core group of Jews who identify enough religiously to join a congregation. The rabbis of these congregations have the opportunity to take the lead with their built-in audiences. Once the group of congregants is educated, outreach can extend to the other millions who do not attend a synagogue, but may hold membership in an agency such as a Jewish Community Center.

PROBLEM: DO NOT SEPARATE YOURSELF FROM THE COMMUNITY

"Have they reached out to us? Maybe one or two [congregations of all faiths] have contacted us. We have reached out to congregations of all types. Some don't even respond." These are the words of one battered women's services director, but her sentiment was echoed by several others.

Since the founding of Safe Havens in Boston, only a handful of synagogues have taken part in this interfaith coalition to learn about and combat domestic violence. In central Massachusetts, the faith community does not participate in the Worcester Intervention Network. In the Berkshires, there is no program in which to participate.

RECOMMENDATION: COMMUNITY COALITIONS

According to experts in the field, early intervention and community coalitions are key to both the prevention and reduction of domestic violence.[12]

Following the successful model developed during the 1990s in Boston to re-
duce juvenile crime,[13] and based on both Boston's Safe Havens and Worcester's WIN programs, every community should develop a collaborative effort
to prevent and alleviate the effects of domestic violence. This campaign
would consist of the police department's domestic violence unit, the district
attorney's office, the Department of Social Services, schools, clergy and their
congregations, and volunteer organizations. Although this collaborative endeavor would not be restricted to the Jewish community, rabbis, their congregations, and the Jewish social service network could use it as an invaluable
resource for education and support in confronting domestic violence.

PROBLEM: OPERATING IN THE DARK

Statistics on the rate of domestic violence in the general community, and
among some minority groups, are readily available from a variety of government sources. However, reliable and valid statistics on the Jewish community are not broken out, and previous studies have been flawed in their
reliance on low-return, self-selected respondents to mass surveys or on interviews with very small numbers of subjects.

RECOMMENDATION: RESEARCH

The national Jewish community should join together to fund a scientifically
designed and executed research study on Jewish family life. Going well beyond the basic data on education levels, intermarriage rates, and synagogue
affiliation found in any number of current studies, the information from a
study such as this could provide the Jewish communal world with a win-
dow into what is really driving the Jewish population of America. If the
leadership of Jewish America is truly concerned about continuity, it must
acknowledge that its enemies are not necessarily always external. In fact, the
information we get from a study of real family life could give us some insight
into why continuity is such a concern.

The social patterns of American Jewry have changed drastically over
the past few generations. In earlier times, as one prominent women's orga-

nization leader told me, "Every woman I talked with said that she got married 'to get out of the house.' I thought I was the only one. My home life was miserable. And, then, it turned out, my husband is a jerk." On the other hand, as another woman pointed out, today we see a very low rate of marriage among young Jews and a high rate of intermarriage among those who do marry. Her perception made me wonder if these trends reflect a desire to escape a repeat of an abusive Jewish childhood home life. I assert that we need to look well beyond the numbers to discover what will make the Jewish community not only survive, but thrive.

FINAL RECOMMENDATION: NEEDS ASSESSMENT

There is no "one size fits all" solution to the misery of domestic violence. The huge New York, Washington, and Los Angeles areas provide kosher shelter and counsel for victims of abuse, but their sheer size provides a measure of anonymity which encourages women to approach them. Jewish victims in smaller cities and towns most likely will never go to the local shelter, even if it has a microwave oven reserved for kosher use.

Therefore, each community must conduct a thorough needs assessment for the region. Then, based on the results, each must prepare a strategic plan for addressing education and outreach as well as collaboration with police and justice officials, local hospitals, and other faith communities. Communities should also take advantage of government faith-based initiative funding to establish a coalition of the above groups.

If I received sixty telephone calls from women willing to talk to me, how many others are out there who are too afraid to call? After all, I only advertised in a limited area and for a short amount of time. What message is the Jewish community sending to these women, and to their abusers, when there is not enough money to help them escape from danger?

If the community wants to keep Jews Jewish it must let them know that the Jewish community is there with help for them. If the community neglects to discuss the problem of domestic violence openly, it implicitly sends its victims to search for help and comfort outside the faith. When they do, they may just decide that they prefer it there.

Appendix A

RESEARCH PROTOCOL

The purpose of this study was to examine the Jewish community as an organization and how it responds to the problem of domestic violence in its midst. I used a multi-methodological approach in gathering data, including structured interviews, demographic information, and archival research. I conducted in-depth interviews with pulpit rabbis, Jewish communal professionals, and lay leaders about their knowledge, attitudes, and opinions regarding spousal abuse, particularly within the Jewish community, and to determine how their particular organizations deal with the problem. At the same time, I conducted interviews with female survivors of abusive marriages. These women were representative of the many streams of Judaism, including Orthodox, Conservative, Reform, Reconstructionist, and one or more *Hasidic* sects. For purposes of comparison, I also contacted other self-identified Jewish women who do not affiliate at all with the Jewish community.

Rabbis, whose names were obtained from the membership list of the Synagogue Council of Massachusetts, were contacted by telephone to solicit participation. I limited this sample to those rabbis who have pulpits and, therefore, more regular contact with congregants than would rabbis who devote their time to teaching or research. The rabbis represented Orthodox, Conservative, Reform, Reconstructionist, Hasidic, and nonaffiliated congregations. Of those rabbis I was able to reach, all but one agreed to talk with me, for a total of thirty-three. Similarly, I obtained communal professionals' and lay leaders' names from the registries of the Jewish Federations of the participating communities as well as from personal contacts with the organizations. The professionals I interviewed individually. The volunteers I met with both individually and in groups, in order to gain historical perspective on the organizations' workings. In all, I spoke with forty-seven volunteers and seven professionals. I also spoke with twenty-eight non-Jewish professionals working in some aspect of domestic violence, including staff in police domestic violence units, attorneys, shelter directors, batterer's program directors, and hospital personnel.

I solicited participation of the survivors using a combination of techniques. First, I placed advertisements in the two major Massachusetts Jewish newspapers. Second, several secular newspapers and synagogue bulletins published press releases about the study. Finally, through a "snowball" recruiting method, directors of women's shelters, other survivors, and rabbis discussed the project with women they knew before forwarding their names to me. As Weitzman discovered in her research on abuse survivors, women were very willing to talk about their experiences in order to help others.[1] Although approximately sixty women called to volunteer for the study, only twenty-five met the criteria I had set for inclusion: (1) that they live in the areas on which I was focusing and (2) that they be either divorced or in the process of divorce. Of those twenty-five, three dropped out before they could participate. That women from as far away as Montreal and Texas had heard about the study and wanted to participate in it was remarkable.

Due to financial restraints, the personal interview segment of the research focused on three areas within the Commonwealth of Massachusetts: the areas served by the Jewish Federation of the Berkshires, in the western part of the state; the Jewish Federation of Central Massachusetts in the middle; and the Combined Jewish Philanthropies in the Greater Boston metropolitan area. Although the beneficiary towns' size may themselves range from tiny to medium, their residents freely travel among them for work, worship, volunteer activities, and recreation. According to Gerald Gamm, who writes about the flight of the Boston Jewish population to the suburbs, Jews are not a place-based people (not surprising, given their history of persecution and exile over centuries).[2] Unlike the Boston Catholics who tend to define themselves by the circumscribed area of their parish, Jews affiliate more according to their interests. Except for the Orthodox communities, which tend to be situated in the neighborhoods immediately surrounding their synagogues, Jews have spread out across the landscape, no longer living in inner-city ghettoes (although it is an open secret that some members of Orthodox congregations live outside the immediate "parish" and drive to the synagogue, perhaps parking out of sight of the more observant congregants).

I also contacted the national offices of Jewish organizations. Included among these were the lay arms of synagogue associations; all organizational members of the Leadership Conference of National Jewish Women's Organizations; and several non-conference member organizations, if their mission statements indicated any concern at all with Jewish survival. Of all, I sought information on whether these organizations had ever issued a policy statement, resolution, or press release on the topic of domestic violence. In addition, I asked whether the organizations had ever addressed domestic violence through any of the following: an annual convention, national educational program, or advocacy campaign.

Finally, to gain a broader perspective on hands-on domestic violence services available in Jewish communities elsewhere, I put out a call to Jewish Family and Children's Services across the country to request information on their programs.

In addition to speaking directly with representatives of rabbinical associations, I conducted archival research to obtain records of the proceedings of their annual conventions. In so doing I could determine if the topic of domestic violence had been covered, and if so, to what extent. In addition, I contacted the rabbinical seminaries of the four main movements in American Judaism—Orthodox, Conservative, Reform, and Reconstructionist—to gain information on curriculum coverage of the topic of domestic violence.

The disadvantage of this exploratory research study is that sample sizes were too small to conduct sophisticated analyses on the quantitative data that I did obtain. On the other hand, the advantage of the qualitative aspect of the research is that, during the course of asking one question, another one frequently arose, often leading both the interviewer and the interviewee in unanticipated directions. Since I was not restricted to analyzing pencil marks on questionnaires, I was able to gather a treasure trove of attitudes and opinions, along with real-life experiences of domestic violence. In the end, I believe this information will prove helpful to communities in addressing issues of domestic violence.

Appendix B

THE BLACK AND BLUE PAGES

A LIST FOR JEWISH RESOURCES ON DOMESTIC VIOLENCE

Many telephone books list the names and telephone numbers of local shelters or domestic abuse hot lines in the front, along with the numbers for police, fire, and emergency medical services. However, as we have discovered, most Jewish women do not avail themselves of general services. Moreover, telephone books do not list specifically Jewish services that would be readily retrievable to somebody in crisis. Finally, since most Jewish communities do not offer such services, one must do some reconnaissance in order to find an agency with a Jewish perspective and with the specific ability to deal with domestic violence. Often the only place to find such a telephone number is in the women's rest room at a synagogue, and that is not consistent throughout the country. Since the abuse incident necessitating a call to a hot line may not occur during the synagogue's operating hours, this presents a problem. Furthermore, as we have previously discussed, abuse victims in small towns may not feel comfortable calling a local hot line or going to a shelter or counselor in their own communities for fear of being recognized.

Resource lists that served as the basis for this research were fairly short. This is only partially due to the fact that they are somewhat dated. Recall that media coverage of domestic violence, too, was practically nonexistent until the 1990s. As awareness of domestic violence increases, more communities are developing programs to deal with it. And, while secular agencies for the most part say that they try to be sensitive to practitioners of a wide variety of religions that come through their doors, many I spoke with really had very little understanding of the unique nature of Jewish family life. But, beyond the fact that domestic violence awareness has only recently increased, the short list appears also to be a function of the narrow view of the distribution of Jews in America. According to the most recently released National Jewish Population Survey, 43 percent of Jews were concentrated in the Northeast.[3] National *Hadassah,* for example, lists twenty-six resources, fifteen in New York alone, making a limited choice for people outside the five boroughs. While JWI listed state and national coalitions and hotlines in their new two-volume guides, that group, too, listed only a handful of local community resources, fewer than in the previous edition of their one-volume handbook.[4] And, although I solicited help from Jewish hospitals and Jewish Family Service agencies across the country, I received only a handful of responses. In the end, between surfing the Internet and networking over the telephone, I believe I have uncovered virtually all the available Jewish resources. As a result, the reader should have a fairly good idea as to the range of services offered by Jewish communities across the country. To those service providers who took my phone calls and responded to my requests for help, thank you.

I am not trying to imply that women should not use non-Jewish services, especially when in crisis. However, having spoken with dozens of survivors, social workers, and activists, and having read the research indicating that Jewish women do not use general battered women's shelters, I felt it would be better to be truthful as to the exact nature of services offered.

What follows is a list of programs with total or partial Jewish content, organized by state.[5] I use the term *partial* very loosely. Some of the shelters listed by Jewish women's organizations as catering to Jewish sensitivities may simply have a microwave oven for their clients who keep kosher or have received donations of toiletries from the local chapter of a national Jewish women's organization. The services offered range from hot line alone to free counseling and legal aid.

Every attempt was made to ensure that telephone numbers were current at the time this book went to press. However, due to frequent changes in area codes and the agencies' occasional change of location, I strongly recommend that, in crisis, an abuse victim waste no time—call 9-1-1.

ARIZONA

LEAH/Let's End Abusive Households
Jewish Family and Children's Service of Southern Arizona,Inc.
Tucson, AZ
(520) 795-0300, ext. 228
The LEAH program makes referrals for shelter services and provides individual and family counseling services for women, men, and children. A support group is available for women who are former or current victims, addressing in a safe and supportive environment the problems related to domestic abuse.

Shelter Without Walls
Jewish Family and Children's Service
Maricopa County, AZ
(480) 994–8477
    Working collaboratively with other community agencies, Shelter Without Walls
provides comprehensive case management, counseling services, employment readiness
training, and assistance with housing, child care, and transportation needs.

CALIFORNIA

Ezras Bayis Warmline
Orthodox Counseling Program
Jewish Family Service
Los Angeles, CA
(323) 761–8810 or (818) 623–0300
    Ezras Bayis offers a twenty-four-hour domestic hot line for Orthodox families.

Family Violence Project
Jewish Family Services
Sherman Oaks, CA
(818) 505–0900 or (310) 858–9344
    Services include individual and group counseling for women and children, re-
ferrals to lawyers, court accompaniment, help in obtaining restraining orders, and
transportation vouchers to shelter. Also, referrals for other shelters, counseling, and
job training are available. Family Violence Project offers two shelter options: (1)
Tamar House, a thirty-day emergency shelter program that accommodates twenty-
six women and children, with both kosher and nonkosher kitchens and mandatory
counseling; and (2) the long-term six-to-nine month program Hope Cottage, which
can accommodate twenty-four women and children. There are no fees for any services. However, women must work while there. One of the criteria for shelter clients is
that women must save 75 percent of their income so that when the program is completed, they will have in hand first and last month's rent. Community education programs are also available.
    The *Nishma* Family Crisis hot line specifically for Orthodox women is staffed by
Orthodox women trained to deal with domestic violence. (*Shabbat* calls are handled
by regular staff.)

Haven House
Pasadena, CA
(626) 564–8880

Founded in 1964, Haven House was the first shelter for battered women in the United States. It provides a hot line, emergency shelter, food, clothing, certified court advocates, transportation, individual counseling, groups, curriculum in high schools on teen dating violence, and a Web site for teens <http://www.itsnotok.org>. The staff makes referrals to lawyers who will provide pro bono services to assist with temporary restraining orders. Counseling is free for shelter residents; community residents pay on a sliding scale. Haven House provides a microwave oven to accommodate Jewish women keeping kosher.

Jewish Family and Children's Service
Long Beach, CA
(562) 427–7916

In collaboration with the Los Angeles Jewish Family Service, Long Beach supports a shelter with a kosher kitchen. Individual and family counseling as well as legal and medical assistance are available on-site. With help from local rabbis, emergency funds are available. The JFS also does educational outreach and therapist education.

Shalom Bayit/Bay Area Jewish Women Working to End Domestic Violence
Oakland, CA
(866) SHALOM–7, toll free for the Bay Area or
(510) 451-SAFE

Services include safety planning; phone and individual counseling; support groups and healing rituals; court accompaniment; holiday programs and adopt-a-family holiday assistance; panels and workshops for the Jewish community on dynamics of violence; in-service trainings for counselors, social workers, attorneys, rabbis and other Jewish professionals, and domestic violence shelter workers; individually tailored support for agencies wishing to help end violence against Jewish women; and strategic planning for congregations and agencies internally combating abuse. Assistance is provided in arranging kosher meals and other services for Jewish residents of battered women's shelters; clients also get help arranging consultations with therapists, attorneys, rabbis, or other service providers. *Shalom Bayit* also offers holiday healing rituals and services for survivors of abuse. Also, teen outreach and education programs for Jewish youth on teen dating violence prevention are available.

COLORADO

CHAI
Community Help and Abuse Information
Denver, CO
(303) 836–1819

CHAI staffs a twenty-four-hour crisis line. Although no therapy is conducted, the staff will make referrals to counselors, rabbis, and lawyers who understand domestic violence. Other services include kosher meals that are sent to secular shelters, crisis intervention, safety assessments, emergency funds for rent, legal services, counseling, and transportation. Community education programs include a teen date abuse prevention program in the Jewish community, a twice-yearly rabbinical council presentation, and participation in an annual women's symposium. Crisis cards are placed in every synagogue, Jewish Community Center, and so forth.

FLORIDA

Jewish Family and Children's Service
West Palm Beach, FL
(561) 684–1991

The Rosenberg program at this JFCS works directly with victims of abuse, offering weekly support services and individual counseling. The KOLOT coalition of volunteers and professionals works in coordination with the Rosenberg program to develop awareness through educational outreach about Jewish domestic abuse.

Shalom Bayit
Miami, FL
(305) 576–1818

Shalom Bayit staffs a hot line and offers up to twelve free individual therapy sessions, support groups, and case management. This service refers to shelters and legal services. Baby-sitters are available to watch children while women are in session. A kosher meal program is made available through Jewish Community Services. Limited emergency funds are available. Another program helps with moving expenses.

Illinois

SHALVA
Chicago, IL
(773) 583–4673

One of the first programs to deal with Jewish domestic abuse in the country, SHALVA offers a twenty-four-hour information and referral hot line for Jewish women, crisis intervention, case management, counseling services, support groups, legal aid, financial assistance, rabbinical advocacy, community education, and prevention programs. (The separate Jewish Children's Bureau provides services to child abuse victims.)

The Weitzman Center
203 N. Wabash Avenue, Suite #2000
Chicago, IL 60601
(312) 444–1777

This new not-for-profit organization provides information as well as referral/resource panels which contain leads to agencies and professionals who are sensitive to the unique aspects of upscale violence and domestic abuse. The Center is currently working on an educational video for national distribution to doctors, lawyers, clergy and other helping professionals to increase awareness about aspects of domestic abuse among overlooked populations, i.e., women who are upper educated and from upper income lifestyles.

Maryland

CHANA
Baltimore, MD
(410) 234–0023 or (800) 991–0023

CHANA staffs a hot line and provides a kosher safe house, counseling, and legal services for Jewish women. Unique to this program is the availability of a private investigator to search for the financial assets of the abusive husband. The first eight counseling sessions are free and then provided on a sliding-fee scale. Legal services are both pro bono and sliding scale, depending on the situation of the client. CHANA will defer payment until after the divorce settlement is final. CHANA also provides Jewish community education. CHANA coordinates with JFS of central Maryland on many services.

MASSACHUSETTS

HAWC

Salem, MA
Hot lines
(978) 281–1135, toll-free for Gloucester or
(978) 744–6841

While not a Jewish shelter, Help for Abused Women and Children (HAWC) will set aside a cabinet in the kitchen for kosher use if the need arises. Individual counseling is available, and support groups, based in the main office and two satellite offices in Lynn and Gloucester, serve twenty-three cities and towns. Advocates work at Salem Hospital and Union Hospital in Lynn as well as at five district courts. Staff personnel also conduct community education in schools about teen dating violence, bullying, and teasing. If there is no vacancy in their shelter, staff will arrange for police to transport, or will give money to the client for transportation, to a hotel room. HAWC works with many communities of faith in outreach.

Kol Isha

Jewish Family and Children's Service
Newton, MA
(617) 558–1278

Domestic violence counseling services include safety planning, court advocacy, and no-cost support groups. Family assistance services offer access to food, clothing, transportation, shelter, medical care, and legal services. Jewish Healing Connections offers spiritual support. Bilingual services are available for Russian- and Hebrew-speaking clients. Community outreach and education training programs are available to Jewish communal professionals, volunteers, and youth. Referrals to community resources include housing and mental health counseling services.

Safe Transitions

Beth Israel Deaconess Medical Center
Boston, MA
(617) 667–8141

Safe Transitions provides services such as group therapy, and referrals to shelters, *Kol Isha,* individual therapists, and to lawyers familiar with and sensitive to Jewish law. The program also trains health care providers to identify and respond to patients experiencing violence in their lives.

Second Step
Newton, MA
(617) 965–3999

Second Step is a transitional shelter for women who have completed the crisis stage at an emergency shelter. There are now two facilities, one with a kosher pantry, one with a full kosher kitchen.

MICHIGAN

Windows
Jewish Family Services
Detroit, MI
(248) 559–1500

Windows offers individual, couples, and family counseling, group therapy, a shelter, and abuse and neglect prevention programs.

MINNESOTA

Jewish Family and Children's Services
Minneapolis, MN
(952) 546–0616

JFCS offers counseling, emergency financial aid, and family-life education programs.

MISSOURI

Jewish Family and Children's Services
Kansas City, MO
(913) 432–9300

JFCS provides counseling and anger management classes. Also, the Jewish Community Domestic Violence Outreach and Education Program, a collaboration of NCJW and SAFEHOME, a domestic violence shelter in Johnson County, conducts programs to raise awareness in the Jewish community of domestic violence. The staff also educates Jewish victims about available services and identifies gaps in services to Jewish victims and develops resources to fill them.

NEW JERSEY

Association of Jewish Family and Children's Agencies
East Brunswick, NJ
(732) 432-7120

The association functions as a referral service for its 145 affiliated Jewish Family and Children's Services around the country. The organization's Web site does list the affiliates and their offerings, but it does not indicate which family services actually provide specific domestic violence services. I suggest you call the individual agency in your locale.

Project Sarah
Passaic, NJ
(800) 883-2323, toll-free hot line (same as *Shalom* Task Force) or
(201) 837-9090 at Jewish Family Service

Project Sarah provides crisis intervention and counseling and access to a kosher safe-house network, with procedures for safety and confidentiality. It also distributes kosher kits and training on Jewish issues to New Jersey shelters. Staff does case consultations and provides training and support for local rabbis to assist in working with victims of domestic violence and educating their congregations. Project Sarah runs training programs for *mikveh* attendants and programs for mental health professionals and volunteers on clinical issues of domestic violence. Community presentations and educational materials are available. Advocacy services for victims include specialized consultations for the Russian-speaking community. Project Sarah is linked with the statewide JFS network.

Rachel Coalition
Florham Park, NJ
(973) 740-1233

The Rachel Coalition staffs a twenty-four-hour crisis intervention hot line and supports an emergency suburban kosher safe house for the MetroWest area. Services include individual and group counseling, transition and housing planning, information and referral services, community outreach and education, access to legal and medical support, and men's support groups.

NEW YORK

Beth Israel Medical Center
Domestic Violence Services
Social Work Department
New York, NY
(212) 420–4054

Part of the rape crisis center at the medical center, Domestic Violence Services employs a social worker in the emergency room to assess the needs of the patient, to be responsible for her safe discharge, and to advocate for her if police are there. The social
worker gives information on getting help with restraining orders and does a follow-up call
within days to offer services to the victim. A program at the hospital trains after-hours
emergency-room volunteers to help refer victims to the right place. Domestic Violence Services conducts training for hospital in-patient and out-patient staff as well as for the community. Beth Israel participates in the Jewish Federation Domestic Violence Task Force.

*Family Violence Prevention Center at the Jewish Board of Family and Children's
Services*
New York, NY
(718) 237–1337, hot line
(888) 523–2769, toll free

In addition to staffing a twenty-four-hour hotline, the Jewish Board of Family and
Children's Services consists of fourteen mental health clinics, all of which provide domestic violence assistance. Also, three shelters accommodate 172 beds in apartments so that
kitchens can be made kosher. Among other services are a men's program for anger management, groups for violent men and Orthodox violent men, individual and group treatment
for women and children, a Jewish support network, counseling service information and
referral, and outreach to yeshivas to teach students about abuse. Payment is on a sliding-
fee scale and insurance is accepted. The Center refers to lawyers. There is limited emergency money available. The New York Legal Assistance Group provides free legal aid.

OHEL Children's Home and Family Services
Brooklyn, NY
(718) 851–6300

OHEL serves a strictly Jewish clientele, some from as far away as Israel. It provides
outpatient service for women deciding whether to leave or stay, or are in the process of
leaving their abusers. The shelter houses up to thirteen family units, all strictly kosher.
Shabbat and holidays are observed. Newly sheltered women are provided with daily individual counseling. Volunteers escort clients to appointments. Among services offered

are group meetings for both case management and support, referral to legal services, and rabbinical help with advocacy in religious courts. Also available are children's support groups and help with locating schools. Limited financial assistance is available. The average stay is six to eight months. OHEL generally does not take emergency cases.

Rockland Family Shelter
Project *Tikva*
New York City, NY
(845) 634-3344

Within the general shelter is Project *Tikva* with specifically Jewish services, including a twenty-four-hour hot line, counseling, and shelter for women and children. *Tikva* provides in-house and drop-in office for individual therapy, court advocacy, free legal consultation on staff, and pro bono lawyers. The shelter provides services to a large local Orthodox community, including Project *Orot*, outreach to rabbis, rabbis' wives, educators, women, law enforcement, mental health professionals, and medical center maternity wards. Orthodox women are directed to an Orthodox woman on staff. Day and evening support groups and individual therapy are available. A Jewish support group was in the process of developing at the time of this writing. A kosher area of the kitchen is available when needed. No emergency funds are available, but the staff has developed links with resources that can help obtain funds.

Shalom Task Force
Brooklyn, NY
(718) 337-3700

The task force operates a toll-free hot line for both New York and affiliated communities throughout the country. Task force staff workers help callers by making referrals to local resources, including shelter, counseling, and rabbis sensitive to violence issues.

Survivors of Domestic Violence Group
Jewish Family Service of Buffalo and Erie County
Amherst, NY
(716) 883-1914

It appears that there is a weekly support group here, but I was unable to find any further information. Call the JFS for more information.

The Transition Center
Far Rockaway, NY
(718) 520-8045

The center provides shelter, group and individual sessions, and referrals to legal services. All apartments within the shelter can be made kosher.

OHIO

Family Violence Prevention Project
Columbus, OH
(614) 358-2530

The project staffs a hot line and provides outreach, education, advocacy, individual counseling on a sliding-fee scale, and referrals to legal services. Limited emergency funds are available. The Project will refer to a general shelter; there are no kosher facilities available.

Project Chai
Jewish Family Service Association of Cleveland
Cleveland, OH
(216) 691-7233

Project *Chai* staffs a twenty-four-hour hot line and provides safe housing, counseling, and referral services for legal, medical, and financial needs. Shelter consists of efficiency apartments in hotels. Jewish Family Service provides a legal justice system advocate (a case manager who will work with a client and her lawyer) and has three lawyers who do pro bono work. Four-week anger management classes are cofacilitated by the JFS and the local batterers' program. (If there is physical abuse the program will not accept the man.) An ongoing eight-week support group is available for clients as long as they like. Art activities are available for children while the mother is in group.

PENNSYLVANIA

Jewish Family and Children's Service
Harrisburg, PA
(717) 233-1681

The JFS mentions "help with domestic violence" as a service. Call for more information.

Jewish Family and Children's Service
Philadelphia, PA
(215) 698-9950

With seven branch offices, JFCS says that any of their clinicians are able to work with domestic violence victims. Their *Sukkat Shalom* domestic violence prevention program offers counseling and case management services, individual therapy, couple sessions when there is no protection order in place (i.e., no physical violence), referrals to shelters, and referrals to lawyers, dentists, gynecologists, and locksmiths. Direct financial help is available to escape danger. The agency will help pay rent, mortgage, or utilities for a limited time if the client is about to lose her home. A grant covers up to ten sessions of counseling. JFCS will accept insurance or will work on a sliding-fee scale. They also provide a thrift store, which offers everything from cars to clothes at discounted prices. There is a small pool of lawyers who will do pro bono work. JFCS will cover court costs but not lawyers' fees. There is also a grant to allow clients to attend college. Camp *Shalom* brings mothers, children, survivors, and volunteers to the Poconos for a summer camp experience. The Miriam Project organizes quarterly holiday get-togethers for the camp participants. Outreach to the community includes public schools and Hebrew schools. Topics include dating violence and conflict resolution. The *Koach* program comprises a group of synagogues that sponsor a client by paying for day care, food scrip, and so forth. The Jewish Education and Vocational Service provides free computer training to help clients obtain future employment.

Jewish Family and Children's Service
Pittsburgh, PA
(412) 422-7200

The JFCS provides individual and family counseling, support groups, court accompaniment, referral to general women's shelters, and medical and legal aid. Also, the agency does community outreach for education. Some funds are available to help victims get away from their abusive homes.

Rachel's Project
Women's Center of Montgomery County
Jenkintown, PA
(215) 885-5020

Ask for "Rachel" for a counselor sensitive to Jewish issues. The Women's Center is a volunteer-staffed organization that provides peer counselors and support groups, assists with protection orders, helps with safety plans, accompanies abuse victims to court, and refers to shelters, therapists, and lawyers. Limited emergency funds are available. Some volunteers are designated as "Rachel" counselors. *Gan Tikva* is a group of Orthodox women, trained by the Women's Center, who help other Orthodox women.

TEXAS

AVDA (Aid to Victims of Domestic Violence)
Houston, TX
(713) 224–9911

Founded with assistance from NCJW in 1980, this agency provides legal assistance to victims of domestic violence and help with divorce and protective orders, accompaniment, and case management. NCJW still contributes to it. AVDA will refer victims to lawyers knowledgeable about *halacha* if requested. All services are free except filing fees. AVDA also sponsors a battering intervention project for abusers on a sliding fee scale. AVDA will conduct outreach education for the general public, therapists, and the religious community.

Jewish Family Service
Dallas, TX
(972) 437–9950

Jewish Family Service provides crisis intervention, safe homes, counseling, and support groups for the victim as well as professional help for the abuser.

Jewish Family Service
Houston, TX
(713) 667–9336

JFS provides individual counseling and referral to shelters (no kosher provisions available), and a speakers' bureau for outreach to the community. Jewish Family Service participates in *Shalom Bayit*: the Houston Jewish Coalition Against Domestic Abuse, an all-volunteer confederation of social workers, rabbis, the JFS, and Jewish women's organizations, that does outreach and education.

WASHINGTON

Project DVORA
Seattle, WA
(206) 461–3240

Project DVORA (Domestic Violence Outreach, Response and Advocacy) provides, free of charge, a safe, confidential, Jewish-sensitive context for getting help. This service also offers community outreach, consultation to professionals, and youth violence prevention education.

NOTES

INTRODUCTION

1. Rabbi Hillel, *Mishna Avot* (2,4), quoted in Joseph Baron, ed. *A Treasury of Jewish Quotations* (Northvale, NJ: Jason Aronson, 1985), 59.

2. I. Epstein, ed., *The Talmud: Tractate Shavuos* (New York: Soncino Press, 1972), 39a.

3. Joseph H. Hertz, ed., *Pentateuch and Haftorahs* (New York: Soncino Press, 1994), 835.

4. Ibid., 501.

5. I. Epstein, ed., *The Talmud: Tractate Shabbos* (New York: Soncino Press, 1972), 54b.

6. Abraham J. Twerski, *The Shame Borne in Silence* (Pittsburgh: Mirkov Publications, 1996).

7. Ibid.

8. Ibid.

9. Ibid., 66.

10. Susan Weitzman, *Not to People Like Us: Hidden Abuse in Upscale Marriages* (New York: Basic Books, 2000).

11. Joseph L. Hertz, *Sayings of the Fathers* (New York: Behrman House, 1945.)

12. Moses Maimonides, *The Guide for the Perplexed* (New York: Dover Publications, 2000).

1: SURVIVORS TELL THEIR STORIES

1. *The Holy Scriptures* (Philadelphia: Jewish Publication Society, 1960), 813.

2. Ibid., 814.

3. U.S. Census Bureau, *Statistical Abstract of the United States: 2000*, 116th ed. (Washington, D.C.: U.S. Census Bureau, 2000).

4. Trish Bonica, *Domestic Violence in Jewish Homes* (Washington, D.C.: Jewish Women International, 2002).

5. Weitzman, *Not to People Like Us.*

6. Ibid.

7. Twerski, *Borne in Silence.*

8. D. B. Berry, *Domestic Violence Sourcebook* (New York: McGraw-Hill, 1995).

9. Weitzman, *Not to People Like Us.*

10. Twerski, *Borne in Silence.*

2: THE MYTH OF *SHALOM BAYIT*

1. Jacob Tam, quoted in Baron, 541.

2. Weitzman, *Not to People Like Us.*

3. P. Tjaden and N. Thoennes, *Full Report of the Prevalence, Incidence and Consequences of Violence Against Women: Findings from the National Violence Against Women Survey* (NCJ 183781) (Washington, D.C.: U.S. Department of Justice, National Institute of Justice, 2000).

4. Ibid., 5.

5. L. W. Hedin and P. O. Janson, "The Invisible Wounds: The Occurrence of Psychological Abuse and Anxiety Compared with Previous Experience of Physical Abuse During the Childbearing Year," *Journal of Psychosomatic Obstetrics and Gynecology* 20, no. 3 (1999): 136–44.

6. Tjaden and Thoennes, p. 4.

7. Domestic Abuse Intervention Project, *The Power and Control Wheel* (Duluth, Minn.: Domestic Abuse Intervention Project, 1999).

8. Ibid.

9. Ibid.

10. D. B. Berry, *Domestic Violence Sourcebook* .

11. Twerski, *Borne in Silence.*

12. Domestic Abuse Intervention Project.

13. G. Bubis, *The Costs of Jewish Living: Revisiting Jewish Involvements and Barriers* (New York: American Jewish Committee, 2002).

14. *Forrest Gump,* film, Hollywood, Calif.: Paramount Pictures, 1994.

15. Domestic Abuse Intervention Project.

16. *Late Night with Conan O'Brien,* television program, National Broadcasting Company (NBC), May 13, 2002.

17. GALs can be appointed by a judge for any number of reasons, but for our purposes here it is to represent the best interests of the children in a divorce case involving abuse.

18. Tjaden and Thoennes, 5.

19. Ibid., 6.

20. Twerski, *Borne in Silence*, 125.

21. Lenore E. Walker, *The Battered Woman* (New York: Harper & Row, 1979), 55–70.

22. Weitzman, *Not to People Like Us*.

23. FBI Web site, *Uniform Crime Reports*, <http://www.fbi.gov/ucr/ucr.htm> (2002).

24. S. Plichta, "The Effects of Woman Abuse on Health Care Utilization and Health Status: A Literature Review," *Women's Health Issues* 2, no. 3 (1992): 154.

25. Tjaden and Thoennes, *Findings from the NVAW Survey*, iv.

26. Pamela Druckerman, "Domestic Violence Among Jews Gets More Attention Since Simpson Case," *Jewish Advocate*, 15 July 1994.

27. Neil B. Guterman, "Confronting the Unknowns in Jewish Family Violence," *Journal of Jewish Communal Service* 70, no.1 (1993): 26–33.

28. B. Giller and E. Goldsmith, *All in the Family: A Study of Intrafamilial Violence in the Los Angeles Jewish Community* (master's thesis, Hebrew Union College and the University of Southern California, 1981).

29. Julie Ringold Spitzer, *When Love Is Not Enough: Spousal Abuse in Rabbinic and Contemporary Judaism* (New York: Women of Reform Judaism, The Federation of Temple Sisterhoods, 1995).

30. J. McCauley et al., "Relations of Low-Severity Violence to Women's Health," *Journal of General Internal Medicine* 13, no. 10 (1998): 687–91.

31. M. B. Mechanic et al., "The Impact of Severe Stalking Experienced by Acutely Battered Women: An Examination of Violence, Psychological Symptoms, and Strategic Responding," *Violence and Victims* 15, no. 4 (2000): 443–48.

32. E. H. Carmen, P. P. Rieker, and T. Mills, "Victims of Violence and Psychiatric Illness," *American Journal of Psychiatry* 141, no. 3 (2000): 378–83.

33. A. O. Rollstin and J. M. Kern, "Correlates of Battered Women's Psychological Distress: Severity of Abuse and Duration of the Postabuse Period," *Psychological Report* 82, no. 2 (1998): 387–94.

34. A. L. Coker et al., "Intimate Partner Violence and Cervical Neoplasia," *Journal of Women's Health and Gender Based Medicine* 9, no. 9 (2000): 1015–23.

35. J. R. T. Davidson, "Recognition and Treatment of Posttraumatic Stress Disorder," *Journal of the American Medical Association* 286, no. 5 (2000): 584.

36. Ibid., 586.

37. A. E. Street and I. Arias, "Psychological abuse and Post-traumatic Stress Disorder in Battered Women: Examining the Roles of Shame and Guilt," *Violence and Victims* 16, no. 1) (2001): 65.

38. Family Violence Prevention Fund. *Confidentiality of Health Records Can Be Life-or-Death Issue for Women Facing Abuse,* <http://endabuse.org/newsdesk/releases> (17 Oct 2000).

39. *Holy Scriptures*, 107.

40. B. B. R. Rossman, "Longer Term Effects of Children's Exposure to Domestic Violence," in *Domestic Violence in the Lives of Children, ed.* S. A. Graham-Bermann and J. L. Edelson (Washington, D.C.: American Psychological Association, 2001), 35–65.

41. A. E. Appel and G. W. Holden, "The co-occurrence of spouse and physical child abuse: A review and appraisal," *Journal of Family Psychology* 12 (1998): 578–99.

42. FVPF, *Confidentiality of Health Records*.

43. Ibid.

44. Ibid.

45. Appel and Holden, "Co-occurrence of Spouse and Child Abuse."

46. Plichta, "Effects of Woman Abuse," 154.

47. Weitzman, *Not to People Like Us.*

48. Hedin and Janson, "The Invisible Wounds," 136.

49. Tjaden and Thoennes, *Findings from the NVAW Survey*, 54.

50. J. Abbott, "Injuries and Illnesses of Domestic Violence," *Annals of Emergency Medicine* 29, no. 6 (1997): 781–85.

51. G. L. Roberts et al., "Domestic Violence in the Emergency Department: I. Two Case-Control Studies of Victims," *General Hospital Psychiatry* 19, no. 1 (1997): 5–11.

52. M. A. Rodriguez et al., "Mandatory Reporting of Domestic Violence Injuries to the Police," *Journal of the American Medical Association* 286, no. 5: 580–83.

53. Bureau of Justice Statistics, *Preventing Domestic Violence Against Women* (Washington, D.C.: Bureau of Justice Statistics, 1986).

54. National Center for State Courts Research, *CPOs: The Benefits and Limitations for Victims of Domestic Violence* (Washington, D.C.: National Center for State Courts Research, 1997).

55. E. S. Buzawa and C. G. Buzawa, *Do Arrests and Restraining Orders Work?* (Thousand Oaks, Calif.: Sage Publications, 1996).

56. S. Adams and A. Powell, *Tragedies of Domestic Violence: A Qualitative Analysis of Civil Restraining Orders in Massachusetts.* (Boston: Office of the Commissioner of Probation, Massachusetts Trial Court, 1995).

57. FVPF, *Confidentiality of Health Records*.

58. American Institute on Domestic Violence, *Training Businesses to Survive the Newest Workplace Security Threat,* <http://www.aidv-usa.com> (2001).

59. Ibid.

60. Ibid.

3: WHAT DOES JEWISH LAW SAY ABOUT ABUSE?

1. Hertz, *Deuteronomy Pentateuch,* 820.

2. Spitzer, *When Love Is Not Enough,* 15.

3. Hertz, *Pentateuch,* 4.

4. I. Epstein, ed., *The Talmud: Tractate Sanhedrin* (New York: Soncino Press, 1990), 37a.

5. *Mekilta* to Exodus 31:13, quoted in Baron, *Treasury,* 275.

6. Elliot Dorff, *Family Violence: A Responsum for the Committee on Jewish Law and Standards* (New York: The Rabbinical Assembly, 1995), 61.

7. Hertz, *Pentateuch,* 501.

8. Ibid., 835.

9. Twerski, *Borne in Silence.*

10. Hertz, *Pentateuch,* 502.

11. Epstein, ed., *Tractate Berachot* (New York: Soncino Press, 1984), 19b.

12. *Zohar, Vayetze,* 164a, quoted in Twerski, *Borne in Silence,* 65.

13. I. Epstein, ed., *The Talmud: Tractate Yebamoth* (New York, Soncino Press, 1984), 62b.

14. Mordecai, in *Tractate Ketuvot,* 185, quoted in Twerski, *Borne in Silence,* 46.

15. *Bereshit Rabbah* 20:18, quoted in Twerski, *Borne in Silence,* 46.

16. Adin Steinsaltz, *The Talmud: Tractate Bava Metzia,* (New York: Random House, 1990), 59a.

17. Ibid., 234.

18. Hertz, *Pentateuch,* 589–92.

19. Twerski, *Borne in Silence,* 46.

20. Ibid., 46.

21. Ibid.

22. *Holy Scriptures,* 922–23.

23. Twerski, *Borne in Silence.*

24. Hertz, *Pentateuch,* 664–67.

25. Maimonides, *Laws of Marital Status* 15:17, quoted in Twerski, *Borne in Silence,* 71.

26. *The Tur, Even Ha'ezer* 154, quoted in Twerski, 71.

27. Twerski, *Borne in Silence,* 65.

28. Naomi Graetz, *Silence Is Deadly: Jewish Tradition and Spousal Abuse* (Northvale, N.J.: Jason Aronson, 1998).

29. *Holy Scriptures,* 710.

30. *Holy Scriptures,* 711.

31. Graetz, *Silence Is Deadly.*

32. Ibid., 93–94.

33. Moses Isserles, *Darkei Moshe, Tur, Even Ha'Ezer,* 154:15, quoted in Graetz, *Silence Is Deadly,* 118.

34. Graetz, *Silence Is Deadly,* 104.

35. Twerski, *Borne in Silence,* 62–63.

36. Hertz, *Pentateuch,* 12.

37. Rabbi Simha in *Or Zarua, Piskei Bava Kama,* sec. 161, quoted in Dorff, *Family Violence,* 7.

38. Rabbi Meir of Rotenburg, *Even Ha-Ezer* 297, quoted in Graetz, *Silence Is Deadly,* 126.

39. Rabbi Meir of Rotenburg, *Even Ha-Ezer* 298, quoted in Graetz, *Silence Is Deadly,* 127.

40. Graetz, *Silence Is Deadly,* 122.

41. Ibid., 123.

42. Twerski, *Borne in Silence,* 65.

43. Graetz, *Silence Is Deadly.*

44. Abraham Paperna, quoted in Graetz, *Silence Is Deadly,* 139.

45. Dorff, *Family Violence,* 44.

46. Ibid., 2.

47. Ibid., 44.

48. Jacob Tam, quoted in Joseph Telushkin, *Jewish Literacy* (New York: William Morrow, 1991), 488.

49. Zangwill, quoted in Hertz, *Pentateuch,* 935.

50. *Rashba Responsa,* part 7, p. 32, no. 477, cited in Graetz, *Silence Is Deadly,* 108.

51. Telushkin, *Jewish Literacy,* 549.

52. Tarfon, quoted in Joseph H. Hertz, *Sayings of the Fathers* (New York: Behrman House, 1945), 45.

53. Telushkin, *Jewish Literacy.*

54. Graetz, *Silence Is Deadly.*

55. *Holy Scriptures,* 143.

56. Ishmael School *Talmud: Arakin,* 15b, quoted in Baron, *Treasury,* 161.

57. *Tosefta, Peah,* 1.2, quoted in Baron, *Treasury,* 460.

58. Mark Dratsch, "Domestic Violence and Halacha," in *Embracing Justice: A Resource Guide for Rabbis on Domestic Abuse,* ed. Diane Gardsbane (Washington, D.C.: Jewish Women International, 2002), 59–66.

59. Dorff, *Family Violence,* 31–32.

60. Dratsch, "Domestic Violence," 64.

61. Hertz, *Pentateuch,* 306.

62. I. Epstein, ed., *The Talmud: Tractate Gittin* (New York, Soncino Press, 1977), 10b.

63. Dorff, *Family Violence*.

64. Twerski, *Borne in Silence*, 35.

65. *Domestic Violence: Battering, the Dynamics of an Abusive Relationship*, police training videotape (Minneapolis: Law Enforcement Resource Center and Minnesota Program Development, Inc., 1997).

66. *The New Mahzor for Rosh Hashanah and Yom Kippur* (Bridgeport, Conn.: Media Judaica, 1976), 514.

67. *Bar Ilan Responsa Project*, part 4, no. 927, quoted in Graetz, *Silence Is Deadly*, 129.

68. Joseph Caro, *bet Yosef, Even ha-Ezer, Hilchot Gittin*, 154:15, quoted in Graetz, *Silence Is Deadly*, 130.

69. Twerski, *Borne in Silence*, 67–68.

70. Graetz, *Silence Is Deadly*, 154.

71. *Holy Scriptures: Habakkuk*, 2:4, 750.

72. Siddur Sim Shalom, *Pirkei Avot* 3:13 (New York: The Rabbinical Assembly and the United Synagogue of America, 1985), 625.

4: The Rabbis and Willful Neglect

1. Steinsaltz, ed., *Bava Metzia*, 33b , 201.

2. Although the focus of this book is on male abuse of females, we recognize the serious, and rising, number of female to male abuse, estimated now by the U.S. government to be about 7 percent of males in intimate relationships. Cited in Tjaden and Thoennes, 26.

3. Dorff, *Family Violence*.

4. Central Conference of American Rabbis, "Violence Against Women" and "Domestic Violence" (New York: Central Conference of Rabbis, 1990).

5. Women of Reform Judaism, The Federation of Temple Sisterhoods, "Resolutions Addressing Spouse Abuse" (New York: Women of Reform Judaism, 1983).

6. Reconstructionist Rabbinical Association, "Ending Domestic Violence" (Philadelphia: Reconstructionist Rabbinical Association, 1991).

7. Rabbinical Assembly Convention Plenum, "Resolution on Domestic Violence" (New York: Rabbinical Assembly Convention Plenum, 1995).

5: Communal Leaders' Response to Abuse

1. I. Epstein, ed. *Talmud: Tractate Shabbos* (New York: Soncino Press, 1972), 54b.

2. *Hadassah,* the Women's Zionist Organization of America, "Stop Domestic Violence" (New York: *Hadassah,* the Women's Zionist Organization of America, 2000).

3. United Jewish Communities, personal communication, September 2002.

4. The Association of Jewish Family and Children's Agencies, personal communication, November 2002.

5. Telushkin, *Jewish Literacy,* 215.

6. Jewish Reconstructionist Federation Web site, <http://www.jrf.org> (November 2002).

7. Union of American Hebrew Congregations Web site, <http://uahc.org/cgi-bin/resodisp.pl?file=violence&year=1991n>.

8. Tjaden and Thoennes, *Findings from the NVAW Survey,* 26.

9. The Leadership Conference includes American Jewish Congress, AMIT Women, Commission for Women's Equality, *Emunah* Women, *Hadassah,* Jewish War Veterans of the USA, Inc., Jewish Women International, *Na'amat* USA, National Council of Jewish Women, National Ladies Auxiliary, Women of Reform Judaism, The Federation of Temple Sisterhoods, Women's American ORT, Women's Branch of the Orthodox Union, and the Women's League for Conservative Judaism.

10. *Hadassah,* the Women's Zionist Organization of America, *Violence Against Women: Domestic Abuse Does Not Discriminate* (New York: *Hadassah,* the Women's Zionist Organization of America, 2000).

11. Julie R. Spitzer, "A Mezuzah Does Not Ward Off Domestic Violence," in Carol Diament, ed., *Jewish Women Living the Challenge* (New York: *Hadassah,* the Women's Zionist Organization of America, 1997), 119–125.

12. *Hadassah,* the Women's Zionist Organization of America, personal communication, September 2002.

13. Diane Gardsbane, ed., *Embracing Justice: A Resource Guide for Rabbis on Domestic Abuse* and *Healing and Wholeness: A Resource Guide on Domestic Abuse in the Jewish Community* (Washington, D.C.: Jewish Women International, 2002).

14. Jewish Women International, personal communication, October 2002.

15. Gardsbane, ed., *Embracing Justice,* 8–9.

16. Na'amat Women Web site, <http://www.naamat.org> (November 2002).

17. National Council of Jewish Women, *STOP Watch* and *Advocacy Tips (New York*: National Council of Jewish Women, n.d.).

18. Twerski, *Borne in Silence,* 68.

19. Tjaden and Thoennes, *Findings from the NVAW Survey.*

20. Extrapolated from figures provided in personal communication with the Jewish Federation of the Berkshires, Fall 2002.

21. Although there has not been a demographic study done in recent years in central Massachusetts, this number was extrapolated from the mailing list of 2,900 households of the Jewish Federation of Central Massachusetts.

22. Based on figures from the *Community Report on the Demographic Study* (Boston: Combined Jewish Philanthropies, 1995).

23. Gary Tobin and Sylvia Barack Fishman, *A Population Study of the Jewish Community of Worcester* (Worcester, Mass.: Worcester Jewish Federation, 1987). This study, while dated, provides the most recent information available.

24. The Melton Center for Jewish Studies Web site, <http://www.cohums.ohio-state.edu/melton/generaldese.htm> (2002).

25. Combined Jewish Philanthropies, *Community Report.*

26. "The Jewish Population of the World," taken from World Jewish Congress (Lerner Publications Co., 1998.) <http://www.us-israel.org/jsource/Judaism/jew-pop.html>.

27. Jewish Family and Children's Services of Greater Philadelphia personal communication, Fall 2002.

28. "The Jewish Population of the World."

29. Ibid.

30. Weitzman, *Not to People Like Us.*

31. Twerski, *Borne in Silence.*

32. Fact Monster Web site <http://www.factmonster.com/ipka/A0004997.html> lists the 2000 U.S. population at about 281,400,000 (Fall 2002).

33. American Jewish Periodical Center. *Jewish Newspapers and Periodicals on Microfilm* (Cincinnati: American Jewish Periodical Center, 1994).

34. Marcia Cohen Spiegel, *Bibliography of Sources on Sexual and Domestic Violence in the Jewish Community,* 2000, <http://www.mincava.umn.edu/bibs/jewish.htm>.

35. Combined Jewish Philanthropies, *Community Report.*

36. Jack Levin, "An Effective Response to Teenage Crime Is Possible—And Cities Are Showing the Way, *The Chronicle of Higher Education* 35 (7 May 1999): 8.

37. Worcester, Mass., Police Department, personal communication, December 2002.

6: CONCLUSIONS AND RECOMMENDATIONS

1. *New Mahzor,* 401.

2. <http://www.uahc.org/shabbat/stt/2shavuot.shtm/> (3 June 2000).

3. *Holy Scriptures,* 227.

4. Ibid., 107.

5. National Association of School Psychologists Web site, *Interview with Russell Skiba,* 18 September 2002, <http://www.nasponline.org/publications/cq303bully.html>.

6. J. Fagan and D. L. Wilkinson, "Social Contexts and Functions of Adolescent Violence," in *Violence and American Schools,* ed. D. S. Elliott, B. A. Hamburg, and K. R. Williams (Cambridge, UK: Cambridge University Press, 1998), 55–93.

7. National Association of School Psychologists Web site.

8. Gardsbane, ed., *Embracing Justice.*

9. David Singer, ed., *American Jewish Year Book* (New York: American Jewish Committee, 2001).

10. United Jewish Communities, *National Jewish Population Survey* (New York: United Jewish Communities, 2000).

11. City University of New York, *American Jewish Identity Survey* (New York: City University of New York, 2001).

12. Law Enforcement Resource Center and Minnesota Program Development, Inc., *Domestic Violence: The Changing Role of Law Enforcement,* police training videotape. Minneapolis: Law Enforcement Resource Center and Minnesota Program Development, Inc., 1997.

13. Levin, "Effective Response to Teenage Crime."

APPENDIX A: RESEARCH PROTOCOL

1. Weitzman, *Not to People Like Us.*

2. Gerald Gamm, *Urban Exodus: Why the Jews Left Boston and the Catholics Stayed* (Cambridge, Mass.: Harvard University Press, 1999).

APPENDIX B: THE BLACK AND BLUE PAGES

1. United Jewish Communities, *Jewish Population Survey.*

2. Gardsbane, ed., *Healing and Wholeness and Embracing Justice.*

3. Some of these agencies were culled from Twerski, *Borne in Silence*; Hadassah, *Violence Against Women*; and Gardsbane, ed., *Embracing Justice.*

GLOSSARY

Agunah: A "chained woman." The state of being chained can result from a husband's failure to give his wife a *get* on divorce, or a husband's disappearance at sea or in war.

Aliyah (plural, *Aliyot*): From the Hebrew, meaning "going up," it signifies an honor one receives to ascend the *bimah* to recite a blessing over the Torah.

Bar mitzvah (feminine, *bat mitzvah*): Literally, son of the commandment. The age at which a child becomes an adult and responsible for fulfilling the commandments of the Jewish faith (thirteen for boys, twelve for girls).

Beit din (plural, *Batei din*): The Jewish court of justice presided over by rabbis, most always Orthodox. Because Jewish law forbade using government courts, Jews brought their civil and criminal matters to the *beit din*. Many Orthodox Jews today continue to let the *beit din* decide their legal disputes. In fact, many rabbis insist that Jews contact police or other criminal justice authorities only if imminent physical danger is present.

Bimah: The raised pulpit in the synagogue. Depending on the tradition of the founding membership, the pulpit can be found either in the front or the center of the sanctuary. It is considered an honor to be seated on the pulpit.

Brit milah: The circumcision ceremony of an eight-day-old Jewish male or of a male converting to Judaism. It is commonly referred to by its Yiddish pronunciation, *bris*.

B'tzelem Elohim: In the image of God.

Eshet chayil: A woman of valor, the ideal Jewish woman, is based on one of the biblical proverbs, portions of which are read before the *Shabbat* meal by the husband to his wife.

Get: A Jewish divorce decree. In order for a divorce to be considered complete, the husband must give his wife a *get*, or any children she may have from a subsequent marriage will be considered *mamzerim*.

Haftarah: A reading from one of the prophetic books of the *Tanach* after the Torah reading on *Shabbat* morning, it has a similar theme to the message of, or even wording in, the Torah portion.

Halacha: From the Hebrew, meaning "the way." *Halacha*, or Jewish canon law, refers to the legal sections of the Talmud, codes of Jewish law, and any *responsa*.

217

Havurah (plural, *Havurot*): Groups of Jews that study, worship, and participate in Jewish life cycle and holiday events together. The *havurah* movement was founded by Mordecai Kaplan, founder of the Reconstructionist movement.

Herem: Excommunication. The *herem* is a method of excluding a Jew from the community for the purpose of reforming his or her behavior. In times when Jews lived in circumscribed villages and neighborhoods, the *herem* was an effective method of controlling behavior.

Hillul HaShem: Desecration of God's name by word or deed.

Huppah: The marriage canopy under which all Jewish weddings take place.

Kallah: A bride.

Kashrut: The body of Jewish dietary laws (*see* kosher).

Ketubah: The Jewish marriage contract. Since ancient times, the groom has given the contract to his bride at the time of their wedding. By signing the *ketubah* the husband promises to provide food, clothing, and conjugal relations to his wife.

Kiddush: Technically the blessing over the wine, the meaning has extended to include the refreshments after a religious service.

Kosher: From the Hebrew word *kasher*, fit, kosher refers to food that is acceptable to eat according to Jewish law. Some people mistakenly believe that the food has been blessed by a rabbi; this is not true. Establishments and manufacturers claiming to serve or make kosher food, however, do have to be inspected to determine that it has been prepared in accordance with standards of the certifying group, which then places its mark on the restaurant, catering hall, or food package.

Lashon hara: Literally "evil tongue," the term is used to denote gossip or slander.

Macher: A big shot, a well-respected member of the community. Often, a big donor to causes.

Mahzor: The High Holy Day prayer book.

Mamzer (plural, *Mamzerim*): A *mamzer* is the offspring resulting from a relationship between a married woman and a man not her husband, or from incest within the forbidden degrees of kinship. In relation to our discussion, a child born to a woman who had not received a *get* would be considered a *mamzer,* and would be forbidden from marrying a Jew.

Mesirah: The principle forbidding Jews from reporting crime to civil authorities, but requiring them to submit their complaints to the *beit din* for judgment.

Mezuzah: The first and second paragraphs of the *Sh'ma*, written by a scribe on parchment, inserted into a small container, and fastened to the doorposts of Jewish homes. The biblical verse instructing the Jews to affix God's words on the doorposts is included in the *Sh'ma*.

Midrash: A form of rabbinic literature usually referring to a method of explaining biblical passages.

Mikveh: The ritual bath, it is used almost exclusively by Orthodox Jews. Women about to be married, and every month following marriage after their menstrual periods, immerse themselves in the waters for spiritual cleansing. Men and women converting to Judaism immerse themselves in the *mikveh.* Some Orthodox men also attend (separately from the women, such as before *Shabbat* or holidays).

Pikuah nefesh: Saving a life, one of the highest precepts in Judaism. With only three exceptions (murder, idolatry, forbidden sexual relations), one may violate Torah law in order to save a life.

Pirkei Avot: Literally, "The Sayings of the Fathers." A tractate of the Talmud consisting of a collection of quotations by several generations of rabbis. Some of the sayings are among the most prominent and popular in use to this day. Included among these is that by Hillel, "Do not unto others what you would not have done unto you," which formed the basis of the Golden Rule.

Rebbetzin: From the Yiddish, meaning "a rabbi's wife." In modern parlance, the term is usually reserved for the wife of an Orthodox rabbi. Most rabbis' wives with whom I am personally acquainted do not care for the term. Of course today, female Conservative, Reform, and Reconstructionist rabbis serve in many pulpits around the country. Would their husbands be called *rebbitzins?*

Shabbat: The Jewish Sabbath, which runs from sundown on Friday to sunset on Saturday.

Shalom Bayit: Peace in the home, an ideal of Jewish family life.

Shanda: A disgrace, embarrassment, or shame, especially before the community. Among the Orthodox, the *shanda* of domestic abuse would harm a child's chance for a good marriage match.

Sh'ma: The central prayer of the Jewish faith that affirms belief in God.

Shoah: The Holocaust, the systematic genocide of 6 million Jews by the Nazis during World War II.

Shofar: A ram's horn, it is blown on the High Holidays and the month preceding them for the purpose of awakening Jews to repentance. It is considered a great honor to be asked to sound the *shofar*, as that person is seen as righteous.

Shtetl (plural, *Shtetlach*): Any of a number of small villages in Eastern Europe. Many American Jews came from such villages.

Shul: Synagogue, from the German for "school." Most often prayer and study occur in the same building.

Takanah (plural, *Takanot*): From the Hebrew, meaning "repair," a *takanah* is an amendment to *halacha* that changes existing law. The purpose of the *takanah* is to remedy a difficulty that arises from the law in the way it is practiced.

Talmud: The compilation of the Oral Law, as distinct from the written text of the Torah. The Talmud consists of sixty-three tractates that record the discussions and arguments among rabbis on subjects ranging from the rules for celebrating *Shabbat* to those on marriage and divorce. The Talmud has two versions, one written by rabbis living in exile after the Babylonian capture of the Holy Temple, the other by rabbis who remained in Jerusalem.

Tanach: An acronym representing the first letters of Torah (the Five Books of Moses), *Nevi'im* (the Prophets), and *Ketuvim* (the Writings).

Tefillot: Prayers.

Teshuvah: Repentance, from the Hebrew, meaning "return." The four stages of *teshuvah* are (1) recognizing that one has sinned, (2) sincerely asking for forgiveness from the person sinned against, (3) righting any wrong done, and (4) resolving never to commit that sin again. It is important to note that God only forgives sins committed against God. God does not forgive sins committed against another person.

Tikkun olam: Repair of the world is the belief that the purpose of Jewish existence on earth is to help perfect it.

Torah: The Five Books of Moses.

Vaad Harabonim: The council of rabbis, usually present in very large Jewish communities; supervises the *beit din, kashrut* certification, and so forth.

BIBLIOGRAPHY

Abbott, J. "Injuries and Illnesses of Domestic Violence." *Annals of Emergency Medicine* 29, no. 6 (1997): 781–85.

Adams, S., and A. Powell. *Tragedies of Domestic Violence: A Qualitative Analysis of Civil Restraining Orders in Massachusetts.* Boston: Office of the Commissioner of Probation, Massachusetts Trial Court, 1995.

American Institute on Domestic Violence. *Training Businesses to Survive the Newest Workplace Security Threat,* 2001 <http://www.aidv-usa.com>.

American Jewish Periodical Center. *Jewish Newspapers and Periodicals on Microfilm.* Cincinnati: American Jewish Periodical Center, 1994.

American Psychological Association. *Violence and the Family: Report of the APA Presidential Task Force on Violence and the Family.* Washington, D.C.: American Psychological Association, 1996.

Appel, A. E., and G. W. Holden. "The Co-occurrence of Spouse and Physical Child Abuse: A Review and Appraisal." *Journal of Family Psychology* 12 (1998): 578–99.

Baron, Joseph L., ed. *A Treasury of Jewish Quotations.* Northvale, NJ: Jason Aronson, Inc., 1985.

Berry, D. B. *Domestic Violence Sourcebook.* New York: McGraw-Hill, 1995.

Blum, J. *Domestic Violence in the North American Jewish Community: Issues and Communal Programs.* New York: Council of Jewish Federations, 1992.

Bonica, Trish. *Domestic Violence in Jewish Homes.* Washington, D.C.: Jewish Women International, 2002.

Bubis, G. *The Costs of Jewish Living: Revisiting Jewish Involvements and Barriers.* New York: American Jewish Committee, 2002.

Bureau of Justice Statistics. *Preventing Domestic Violence Against Women.* Washington, D.C.: Bureau of Justice Statistics, 1986.

Buzawa, E. S., and C. G. Buzawa. *Do Arrests and Restraining Orders Work?* Thousand Oaks, Calif.: Sage Publications, 1996.

Carmen, E. H., P. P. Rieker, and T. Mills. "Victims of Violence and Psychiatric Illness." *American Journal of Psychiatry* 141, no. 3: 378–83.

Carnay, Janet, Ruth Magder, Laura Wine Paster, Marcia Cohn Spiegel, and Abigail Weinberg. *The Jewish Woman's Awareness Guide*. New York: Biblio Press, 1992.

Cavanagh, Michael E. "The Myths of Relationship Abuse." *Journal of Religion and Health 33*, no. 1 (1994): 45–50.

Central Conference of American Rabbis. "Violence Against Women" and "Domestic Violence." New York: Central Conference of American Rabbis, 1990.

City University of New York. *American Jewish Identity Survey*. New York: City University of New York, 2001.

Cohen Spiegel, Marcia. *Bibliography of Sources on Sexual and Domestic Violence in the Jewish Community*, 2000, <http://www.mincava.umn.edu/bibs/jewish.htm> (11 April 2000).

Coker, A. L., M. Sanderson, M. K. Fadden, and L. Pirisi. "Intimate Partner Violence and Cervical Neoplasia." *Journal of Women's Health and Gender Based Medicine 9*, no. 9 (2000): 1015–23.

Combined Jewish Philanthropies. *Community Report on the Demographic Study*. Boston: Combined Jewish Philanthropies, 1995.

Cwik, Marc S. "Peace in the Home? The Response of Rabbis to Wife Abuse Within American Jewish Congregations." *Journal of Psychology and Judaism* 20, no. 4 (1996): 279–348 and 21, no. 1 (1997): 5–81.

Davidson, J. R. T. "Recognition and Treatment of Posttraumatic Stress Disorder." *Journal of the American Medical Association* 286, no. 5 (2000): 584–88.

Diament, Carol, ed. *Jewish Women Living the Challenge*. New York: *Hadassah,* the Women's Zionist Organization of America, 1997, 119–125.

Domestic Abuse Intervention Project. *The Power and Control Wheel.* Duluth, Minn.: Domestic Abuse Intervention Project, 1999.

Dorff, Elliott. *Family Violence: A Responsum for the Committee on Jewish Law and Standards of the Rabbinical Assembly.* New York: The Rabbinical Assembly, 1995.

Dratsch, Mark. "Domestic Violence and Halacha." In *Embracing Justice: A Resource Guide for Rabbis on Domestic Abuse*, ed. Diane Gardsbane, 59–66. Washington, D.C.: Jewish Women International, 2002.

Druckerman, Pamela. "Domestic Violence Among Jews Gets More Attention Since Simpson Case." *Jewish Advocate*, 15 July 1994.

Engeldinger, Eugene A. *Spouse Abuse: An Annotated Bibliography of Violence Between Mates.* Metuchen, N.J.: Scarecrow Press, 1986.

Epstein, I., ed. *The Talmud: Tractate Berachot.* New York: Soncino Press, 1984.

———. *The Talmud: Tractate Gittin.* New York: Soncino Press, 1977.

———. *The Talmud: Tractate Sanhedrin.* New York: Soncino Press, 1990.

———. *The Talmud: Tractate Shabbos.* New York: Soncino Press, 1972.

———. *The Talmud: Tractate Shavuos.* New York: Soncino Press, 1972.

———. *The Talmud: Tractate Yebamoth.* New York: Soncino Press, 1984.

Fact Monster Web site, <http://www.factmonster.com/ipka/A0004997.html>.

Fagan, J., and D. L. Wilkinson. "Social Contexts and Functions of Adolescent Violence." In *Violence in American Schools,* ed. D. S. Elliott, B. A. Hamburg, and K. R. Williams, 55–93. Cambridge, UK: Cambridge University Press, 1998.

Family Violence Prevention Fund. Confidentiality of Health Records Can Be Life-or-Death Issue for Women Facing Abuse, 2000, <http//endabuse.org/newsdesk/releases.php3?/Search=Article&ID=17> (17 October 2000).

FBI. *The Structure of Family Violence.* Washington, D.C.: Federal Bureau of Investigation, 1998.

———. *Uniform Crime Reports,* 2000 <http://www.fbi.gov/ucr/ucr.htm> (16 December 2002).

Forrest Gump. Film. Hollywood, Calif.: Paramount Pictures, 1994.

Frishtik, Mordechai. "Physical and Sexual Violence by Husbands as a Reason for Imposing a Divorce in Jewish Law." *The Jewish Law Annual* 9 (1991): 145.

———. "Violence Against Women in Judaism." *Journal of Psychology and Judaism* 14 (1990): 131–53.

Gamm, Gerald. *Urban Exodus: Why the Jews Left Boston and the Catholics Stayed.* Cambridge, Mass.: Harvard University Press, 1999.

Gardsbane, Diane, ed. *Embracing Justice: A Resource Guide for Rabbis on Domestic Abuse.* Washington, D.C.: Jewish Women International, 2002.

———. *Healing and Wholeness: A Resource Guide on Domestic Abuse in the Jewish Community.* Washington, D.C.: Jewish Women International, 2002.

Giller, B., and E. Goldsmith. "All in the Family: A Study of Intrafamilial Violence in the Los Angeles Jewish Community." Master's thesis, Hebrew Union College and the University of Southern California, 1983.

Gittelsohn, R. B. *The Extra Dimension: A Jewish View of Marriage.* New York: Union of American Hebrew Congregations, 1983.

Graetz, Naomi. *Silence Is Deadly: Jewish Tradition and Spousal Abuse.* Northvale, N.J.: Jason Aronson, 1998.

Guterman, Neil B. "Confronting the Unknowns in Jewish Family Violence." *Journal of Jewish Communal Service* 70, no. 1 (1993): 26–33.

Hadassah, the Women's Zionist Organization of America. *Stop Domestic Violence.* New York: Hadassah, the Women's Zionist Organization of America, 2000.

———. *Rape as a Hate Crime in War and Peace.* New York: Hadassah, the Women's Zionist Organization of America, 2000.

———. *Violence Against Women: Domestic Abuse Does Not Discriminate.* New York: Hadassah, the Women's Zionist Organization of America, 2000.

Hedin, L. W., and P. O. Janson. "The Invisible Wounds: The Occurrence of Psychological Abuse and Anxiety Compared with Previous Experience of Physical

Abuse During the Childbearing Year. *Journal of Psychosomatic Obstetrics and Gynecology* 20, no. 3 (1999): 136–44.

Hertz, Joseph H., ed. *Pentateuch and Haftorah*. Brooklyn, N.Y.: Soncino Press, 1994.

————. *Sayings of the Fathers*. New York: Behrman House, 1945.

Holt, V. L., M. A. Kernie, T. Lumley, M. E. Wolf, and F. P. Rivara. "2002 Civil Protection Orders and Risk of Subsequent Police-Reported Violence." *Journal of the American Medical Association* 288 (no. 3): 589–94.

The Holy Scriptures. Philadelphia: Jewish Publication Society, 1960.

Jacobs, Lynn, and Sherry Berliner Dimarsky. "Jewish Domestic Abuse: Realities and Responses." *Journal of Jewish Communal Service* 68, no. 2 (1991–1992): 94–113.

Jewish Reconstructionist Federation Web site, <http://www.jrf.org>.

Jewish Theological Seminary of America. "Know Whom You Put to Shame, For in the Likeness of God Is She Made." High Holy Day Message, 5753, September 1992.

Jewish Women International. *Resource Guide for Rabbis on Domestic Violence*. Washington, D.C.: Jewish Women International, 1996.

Late Night with Conan O'Brien. Television program. National Broadcasting Company (NBC), May 13, 2002.

Law Enforcement Resource Center and Minnesota Program Development, Inc. *Domestic Violence: Battering, the Dynamics of an Abusive Relationship*. Police training videotape. Minneapolis: Law Enforcement Resource Center and Minnesota Program Development, Inc., 1997.

————. *Domestic Violence: The Changing Role of Law Enforcement*. Police training videotape. Minneapolis: Law Enforcement Resource Center and Minnesota Program Development, Inc., 1997.

Levin, Jack. "An Effective Response to Teenage Crime Is Possible—And Cities Are Showing the Way. *The Chronicle of Higher Education* 35 (7 May 1999): B10–11.

Linzer, Norman, Irving Levitz, and David Schnall, eds. *Crisis and Continuity: The Jewish Family in the 21st Century*. Hoboken, N.J.: KTAV Publishing House, 1995.

McCauley, J., D. E. Kern, K. Kolodner, L. R. Derogatis, and E. B. Bass. "Relations of Low-Severity Violence to Women's Health. *Journal of General Internal Medicine* 13, no. 10: 687–91.

Maimonides, Moses. *The Guide for the Perplexed*. New York: Dover Publications, 2000.

Mechanic, M. B., M. H. Uhlmansiek, T. L. Weaver, and P. A. Resick. "The Impact of Severe Stalking Experienced by Acutely Battered Women: An Examination of Violence, Psychological Symptoms, and Strategic Responding." *Violence and Victims* 15, no. 4 (2000): 443–48.

The Melton Center for Jewish Studies Web site, <http://www. cohums.ohio-state.edu/melton/generaldesc.htm>.

Miller, Mary Susan. *No Visible Wounds: Identifying Nonphysical Abuse of Women by Their Men.* Chicago: Contemporary Books, 1995.

Moriarty, Lynn. "Addressing Domestic Violence Within the Jewish Community." *Journal of Jewish Communal Service* 73, no. 2/3 (1996–1997): 174–80.

Na'amat Women Web site, <http://www.naamat.org>.

National Association of School Psychologists Web site. *Interview with Russell Skiba,* 18 September 2002, <http://www.nasponline.org/publications/cq303bully.html>.

National Council of Jewish Women. *Advocacy Tips.* New York: National Council of Jewish Women, n.d.

_____. *STOP Watch.* New York: National Council of Jewish Women, n.d.

The New Mahzor for Rosh Hashanah and Yom Kippur. Bridgeport, Conn.: Media Judaica, 1976.

Parker, B., J. McFarlane, K. Soeken, C. Silva, and S Reel. "Testing and Intervention to Prevent Further Abuse to Pregnant Women." *Residential Nursing Health* 22, no. 1 (1999): 59–66.

"*Pirkei Avot,* The Sayings of the Fathers." In *Siddur Sim Shalom: A Prayerbook for Shabbat, Festivals, and Weekdays,* ed. J. Harlow. New York: United Synagogue of America, 1985, 602–665.

Plichta, S. "The Effects of Woman Abuse on Health Care Utilization and Health Status: A Literature Review." *Women's Health Issues* 2, no. 3 (1992): 154–63.

Rabbinical Assembly Convention Plenum. "Resolution on Domestic Violence." New York: Rabbinical Assembly Convention Plenum, 1995.

Reconstructionist Rabbinical Association. "Ending Domestic Violence." Philadelphia: Reconstructionist Rabbinical Association, 1991.

Reich, Lisa W. "Shalom Task Force: A Grassroots Community Response to Family Violence. *Viewpoint* (1997): 49–50.

Roberts, G. L., J. M. Lawrence, B. I. O'Toole, and B. Raphael. "Domestic Violence in the Emergency Department: I. Two Case-Control Studies of Victims." *General Hospital Psychiatry* 19, no. 1 (1997): 5–11.

Rodriguez, M. A., E. McLoughlin, G. Nah, and J. C. Campbell. "Mandatory Reporting of Domestic Violence Injuries to the Police." *Journal of the American Medical Association* 286, no. 5 (2000): 580–83.

Rollstin, A. O., and J. M. Kern. "Correlates of Battered Women's Psychological Distress: Severity of Abuse and Duration of the Postabuse Period. *Psychological Report* 82, no. 2 (1998): 387–94.

Rossman, B. B. R. "Longer Term Effects of Children's Exposure to Domestic Violence." In *Domestic Violence in the Lives of Children,* ed. S. A. Graham-Bermann and J. L. Edelson, 35–65. Washington, D.C.: American Psychological Association, 2001.

Rovella, David E. "Hasidic New York Enclave Shaken by Lurid Case: Domestic Violence Triggers Debate over the Divorce Laws of Orthodox Judaism." *The National Law Journal* 19, no. 9 (1996): 10.

Scarf, Mimi. *Battered Jewish Wives*. Lewiston, N.Y.: Edwin Mellen Press, 1988.

Singer, David, ed. *American Jewish Year Book*. New York: American Jewish Committee, 2001.

Spitzer, Julie Ringold. *When Love Is Not Enough: Spousal Abuse in Rabbinic and Contemporary Judaism*. New York: Women of Reform Judaism, The Federation of Temple Sisterhoods, 1995.

Stedman's Medical Dictionary, 22nd ed. Baltimore, Md.: Williams & Wilkins, 1972.

Steinsaltz, Adin, ed. *The Talmud: Tractate Bava Metzia*. New York: Random House, 1990.

Strauss, Murray A., Richard J. Gelles, and Suzanne K. Steinmetz. *Behind Closed Doors: Violence in the American Family*. Garden City, N.J.: Anchor/Doubleday, 1980.

Street, A.E., and I. Arias. "Psychological Abuse and Post-traumatic Stress Disorder in Battered Women: Examining the Roles of Shame and Guilt." *Violence and Victims*, 16, no. 1 (2001): 65–78.

Telushkin, Joseph. *Jewish Literacy*. New York: William Morrow, 1991.

Tjaden, P., and N. Thoennes. *Full Report of the Prevalence, Incidence and Consequences of Violence Against Women: Findings from the National Violence Against Women Survey* (NCJ 183781). Washington, D.C.: U.S. Department of Justice, National Institute of Justice, 2000.

Tobin, Gary, and Sylvia Barack Fishman. *A Population Study of the Jewish Community of Worcester*. Worcester, Mass.: Worcester Jewish Federation, 1987.

Twerski, Abraham, J. *The Shame Borne in Silence*. Pittsburgh: Mirkov Publications, 1996.

Union of American Hebrew Congregations. Violence Against Women. Resolution at the 61st General Assembly. Reprinted on Web site <http://uahc.org/cgi-bin/resodisp.pl?file=violence&year=1991n>.

United Jewish Communities. *National Jewish Population Survey*. New York: United Jewish Communities, 2000.

United Synagogue of Conservative Judaism. "Judaism and Domestic Violence." A United Synagogue resolution implementation packet, February 1995.

U.S. Census Bureau. *Statistical Abstract of the United States: 2000*, 116th ed. Washington, D.C.: U.S. Census Bureau, 2000.

Walker, Lenore E. *The Battered Woman*. New York: Harper & Row, 1979.

Weiss, Elaine. *Surviving Domestic Violence: Voices of Women Who Broke Free*. Salt Lake City: Agreka Books, 2000.

Weitzman, Susan. *Not to People Like Us: Hidden Abuse in Upscale Marriages*. New York: Basic Books, 2000.

Women of Reform Judaism, The Federation of Temple Sisterhoods. Resolutions Addressing Spouse Abuse (New York: Women of Reform Judaism, 1983).

INDEX